THE COMPLETE PRACTICAL GUIDE TO

STENCILING
AND STAMPING

THE COMPLETE PRACTICAL GUIDE TO

STENCILING
AND STAMPING

160 INSPIRATIONAL AND STYLISH PROJECTS WITH EASY-TO-FOLLOW
INSTRUCTIONS AND ILLUSTRATED WITH 1500 STUNNING STEP-BY-STEP
PHOTOGRAPHS AND TEMPLATES

HOW TO DECORATE AND PERSONALIZE YOUR HOME WITH BEAUTIFUL
STENCIL AND STAMP TECHNIQUES FOR INTERIORS, FURNITURE, STORAGE,
FABRICS, CHINA AND ACCESSORIES

LUCINDA GANDERTON, STEWART WALTON & SALLY WALTON

LORENZ BOOKS

CONTENTS

INTRODUCTION

Stencilling and stamping are each simple painting skills and enduringly popular art and craft forms that can be used to effect to transform every surface of the home, including floors, walls and windows as well as fabrics and accessories. Different paints are used depending upon the surface to be decorated, but with each technique, large or small-scale items are decorated in the same way. The stamps, stencils and paint quantities are scaled up or down according to the amount of space to be covered. Both craft skills can be mastered quickly and easily; the level of complexity is dictated by the size and scale of the stencils or stamp designs and the surface area on which you choose to work.

STENCILLING

Versatile, adaptable, stencilling is an age-old technique that has evolved alongside changing tastes and fashions in interior decor, from Victorian Gothic to Bloomsbury bohemian. Like many craft skills, the technique was honed among the working classes to add colour and decoration to homes in imitation of the decorating techniques employed in grand town and country houses. The technique is currently enjoying a resurgence of popularity in recent years. New techniques and images are constantly being developed to fit in with current styles, and creating a decorative panel for a wall or floor, for example, is viewed positively as adding individuality to our homes.

After a decade of minimalism and plain walls, colour and pattern are once again finding their way back into our homes and interiors, and today's home designers are now reinterpreting traditional stencilling in an exciting new way. Just as modern wallpaper is designed to be used creatively on a single wall, for example, or within a decorative panel, to add an element of colour so too are stencils designed. The most up-to-date stencils are both bold in design and they are graphic, with an unmistakably 21st-century look. The wide range of colours available or to mix means that you have total control over the pattern and colour choice in a way that was never available before.

Stencilling is straightforward, easy to put into practice and above all, great fun to do. The beauty of it, and much of the reason for its continued popularity, is that it is possible to achieve professional-looking results very quickly and easily, without having any previous experience of the craft. (Beginners may want to practise first on small-

ABOVE: This bright and colourful rose stencil can be applied quickly to transform a plain piece of fabric.

scale or repeat projects.) Once the space to be decorated is marked out, the stencilling can be applied as time allows. Some projects may take days to build up the tones and shades of colour, or the layers of pattern. Others may be completed in hours. There is great satisfaction in peeling back a stencil to reveal a crisply detailed one-off image, and also in building up a pattern or border from a repeated motif.

STAMPING

Unlike stencilling, rubber stamping is a relatively new craft which developed from the humble office rubber stamp. However, as fashions go, stamping has captured the public imagination and made an unmistakable impression on the craft and home decorating market. Wonderfully simple, yet stunningly effective, stamped designs can be used to transform anything from entire walls to greetings cards and sheets of giftwrap; to create a theme for a whole room, or to provide original accessories for an eye-catching display.

The equipment that you need to buy is a stamp, a roller and some ink, or paint, depending upon the surface and scale of the area to be decorated. Commercial stamps are readily available, either made of rubber and adhered to a wooden block for ease of handling, or without the wooden block, so that the stamp will bend easily around curved surfaces. Stamps can even

ABOVE: *This stylized tree makes a bold feature on a pastel wall.*

BELOW RIGHT: *Plain cushions are quickly transformed with a simple stamped motif.*

BELOW LEFT: *A single chair is stencilled with simple floral designs and a single complementary colour scheme.*

be purchased as outlines that are designed to be filled in with your choice of paint colours. Ready-made designs range from simple and traditional motifs such as fleur-de-lys, diamonds and crowns, to contemporary, artistic pieces that can be used singularly to add an artistic statement to a small item.

However, there are plenty of other stamp sources. It is possible to create your own stamps using potatoes, erasers, sponges, linocuts, and found objects such as feathers. With the stamp and paint to hand, fabric, wood, stone, walls, floors, tiles and plastic can all be transformed quickly and easily. Repeat

motifs on different accessories using the same colour to co-ordinate the theme of a room, or build up a single image using one motif to create a unique artistic piece of work on a wall, such as a large stylized tree.

LEFT: An old cabinet that has seen better days is a good choice for a makeover and could inspire more ambitious projects.

Under chapter headings from "Walls and Surfaces" and "Furniture and Storage" to "Fabrics" and "Home Accessories" you will find a wealth of ideas to create for your home, and garden, and as gifts for your friends and family. Choose from cushions, throws, bedspreads, lampshades, tiles, floors, walls, borders and friezes, t-shirts, scarves, ceramics and glassware.

None of these decorative ideas need be costly, particularly at a time when salvage and recycling are key trends. Much early American folk-art stencilling, for example, was a thrifty way of recreating the wallpaper and rugs that were prohibitively expensive in the New World, and a stamped design on sanded boards or a painted floor cloth can still be a very stylish alternative to a carpet. Many of us have a slightly shabby piece of furniture, tucked away in a spare

USING THIS BOOK

Here is a comprehensive technical guide and an invaluable resource for everybody who is interested in stencilling and stamping, from the complete novice to the experienced crafter and every level of ability inbetween. The practical introductions to each chapter cover everything you will need to know about cutting a stencil from card or plastic, or making a stamp from your own choice of material. The different methods of applying colour by brush, roller or sponge to create various painted effects are all included. Simple skills will help the beginner to get started, and for those with more experience there is a wealth of information on blending colours and creating different paint effects and looks for your home.

Each chapter begins with a fascinating survey of stamping or stencilling styles. Stencilling has a long history and the styles of home decor it has embraced are many and varied. Stamping is relatively new, but it too, has been applied to create different styles. All are reflected in the projects in this book, together with basic lessons in pattern making. The following chapters show you how to put all this information into practice and illustrate the vast potential of stencilled and stamped ornament in modern interior decoration. The inspirational ideas range from sheets of wrapping paper that can be finished in an afternoon to room schemes that may take weeks to complete.

RIGHT: Gilding and highly ornamental oriental designs are currently making a come-back in interior decor fashions.

room, that can be revamped with a fresh coat of paint and a few well-chosen stencils or stamps, or a plain throw or bedcover that can be given a new lease of life with a scattering of motifs. For those for whom time is short, or where small-scale items are appealing, decorating gift wrap and stamping greetings cards may offer a good introduction.

GETTING STARTED

Stencilling and stamping do not require much outlay of time or money for basic and small-scale projects. Large-scale room schemes will take more preparation work, and it is essential that this stage is done thoroughly if you are to have a professionally finished room in which you can live happily for several years.

You may have some of the tools and art materials that are required for stencilling and stamping already around the house. Brushes, rulers, paint palettes and string are a few of the everyday items you will be using to plan and prepare your project. Acrylic paints, which are used for many projects, are relatively inexpensive and are readily available in home decorating and craft supply stores. These offer a professional finish to the amateur. Spend time choosing and mixing the correct toning colours and quantites of paint before you begin. New innovations such as the heat pen and easy-to-cut acetate have speeded up the process of making stencils from the days when they were hand cut from sheet metal, and photocopying templates saves time as well as ensuring that the repeat patterns are identical.

Once you have chosen and made your first stencil or stamp, spend a little time experimenting with paint techniques and develop a few ideas of your own. By practising first on scrap paper you will learn how much paint to apply to get an even coverage. Bear in mind though that different surfaces, such as wood or plaster, absorb paint at different rates and each project will need to be assessed individually. Fabric will absorb more paint than a tiled wall, for example, so if you have a spare sample of the fabric you intend to use, practise on this first.

All the projects featured in the book have concise instructions, which are fully illustrated with step-by-step photographs: you can follow these to the letter to copy the project exactly, learning how to build up layers of colour and tone, or use your own imagination to interpret the design motifs as you wish. Whatever your choice, no two people will ever interpret a project in the same way.

BELOW: Inexpensive candles can be given an instant decorative treatment with a stencil and gold spray paint.

STENCILLING

STENCILLING STYLES

The sheer versatility of stencilling means that it has appeared in many different guises over the years, and historic stencilling ranges from the purely functional to the highly decorative. Reverse stencil hand prints have been found in prehistoric cave dwellings, Egyptian tombs had stencilled patterning and Japanese fabrics were stencilled with "katagami" – resist floral designs. In the 1920s Mariano Fortuny recreated renaissance patterns on stencilled velvet and embellished them with Venetian glass beads. In more recent times it was even used as a propaganda medium by Italian fascists and Basque separatists, and hijacked by graffiti artists in both Europe and America, whose paintings have developed into popular street art.

PRACTICAL STENCILLING

Today stencilling is thought of as a purely decorative craft, but its origins are rather more utilitarian. In the early days of printing, it was the quickest and most effective method of colouring black-and-white wood block engravings and transferring designs on to fabric. Stencilled lettering has long been a quick method for manufacturers to transfer information on to packaging. The Shaker community used tin sheets pierced with fine lettering to label the vegetable seeds harvested from their fields and, in the 19th century, Italian fruit growers from the Mediterranean port of Sorrento developed the stencilled labels on their lemon crates into a fine art. Even today, stencils are used to mark crates of whisky in Scottish distilleries and wooden boxes of salted pilchards in Penzance, at the far west tip of England.

Stencilled design has also been used for adding pattern to domestic pottery, especially in France and Eastern Europe. Hungarian and Czech bowls of the mid-20th century were embellished with spot or border designs of flower baskets, fruit, vines and animals, in rich folk-art style. These designs were transferred by painting a coloured slip glaze through a stamped tin stencil, specially shaped to fit within the biscuit-fired dish. Three or more stencils could be used to build up the most detailed patterns. As technology advanced, the airbrush replaced the stencil brush, giving a smoother surface to the colour. The trompe l'oeil plate project is a witty re-interpretation of these popular ceramics.

AMERICAN FOLK ART

Stencilled interiors reached their peak of popularity and expertise along the Eastern seaboard of the United States in the early 19th century. The elaborate wallpapers and woven carpets that settlers had enjoyed in Europe were no longer available, and home owners looked to paint as a way of creating decorative effects. Stencilling became a recognized trade and itinerant artists, such as J. Gleason of Rhode Island and Moses Eaton in New England, would travel from house to house, adding stencilled pineapples, garlands, swags and hearts to marbled and wood-grain effects.

ABOVE: Stencilling allowed poorer people to copy styles found in grander homes and public buildings across Europe.

OPPOSITE: Floral motifs are always popular.

Colour schemes, as now, depended largely on the taste of individual clients and ranged from subtle grey walls with simple repeated patterns to sunshine yellow with red and green flowers. Nowadays we go to great lengths to ensure patterns match exactly and that all our repeats line up, but surviving folk art walls were painted with a great panache that reveals a careless disregard for accuracy, visible brush marks and the occasional smudge.

VICTORIAN GOTHIC

The Victorians used stencilling to add formal decoration to the interiors of public buildings such as churches, synagogues, stations, art galleries and town halls. Many of these original schemes have been refurbished to dazzling effect. As much surviving Victorian needlework and paintwork has faded over the decades, it is useful to remember just how bright the original threads and paints actually were. A recently discovered stencilling scheme of 1863 by Alexander Thomson (the leading Scottish architect of his day) shows a surprisingly bright range of colours: Pompeiian red, bottle green and gold leaf. He included an eclectic combination of neo-classical, Asian and Egyptian motifs on the murals and borders of Lilybank House in Glasgow. Restoration work on London's Midland Hotel, built at the height of the railway boom, has revealed complex multicoloured stencilling schemes that originally extended down long corridors and across vaulted ceilings. Most of these were painted over by succeeding generations, for whom such intense pattern proved difficult to live alongside.

ARTS AND CRAFTS

At the end of the 19th century, a new aesthetic movement transformed the decorative arts. Art nouveau, and the subsequent Arts and Crafts movement, was a fresh way of looking at natural subjects. Building on the inspiration of artists such as William Morris and the arts of Eastern cultures, the slavish realism and overblown ornamentation of the Victorian era was simplified into flowing, graceful forms. The stylized, two-dimensional patterns of this era were ideally suited to stencilling and with the growing enthusiasm for crafts, particularly among women, it became a highly popular method of decorating the home.

The advent of electric lighting meant that rooms were lighter and brighter than they had ever been, and the fussiness of the parlour

ABOVE: The organic forms and patterns of the art nouveau period make excellent stencil designs for tiles, walls and borders.

RIGHT: The repeated paisley pattern creates a wallpaper effect in this small study.

was gradually replaced by pale walls and uncluttered surfaces. The epitome of this new look was Charles Rennie Mackintosh's unique "Glasgow Style". Considered radical at the time, his elegant interiors are the precursor of late 20th century minimalism. He used stencilling as an unobtrusive way to add flat colour and pattern to canvas chair backs, bed hangings and upholstered seating. His favourite motifs of roses and sinuous plant forms have been much imitated and reproduced.

In America at the same time, larger scale stencils in a slightly softer style became highly popular. Continuous border designs encircled rooms, running both above and below plate and dado (chair) rails, and large friezes filled

the deep areas below picture rails. Single stencils, repeated motifs and overall patterns were all used, and stylized flora and fauna – birds, fish, insects and animals – were a favourite theme.

ART DECO

As the soft lines of art nouveau gave way to the more angular shapes of art deco, so stencilled patterns changed. *The Practical Guide to Stencilling* by Frank Gibson, published in 1926, featured an array of motifs and all-over designs including the characteristic sunray pattern. Other enduring stencil designs – many of which appear in modern form in this book – included were Greek key borders, twining vines and bunches of grapes, fleurs-de-lys,

ABOVE: Pale light blues and candy tones are popular contemporary colours.

ABOVE RIGHT: Focusing the attention on one wall is a modern use of stencils – use large single motifs, such as this branch of delicate orange blossom.

butterflies and (at the time when Tutankhamun's tomb was causing a sensation) an Egyptian scarab. The most intricate of all is a detailed reproduction of the willow pattern plate design in traditional blue and white.

Gibson's book suggests a wide range of textiles considered suitable for stencilling, which provide an interesting insight into the wide range of domestic linens to be found in an ordinary household. They include not just table cloths, but also runners, napkins and mats. Some of the decorated items are still to be found and many of them are still subjects for stencilling: lampshades, cushions, curtains and picture frames. Others – collar boxes, shaving paper holders, bookcase curtains and mantel borders – are now obsolete, but the idea of stencilling garden paling is charming and one that could be copied for a cottage-style plot.

SWEDISH STYLE

One of the most influential decorating styles of recent years derives from the Gustavian look of 19th-century Sweden. The short days and long winters of Scandinavian countries mean that people spend a lot of time indoors, and interior colour schemes are predominantly pale in tone: cream, light blue and sage green provide the backdrop for highlights of dusky pink, cherry red and the favourite blue.

Artist Carl Larsson's book *My Home* introduced this style to a wider audience, who relished the detailed paintings of his wife and children in a house decorated with simple furniture, striped and checked fabric, and restrained stencilling. Small florals, looped ribbon bows, hearts and wheatsheaves all echo the embroidery designs of the period and region and were used on walls, floors and furniture. Any stencilling done in this style should be done in pale colours and gently aged by rubbing it lightly with abrasive paper to give an authentic look.

CONTEMPORARY STENCILS

Interior design of the 1980s tended towards the flouncy and floral, and gave stencilling a reputation as fiddly and over-decorated. Since then, there has been a great turnaround in style. "New vintage" effects pay homage to the past, but are to be found in bright, clear shades with none of the fussiness of their original inspiration. Drawing on a wealth of historic decorative styles, new designers are reworking antique motifs such as oriental blossoms, paisleys and lace patterns in a bold, graphic manner, using new colours and shades.

The primary colours, flamboyant flowers and geometric patterns of 1970s wallpaper have already made a comeback, and they look more at home within the proportions of modern loft-style apartments and open living spaces than they ever did in suburban bedrooms and sitting rooms. These patterns are filtering through to stencil design, such as in the form of pop-art style canvases. By playing with scale – enlarging a single flower to cover a cushion – interior designers are creating a new, modern look.

STENCILLING BASICS

The appeal of stencilling as a decorative technique lies in its immediacy. Getting started is easy, as it requires only a few basic materials and items of equipment, and no special painting skills. Even a complete beginner can achieve stunning results in a short time. The following pages show you how to make a stencil and how to use it, and suggest ways in which you can produce your own individual interpretations of the designs in the book to suit your own style and interior decoration.

ABOVE: Making sketches and transferring your designs to stencil card or acetate can be very rewarding.

LEFT: Stencil brushes are available in many shapes and dimensions. It is important to clean them after every session to keep them in good condition.

STENCILLING EQUIPMENT

Making a stencil is a straightforward process that does not entail buying a huge amount of equipment. Some of the items you may already have around the house, and others are readily available from good art and craft suppliers. As with any other creative task, it is worth investing in the best tools for the job, in order to achieve a professional result. If you plan to make a lot of acetate stencils, for example, using a heat knife will save a great deal of time and a self-healing cutting mat is essential for safe stencil making.

MEASURING AND MARKING EQUIPMENT

Accurate measuring is important when planning the final position of a stencil. You may need to mark up a wall, box lid or greetings card with registration marks – and when drawing up the stencil itself. Set squares (triangles) give accurate corners and right angles and a metal ruler has a dual role, for measuring and as a straight edge to guide the knife when cutting straight lines within a stencil. Graph paper can be used for planning more formal designs and enlarging a template if you do not have access to a photocopier.

A retractable tape measure is essential for marking up a wall scheme or other large surface, but a dressmaker's measure will do for smaller areas. Light pencil marks and guidelines on wood, walls or paper can easily be removed with an eraser when the paint is dry. Water-soluble or fading fabric marking pens can be used to mark up fabric.

TRACING AND TRANSFERRING EQUIPMENT

Traditional orange or yellow stencil card is treated with linseed oil (which gives it its characteristic smell) to make it pliable, easy to cut and waterproof. Use a sheet of carbon paper or tracing paper (and a soft pencil) and a ballpoint pen to copy a design on to the card. If you are using clear or semi-transparent acetate, there is no need to transfer the design before cutting out. Adhesive stencil film

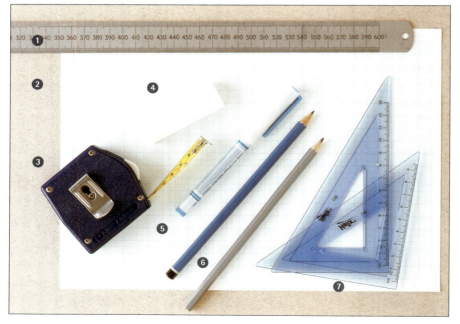

LEFT: Measuring and marking equipment: *1 metal ruler, 2 graph paper, 3 tape measure, 4 eraser, 5 fabric marking pen, 6 pencils, 7 set squares.*

RIGHT: Tracing and transferring
equipment: 1 *adhesive stencil film, 2
stencil card, 3 acetate, 4 carbon paper,
5 tracing paper, 6 hard pencil, 7 soft
pencil, 8 ballpoint pen.*

used for airbrushing and other
graphic work is ideal for intricate
one-off stencils on glass or
ceramic surfaces. The design can
simply be traced through it with
a sharp hard pencil.

FIXING AND CUTTING EQUIPMENT

If you only intend to make one or
two stencils you can cut them on
to a piece of thick card (stock), but
this tends to blunt any knife quite
quickly. Alternatively, a durable
self-healing cutting mat will prove
invaluable, as it protects the blade
and is much safer. If you need
extra stability, fix your tracing
paper or acetate on to the mat
with low-tack masking tape, which
will not damage either surface,
and a coating of spray mount,
which is a light adhesive that can
easily be repositioned and does not
leave any residue.

When cutting out, you should
always work with a sharp blade,
which will give a cleaner line and
is easier to use. Choose a snap-off
knife, which has a supply of new
tips, or a craft knife into which
new blades can be fitted. A heat
knife melts quickly through plastic
and speeds up the process: always
place a sheet of glass over the
design being traced.

RIGHT: Fixing and cutting equipment:
*1 self-healing cutting mat, 2 spray mount,
3 heat knife, 4 low-tack masking tape,
5 snap-off knife, 6 craft knife.*

BRUSHES AND PAINTS

There are various different methods of applying colour to a stencil and many different types of paint that can be used. Small pots of creamy oil-based colour and oil crayons are specially made for use with stencils, but water-based acrylics are easy to use and can be bought from any good art or craft supplier. Special stencil brushes are, however, an essential purchase and the initial outlay of buying a range of several different sizes will prove worthwhile. With care, they will last you for years.

BRUSHES

Stencil brushes are short-handled and their round flat heads are densely packed with firm bristles to let you control the flow of paint. Sizes range from about 5mm to 4cm/¼in to 1½in. Smaller brushes are intended for detailed areas and big ones will cover large areas very quickly. Some have short, stiff bristles for stippling and others are slightly longer and more flexible for a softer, swirled effect. It is worth investing in a good set of stencil brushes. Do not let your brushes or sponges dry out or they will be ruined. It is important to keep your equipment in good condition.

Decorator's brushes are for painting in backgrounds and colour washes. Choose a size to suit your needs. Artist's brushes are used for adding fine details. A sponge roller is another quick way to apply flat colour, while a natural sea sponge, which is better than an artificial one, will produce interesting textures.

RIGHT: Brushes and paints: *1 Stencil brushes in different sizes, 2 decorator's brushes, 3 fine artist's brushes, 4 sponge roller, 5 natural sea sponge, 6 artist's acrylic paint, 7 emulsion (latex) paints, 8 spray paint, 9 fabric medium, 10 paint tray, 11 emulsion (latex) paint swatches.*

PAINTS

Emulsion (latex) paint is used for painting plastered or paper-covered walls. Sample pots (in the same colour range as the room scheme) are a good source of historic and unusual colours for stencilling. Artist's acrylic paint comes in tubes and acrylic craft paint in pots. The latter is very versatile and can be mixed with fabric medium for use on textiles or texture gels to give a variety of three-dimensional effects. Glass and ceramic paints can be used for stencilling, but have to be baked in a hot oven to fix the colour.

Spray paint is fast and easy, and any aerosol from car colour to granite-effect craft spray can be used for stencils. A paint tray or ceramic palette will keep colours separate and is useful for mixing shades with a brush, but a saucer or tile serves the same purpose and is more useful for sponging.

CREATING STENCILS

A stencil is a negative image of a finished design. The basic shapes that form the image are cut from stencil card or acetate and the links that are left between the spaces are called "ties".

CARD STENCILS

Stencil card – lightly oiled Manila board – is strong and durable. It is particularly useful if you are going to repeat a design many times. Plastic stencil film is less long-lasting but quicker to use and easy to cut.

It also saves time when working on multi-layered or continuous designs. Using a heat knife (a pointed tool, which melts through the plastic) will speed up the stencil-making process even further.

Using tracing paper

When transferring a design with tracing paper use this method for an actual-size template. Fix tracing paper over the design with low-tack masking tape, then draw over the outlines using a sharp pencil. Remove the tape and turn the paper over. Rub the back of the lines with a soft pencil. Turn the paper and tape it centrally to a piece of stencil card, then redraw the shapes with a ballpoint pen.

Using carbon paper

When transferring a design with carbon paper, enlarge or reduce the template to the required size on a scanner or a photocopier. Place the copy centrally on the stencil board and slip a piece of carbon paper, face down, underneath. Tape the edges securely to the stencil board with low-tack masking tape. Draw carefully around each outline with a ballpoint pen, pressing firmly but smoothly.

Cutting out

Tape the stencil card securely to a self-healing cutting mat or a piece of thick card (stock) with low-tack masking tape. Using a sharp-bladed craft knife, cut along each line at a time within the shapes. It is much easier to start with the largest elements of the stencil, then tackle the more detailed, intricate areas. Always cut towards yourself turning the board with your free hand as necessary, but with care, to create smooth curves. Don't worry if you slice through a tie (one of the card "bridges" that link the cut out shapes): they are easily repaired with adhesive tape.

PLASTIC STENCILS

The benefit of using plastic stencils such as acetate is that you do not have to transfer the design but can cut the shape out directly.

Preparing to cut

Place a sheet of glass (tape the edges if they are rough) over the page of the book or photocopy you have chosen. Cut a piece of plastic at least 5cm/2in larger all round than the design and tape it to the glass with low-tack masking tape. Peel this off carefully when the stencil is complete. For extra security, you can lightly spray the back with spray mount.

Using a craft knife

Always use a sharp craft knife to cut around each element within the design as for a card stencil, but take extra care because the blade is more liable to slip on the smooth surface of the glass than it is on card. Remove the tape, lift the design and check that nothing has been missed out. Neaten any rough edges with the knife or a small pair of curved blade scissors.

Using a heat knife

When cutting out with a knife, read the manufacturer's instructions carefully before starting and practise on an offcut or spare piece of acetate to get the hang of using the knife before you start. Always use a sharp blade to give a cleaner line and make sure the blade is secure. Trace the point of the knife steadily around each outline, without pressing too hard and keeping an even pressure. If you work too slowly the line will be too wide so trace each element smoothly in a single motion.

APPLYING COLOUR

There are several different ways of colouring in a stencil with acrylic paints. You can use a brush, sponge or foam roller and each will produce its own individual look. Take inspiration from the suggestions shown here, then test each tool to see which effects best suits your style of work and decorative theme.

BRUSH EFFECTS

A single stencil can be used in many ways by applying paint in different colours and textures. The examples on the next few pages show you how to create just some of the many possible paint effects. Experiment and try them out before you start work on an actual project. Start off by securing the stencil to the surface being decorated with masking tape (use the low-tack version which will not damage the background) or spray mount. This adhesive keeps the whole stencil flat, reducing the risk of paint seeping under the edges, but should only be used in a well-ventilated space. Wipe the stencil clean of paint and glue when you have finished working. An acetate stencil can be washed in soapy water and dried on kitchen paper.

Using a stencil brush

Dip the flat tip of the stencil brush into a saucer of paint, then remove the surplus by rubbing the bristles on to kitchen paper in a circular motion. Avoid overloading: it is better to apply two light coats of paint rather than one heavy one. Always wash the bristles in warm soapy water when the paint builds up and when changing colours – a quick blast from a hairdryer will speed up the drying process.

Blocked colour

Always hold the brush lightly at right angles when stencilling, so that the paint will not get underneath the stencil itself and smudge the outline. Load the brush and dab it up and down within the stencil. You should be making a tapping movement rather than sweeping the brush as when painting. Build up the paint gradually to produce a solid block of colour and wait until it is dry before removing the stencil.

Stippled colour

This technique can be used to create differently shaded elements within a stencil to give the finished design an almost three-dimensional appearance. Block the colour as above for the darkest parts (around the outer edge of the petals in this example) and apply the same colour much more sparsely to the lighter areas. Take time to build up layers of colour and rework the stencil until you are pleased with the result.

Using more than one colour

If you are using two or more colours on a stencil, it is important to use just one paint at a time, changing or washing the brushes in between use to keep the elements distinct and the colours clean. If the different coloured sections are adjacent, use strips of low-tack masking tape or a piece of paper to protect the areas that are not being painted.

Multicoloured stippling

It is possible to create a huge range of textures and great depth of colour by applying several colours to a stencil. Here the outside edges of the petals have been stippled in solid pink, which fades through to a soft orange. In contrast, the star-shaped flower centre is more solid and the dense colour of the leaves is broken up with pink stippling.

Dry brushing

As its name suggests, this paint effect uses only a very small amount of paint. Load the stencil brush, then wipe most of the paint off on to kitchen paper. Fill in the shapes with light, straight strokes, allowing a little of the background colour to show through as you apply each successive layer. Here, all the strokes have been made from the centre outwards.

Using a sponge

Sponging is a good way to fill a large or small stencil with interesting texture. You can use a synthetic household sponge for dense colour, but natural sponges give a more open and varied effect. Dip the sponge into the paint, remove the excess by dabbing it on to newspaper or kitchen towel then dab it lightly over the stencil.

Using a roller

Sponge rollers can be used to apply a coat of a single colour or, as here, to produce subtly blended effects. Put a blob of each paint in a saucer, in a short line. Push the dry roller over the paint and roll it backwards and forwards until the edges are blurred, then roll it over the stencil.

Stippling from the edges

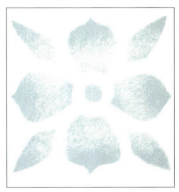

Using a very dry stencil brush (dab most of the paint off the bristles before you start), stipple from the outside of the design, working inwards. By the time you get to the centre, there should be hardly any paint left on your brush, ensuring a very soft paint effect in this area.

PAINT EFFECTS

A stencil brush, versatile as it may be, is not the only way to apply paint through a stencil. Sponging and rolling are both very quick and effective alternative techniques, particularly if you are going to repeat the design across a large area, such as a wall. As with brush effects, it is a good idea to have several sponges or brushes to hand when working on a stencil that uses more than one colour. Pour a small amount of each paint into a separate saucer so that the colours do not become mixed and keep each to hand.

Sponge effect

The open texture of a natural sponge makes it ideal for building up layers of colour. The holes within it produce round or oval spaces within the paint surface, which means that the previous layers are still visible. Try not to cover the background completely as a few white speckles make the finished design look bright and lively.

Sponge roller effect

Sponge rollers – cylinders of sponge fixed on to a plastic handle – come in widths from 2.5cm/1in up to 15cm/6in. Use narrow ones for details and wider ones for applying a first coat to the stencil or covering bigger spaces. When working on a multicoloured design, mask off the areas that are not to be painted, because the roller is not as precise as a brush.

Adding a drop shadow

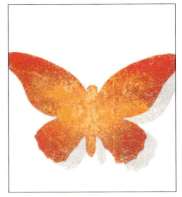

A drop shadow is a deceptively simple way of giving a sophisticated feeling of depth to a flat motif. Decide where the finished design is to go, then position the stencil slightly below and to the right of that position. Stipple the right-hand side of the design lightly in grey paint. When dry, stencil the main design above and to the left of the shadow.

Adding texture

There are several different texture gels available from good craft stores, all designed for use with artist's acrylic paints. The gels range from ground pumice stone to very small plastic balls, or metallic glitter. They are stirred into the paint, which is then stippled thickly on to the stencil. A simple do-it-yourself grainy texture can, however, easily be produced by adding grains of sand to acrylic paint or using powdered multipurpose filler.

SPECIAL PAINTS

Several of the projects in this book
use artist's acrylic paint, which has
many advantages. It is relatively
cheap and economic to use,
readily available, and it comes in
a wide spectrum of colours and
can be mixed to create myriad
others. It also dries quickly and
can be washed from brushes,
rollers or sponges with warm,
soapy water. There are, of course,
many alternatives, each of which
has its own individual character
and purpose. Some of them are
illustrated here and once you
have tried them, search the
shelves of your local art store
and experiment with glitter paints,
wax crayons, oil sticks, translucent
glass paints or watercolours.

Using spray paint

When using an aerosol it is important
that you mask off the surrounding area
completely with sheets of newspaper.
However carefully you spray the paint,
small particles inevitably hover in the air
and will mark any background that has
not been covered. You should also work
in a well-ventilated room or outdoors.

Spray paint effects

Mask off with card or masking tape all
the parts of the stencil that are not being
used before applying the first colour.
Press the button and move the can across
the surface a few times. Build up several
thin layers of paint, rather than one thick
one, which will form a pool and seep
under the edges of the stencil.

Fabric paint

Wash and press the fabric or garment
before stencilling to remove any residue
from the manufacturing process. Tape
a length of spare fabric on to a pad of
newspaper (to absorb any excess paint
that goes through the fabric), or insert
a piece of card (stock) inside a garment
to protect the back. Once it is dry, heat-
fix the paint according to the
manufacturer's instructions.

Ceramic paint

Adhesive stencil film, used by graphic
artists, is very useful when painting on
glass or ceramic surfaces. Trace the
design in pencil, then remove the
backing and stick the film to a clean
surface. Use a sharp craft knife to cut
out the shapes, and apply the paint
sparingly with a brush, sponge or roller.
The finished object should then be fired
by baking it in the oven, as instructed by
the manufacturer.

Metallic wax

This creamy wax, used by gilders and
picture framers, comes in a range of
metallic shades from pale platinum and
gold through to bronze and pewter. Apply
it by wrapping your forefinger in a piece
of soft cloth and rubbing your fingertip
over the surface of the wax. Transfer it to
the stencil by rubbing in small circles until
the surface appears burnished. More than
one colour can be applied for a luxurious
effect: apply the lightest shade first.

REGISTRATION MARKS

If a stencil has more than one component, the two parts must line up exactly. This is easy with acetate stencils, as the first layer of paint will be visible. It is more difficult with card stencils, so registration marks – small crosses or notches – cut into both stencils in the same position are used. They are transferred by pencil and the overlay is positioned so that the lines show through the second set of registration marks. Use them also for a repeated border where the motifs overlap to create the finished design.

BORDERS AND TWO-LAYERED STENCILS

Elegant stencilled borders provide the finishing touch in a room. They are ideal for creating "frames" and panel effects. Use them to define space, such as a dado (chair) rail or to create a painted border around a floor.

Using a card stencil for a border

Each repeated motif should be positioned at the same level. Once you have transferred the stencil on to card, draw a line along the bottom edge of the design, continuing it out to the left and right edges. Draw a line and match the two up for each repeat. Transfer the registration marks at the beginning and end of each repeat on to the card and cut notches at these points. Transfer the second notch on to the surface with a pencil "V" and match the first notch up to this point each time the stencil is used.

Using acetate for a border

Clear sheets of acetate are much easier to use than card when stencilling borders. You can line them up by eye, rather than by using registration marks. It is still, however, important to draw a baseline on to the surface so that the stencil will be straight and horizontal. For two-layered stencils, the design can be lined up by eye. You can also transfer the registration marks with a waterproof pen and make small slits along them. Pencil a cross within these marks when the first layer has been finished and match the second stencil to them.

Two-layered stencils

When transferring the two elements that make up the design on to stencil card, draw in the cross-shaped registration marks. Carefully cut out each stencil, then rule in pencil lines to join up the four crosses, making a rectangle or square. Snip out the corners to make right-angled notches. Before removing the first stencil, make a two-sided pencil mark like an arrow tip along each corner. Position the second stencil within these marks and it will then be aligned precisely to the first.

ONE-OFF AND REVERSE STENCILS

Stencil-making does not always have to be time-consuming and formal, nor does it require specialist equipment. These one-off techniques show that stencilled decoration can also be spontaneous and unstructured. Use them for stationery or paper projects such as greetings cards or wrapping paper, or let your imagination run wild and stencil lacy patterns on to a silk scarf or a flurry of leaf outlines across a wall. Instead of starting with a negative image, as with a regular stencil, reverse stencils are in fact positive images, with outlines defined by the paint. Found natural objects, such as ferns or dried, pressed leaves, are a good source of unexpected shapes, or try using lace or paper doilies. Test your ideas on scrap paper.

Using leaves

Collect a selection of interestingly shaped autumn leaves and press them under a heavy book overnight. To use them as stencils, hold the leaf down with the fingers of one hand or fix to the surface with a reusable putty adhesive and block in colour around the edge, using a wide brush loaded with paint.

Using lace

Use a brush or aerosol spray paint to transfer the intricate designs of woven lace without distorting the fabric. Fix the lace on to the surface to be decorated with spray mount and mask off the surrounding area. Spray two or more light coats of paint across the surface, using even strokes, until the pattern is well defined.

Paper cuts

Simple, symmetrical designs that are going to be used just once can be cut from thin coloured paper. Fold the paper in half vertically and draw one side of a heart along the crease with a pencil. Cut out the shape with sharp scissors and flatten out the paper, then stencil as usual. Once you have mastered this quick and versatile technique, you could go on to make more complex designs, such as paper snowflakes, Christmas trees, or chains of little figures.

VARIATIONS ON A THEME

The stencils that appear in this book have each been designed with a specific project in mind – a complex wall treatment, a kitchen curtain, a cushion or a simple greetings card. All of them, however, can be altered and reinterpreted endlessly. There are many ways in which you can vary colour schemes, invert or reverse the motif, change the spacing, enlarge or reduce the design, or print it on an unexpected surface. You could overprint the same design too. Here are some ideas for creating different layouts and patterns. Use a little imagination, and you will be able to come up with countless variations of your own.

Positive and negative images

The negative image on the left – a pale flower branch in a single colour on a very dark green background – is a graphic design. It is, in fact, exactly the same design as the delicate spray on the right – a positive image that has been stencilled more conventionally in colour on white paper. Light-on-dark images always have strong visual impact. Try stencilling a white pattern on a pastel background for a more subtle, but still unusual look.

Mirror image

Any stencil design that is not symmetrical can be flipped over to create its mirror image. Paint the first motif as usual. Clean off any surplus paint from the stencil and leave it to dry. Turn it over, line up the stencil carefully opposite the first motif, and block in the second motif. This is a good way to create a simple border, by stencilling pairs of reversed motifs above a dado (chair) rail or below a ceiling coving (cove molding).

Repeating around a point

This pattern, in which a roughly square design has been repeated four times around a centre point, is reminiscent of a tiled wall. It can be copied with any symmetrical stencil. Draw two lines that intersect at right angles, then two more at 45 degrees to the first pair. Mark the base of the first motif, close to the centre point, then line the stencil up along the diagonal line. Stencil three more motifs on the diagonals, ensuring that they all start at the same distance along the lines.

Random repeats

A small, self-contained motif like this butterfly or a floral motif can be repeated at random across the surface. Use a single colour, or stencil each one in a different shade to produce a lively, interesting pattern, which would work equally well on a wall or on fabric.

Changing sizes

This pattern uses a pretty Japanese flower, which has been enlarged to make a bigger stencil. The combination of the two sizes gives vitality to the design, and shows just how many different ways there are of using a very simple motif to produce a sophisticated result.

Rotating with blocked leaves

Using a very dry brush with a tiny amount of paint, rotate the bristles in a circular motion. This rotating action leaves enough paint on the surface for a lighter, softer look than a block application. Use the same effect in a darker colour on the inside of the petals.

Rotating and soft shading

Using a very dry brush with a tiny amount of paint, place your brush on one side of the stencil and rotate the brush in small circles. Repeat this action, using a slightly darker colour on the edges of the stencil, to create the effect of soft shading.

Rotating and shading in two colours

This is a similar effect to rotating and soft shading, but is more directional. Using a very dry brush with a tiny amount of paint, place your brush in the centre of the flower and rotate the bristles slightly outwards. Repeat this action, using a slightly darker colour.

HALF-DROP REPEATS

A regular repeated design looks
very effective on a large expanse
of wall, giving the illusion of a
printed wallpaper pattern. Stencil
a few motifs roughly on to sheets
of paper, cut them out and tape
them to the wall before you begin,
to get an idea of the finished look.

The framework for the pattern
should be measured up very
carefully, especially in older
houses where walls and windows
may not be perfectly straight. Start
by marking a vertical line down
the left edge of the wall using
chalked builder's string and bear
in mind any fixed architectural
features such as light fittings,
chimney breasts (fireplace
projections), architraves (trims),
alcoves and corners that you will
need to work around.

1 To mark up the wall, decide how far apart the motifs are to lie, horizontally and
vertically. Cut a rectangle of card (stock) to these measurements and draw two
lines to divide it into quarters. Cut a notch at each end of the lines. Use the card as a
guide to draw a light pencil grid across the wall.

2 To stencil a half-drop repeat: in the same way, draw two
lines across the stencil and notch the ends. Use these
marks to match the stencil to the grid. Stencil in the first
horizontal row of motifs, then position the next row in the
spaces below. Continue until the wall is covered.

3 To make half-drop repeats on fabric, mark a grid on to
fabric, decide how far apart the motifs are to be, then fold
and press lightly along these lines. When the fabric is opened
out these lines will appear as creases, which will disappear when
the fabric is pressed once again.

PREPARING AND FINISHING

As with any home decorating project, whether it is painting an old wooden chair or putting a new paint effect on a wall, time invested in preparation pays off by giving you a professional result at the end. Don't be in too much of a hurry to start, plan carefully and work in an orderly way. Collect together all the equipment and tools you will need, including the cleaning materials for tidying up afterwards and a stack of old newspaper to protect the floor or work surface. An overall or smock will protect your clothes.

PREPARING WALLS

If you are working on a freshly plastered wall, make sure that it is completely dry before painting it with emulsion (latex) paint in your desired base colour. However clean they appear, previously decorated surfaces should always be washed down well with detergent or sugar soap to remove accumulated dust and grease. If you wish your stencils to have a more textured background than that which is given by flat emulsion paint, try using one of these simple paint effects on the wall.

Most modern acrylic paints are tough and waterproof, but your finished stencils may need to be sealed, especially in humid areas such as kitchens and bathrooms, or if they are in rooms which receive lots of wear and tear such as hallways and landings. Leave the painted surface to dry thoroughly for a week, then seal with matt (flat) varnish.

PREPARING WOOD

New or unprimed wood should be sanded down with medium- and then fine-grade abrasive paper. When the surface is smooth, wipe it over with a damp cloth to remove any residual dust and leave to dry. If you wish to darken the natural colour, use a wood stain, diluting it with water for a lighter shade and painting it in long strokes along the grain. Otherwise, prepare with a clear wood sealer. Water-based sealants are easier to use and do not have the yellowish hue of their oil-based equivalents. When the stencilling is complete, apply two coats of water-based varnish to give a hardwearing finish to the wood.

Colour washing

This can be done with a light paint on a darker background or vice versa, or for a more subtle look with two very closely toning colours. Dilute the second coat with water, adding more water for a lighter colour, then paint it on the wall using loose brushstrokes painted in one or many directions, or use a wide roller.

Sponging

Using a natural sea sponge creates an open texture and is a quick way to cover a large surface. Wash and rinse the sponge, then squeeze out the excess moisture. Dip it into a saucer of diluted emulsion (latex) paint then dab it on to the wall in a circular pattern or straight lines, depending on the effect required.

ABOVE: Always sand new or unprimed wood before stencilling to create a key.

WALLS AND SURFACES

Whether you wish to recreate an American folk art interior, paint an Indian-inspired paisley design to imitate wallpaper or add a bold one-off mural to your living space, a plain-coloured wall provides the perfect backdrop for large-scale stencilled design. This chapter also includes borders for walls and floors, a clever trompe l'oeil row of plates and ideas for enhancing architectural features such as fireplaces and windows.

ABOVE: These pretty faux plates add interest behind a plain country kitchen shelf.

LEFT: A repeated border adds style and individuality to simple white-washed floorboards.

GREEK URNS

Classic Greek urns softly outlined under a warm terracotta colourwash have a strong Mediterranean feel. The stencilling is worked in clear varnish so that the top colour slides over without adhering, leaving very subtly coloured motifs. Arrange the urns randomly over the wall for an informal and rustic finish. This effect works well in a kitchen or dining room and on slightly uneven walls. You can try different colour combinations or use a stronger coloured emulsion (latex) paint to create a bolder look. Other classic motifs include scrolls, abstract geometric shapes, formal decorative borders, animals, marine life, fruits, flora and fauna.

You will need

- emulsion (latex) paints in cream and terracotta
- large household sponge
- acetate sheet
- craft knife and self-healing cutting mat
- masking tape
- stencil brush
- satin acrylic varnish
- wallpaper paste
- clean cotton rag

1 Working in rough, sweeping strokes, rub a base coat of cream emulsion (latex) paint over the wall using a sponge. Trace the urn template at the back of the book and cut a stencil from acetate sheet using a sharp-bladed craft knife and cutting mat. Tape it to the wall and stencil with varnish. Reposition the stencil and cover the wall with randomly arranged urns.

2 Make up the wallpaper paste following the manufacturer's instructions on the pack. Mix one part terracotta emulsion with one part paste. This will make the colourwash slimy and slow down the drying time, preventing "joins" in the finished colourwash. Using a clean household sponge, dab lumps of the mixture over about 1m/3¹/₄ft square of the wall.

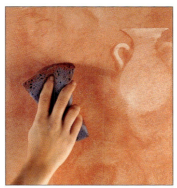

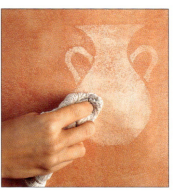

3 Immediately rub the wall in a clockwise circular motion to blur the sponge marks.

4 Continue dabbing on paint and blurring with the sponge to cover the whole wall. The varnished urns should be revealed underneath the colourwash.

5 If the urns are not clear enough, use a slightly damp rag and your index finger to rub off a little more colourwash from the varnished shapes. This can be done even after the wall has dried.

ABOVE: Experiment with other colour combinations. Try colourwashing duck-egg blue emulsion (latex) paint over a beige emulsion background as an alternative.

RIGHT: The stencils are placed at random and the effect is very subtle.

TROMPE-L'OEIL PLATES

A shelf full of decorative painted plates adds a witty touch to a kitchen corner. Follow these plate designs or translate your own patterned china into stencils to give a co-ordinated look. Why not add some individual plates to the wall as well?

You will need

- tracing paper and pen
- stencil card
- pencil
- ruler
- craft knife and self-healing cutting mat
- 23cm/9in diameter plate
- pair of compasses
- spray mount
- brown wrapping paper or newspaper
- masking tape
- spray paints in white, cream, a range of pinks and mauves, light green, dark green, red, blue and grey
- protective face mask

1 Cut three pieces of stencil card 30cm/12in square. Mark the centre of each card by measuring the centre of each edge and ruling a horizontal and a vertical line across each card to join the marks.

2 Draw a line 3.5cm/1¼in in from all four edges of each card. Place the plate in the centre of the card and draw around the edge. Cut out the plate shape from the first piece of stencil card (stencil 1).

3 Using a pair of compasses, draw a circle from the centre point about 4cm/1½in from the edge of the plate on the two remaining pieces of yellow stencil card.

4 Trace or photocopy the plate template at the back of the book to the desired size and carefully transfer the floral design to the second piece of stencil card.

5 Cut out the design using a craft knife and cutting mat. Cut out the smaller areas first and the larger areas last (stencil 2). On the third piece of stencil card, cut out the inner circle (stencil 3).

6 Draw a faint horizontal pencil line on the wall and put two marks 30cm/12in apart on the line to act as a guide for positioning the stencils. Spray the back of the plate stencil (1) with spray mount and place in position on the wall. Press down firmly to ensure a good contact. Mask off the surrounding area with paper and masking tape, leaving no gaps. Wearing a protective face mask, spray white and cream spray paint on to the stencil. Remove the masks and stencil.

7 Attach the flower stencil (2) to the wall with spray mount, lining it up with the marks on the wall. Mask off the surrounding area. Stick small pieces of masking tape over the leaves on the stencil. Wearing a protective face mask, spray the flowers with pinks and mauves, applying a fine layer of paint in short sharp puffs. Try each paint colour on the mask surrounding the stencil to test the colour and to make sure that the nozzle is clear.

8 Remove the masking tape from the leaves. Fold a small piece of stencil card in half and use it to shield the rest of the stencil from any spray paint. Spray the leaves using light and dark green paints, trying not to get too much green on the flowers.

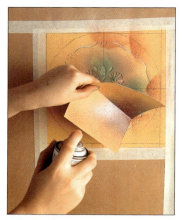

9 Cut a small hole in a piece of stencil card and use it to spray the centres of the flowers green.

10 Hold the shield of card around the dot designs on the border, and spray each one with red paint. Spray blue paint over the wavy lines on the border. Again, do not apply too much paint. Remove the masks then carefully remove the stencil.

11 Spray the back of the last stencil (3) with spray mount and position it on the wall. Mask off the surrounding area as before. Spray a fine mist of grey paint over the top left-hand side and bottom right-hand side of the plate design to create a shadow. Aim the nozzle slightly away from the stencil to ensure that hardly any paint hits the wall. Remove the masks and stencil.

12 Reposition stencil 1 on the wall and spray a very fine mist of blue paint around the edge of the plate. Repeat all stages along the edge of the shelf length.

RIGHT: The design for these trompe l'oeil plates can be adapted to the colour scheme in your kitchen or to match your own crockery.

KITCHEN ALCOVE

Stencil rows of china crockery and glassware along shelves to create a trompe l'oeil effect. Because the design is minimal this stencil would also make a great backdrop to a set of real shelves in a kitchen alcove. You can use emulsion (latex) paints to suit your own kitchen colour scheme or follow the colourways given here.

You will need

♦ masking tape
♦ spirit level
♦ tracing paper and pen
♦ acetate or stencil card
♦ craft knife and self-healing cutting mat
♦ soft pencil
♦ ceramic tile
♦ flat paintbrush
♦ stencil brush
♦ emulsion (latex) paints in dark sage green and cream
♦ eraser

1 Stick a length of masking tape across the wall to designate the top shelf. Check the level with a spirit level and adjust if necessary.

2 Stick a length of masking tape immediately above and below the first tape. Peel off the first tape. Mask the position of two more shelves 18cm/7in apart below the top shelf. Check the position of the shelves with a spirit level as before. Tape vertically across the ends of the shelves.

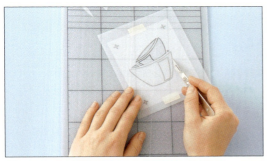

3 Trace the glassware and crockery templates at the back of the book. Cut out using a craft knife and cutting mat. You will need two stencils for each item – the glassware or crockery then the highlights.

4 Apply a thin coat of dark sage green paint on a ceramic tile with a flat paintbrush. Dab at the paint with a stencil brush and stencil the shelves holding the stencil brush upright and moving it in a circular motion.

5 Leave the paint to dry completely then carefully pull off the low-tack masking tape to reveal the straight edges of the shelves. You are now ready to stencil the glassware and the crockery.

6 Tape the bottle stencil to the wall, placing the lower registration marks on the lower edge of the top shelf. Mark the top registration marks and the top of the lower registration marks on the tape with a soft pencil. Stencil in the bottle.

7 Remove the stencil when it is completely dry. Tape the bottle highlight stencil to the wall, matching up the registration marks. Stencil the highlight in cream paint. Remove the stencil.

8 Tape the glass stencil to the wall, matching the lower right-hand registration mark of the bottle with the lower left-hand registration mark of the glass. Stencil the glass in dark sage green. Remove the stencil then stencil the highlight in cream.

9 Move the glass stencil along the wall, taping it in place matching the right-hand registration marks of the first glass with the left-hand registration marks of the second glass. Stencil the second glass and highlight as before. Continue stencilling a row of three glasses along the shelf always matching the registration marks.

10 Tape the cup stencil to the wall above the middle shelf, marking the registration marks as before. Stencil the cup in dark sage green then the highlight in cream. Move the stencil along the wall to work a row of three cups, matching the right-hand registration marks of the last cup with the left-hand registration marks of the next cup.

11 Tape the pot stencil to the wall above the bottom shelf, marking the registration marks as before. Stencil the pot in dark sage green. Leave to dry then remove the stencil. Tape the pot highlight stencil to the wall matching the registration marks. Stencil the highlights in cream paint. Remove the stencil.

12 Move along the bottom shelf to tape the bowls stencil to the wall above the bottom shelf, matching the lower right-hand registration mark of the pot with the lower left-hand registration mark of the bowls. Stencil the bowls in dark sage green then the highlights in cream. Erase the registration marks when complete.

FRENCH COUNTRY KITCHEN

This curtain design is adapted from the pattern on a French Art Deco soup bowl found in a fleamarket in Brussels. The flower design is also echoed in the hand-stencilled tiles and teams perfectly with the simple chequerboard border for a country look.

1 Press the muslin (cheesecloth) to remove any creases, then fold it lengthways in accordion-style folds. Press lightly to mark the creases, then fold it widthways in accordion-style folds and press again. These squares will act as a guide for positioning the motifs. Cover the work surface with newspaper and tape down the muslin so that it is taut.

2 Trace the three floral templates and the border template at the back of the book and cut out the stencils from stencil card using a craft knife and cutting mat. Spray the back of one stencil with spray mount and, starting at the top right, lightly stencil the first motif.

3 Alternating the stencils as you work, stencil flowers in every other square over the whole curtain, leaving 15cm/6in free at the lower edge.

4 Stencil the blue chequerboard border along the bottom, lining up the stencil each time by matching the last two squares of the previous motif with the first two of the next stencil. Press the fabric well using a pressing cloth and iron.

5 Press under and slip-stitch a 1cm/½in double hem around the sides and lower edge of the curtains. Make a 2.5cm/1in double hem along the top edge.

6 Measure the top edge of the curtain and, using dressmaker's chalk, mark it into sections about 20cm/8in apart. Cut a 25cm/10in piece of cotton tape for each mark. Fold the first piece of tape in half and stitch to the back of the first mark. Sew a button on to the front of the curtain to anchor the tape. Repeat all the way along the edge then tie the finished curtain on to the curtain pole in bows.

7 For the tiles, cut a piece of stencil card to fit the tile. Cut out the three floral stencils using a craft knife and cutting mat.

8 Cover the work surface with newspaper. Using red spray paint, spray over the stencil lightly and evenly. Leave to dry, then remove the stencil.

RIGHT: The co-ordinating tiles can be used individually as pot stands or set in the wall among plain white tiles.

HERALDIC DINING ROOM

L end an atmosphere of medieval luxury to your dining room with richly coloured red, blue and gold walls and traditional heraldic motifs stencilled in the same deep tones. Gilt accessories, heavy fabrics, brocades and a profusion of candles team well with this decor. All that remains is to prepare a sumptuous banquet.

ABOVE: Richly coloured walls and heraldic motifs are stencilled in the same deep tones to lend an atmosphere of luxury.

1 Using a large household or decorator's sponge, rub camel emulsion (latex) paint all over the wall. Leave to dry.

2 Repeat the process using a generous amount of deep red emulsion so that it almost covers the camel, giving a slightly mottled effect. Leave to dry.

3 Using a ruler and spirit level, draw a light pencil line at dado (chair) rail height. Stick a line of low-tack masking tape just above it.

4 Sponge deep purple emulsion all over the wall below the masking tape to give a slightly mottled effect. Leave to dry completely, then remove the masking tape.

5 Trace the heraldic templates at the back of the book and cut the stencils from acetate sheet using a sharp-bladed craft knife and cutting mat. Secure the rose stencil above the dividing line and stencil in purple emulsion, using a stencil brush. When it is dry, position the fleur-de-lys stencil next to the rose and stencil in camel emulsion. Continue to alternate the stencils around the room.

6 Place the highlighting stencils over the painted motifs and, using a stencil brush, add purple highlights to the camel fleurs-de-lys and camel highlights to the purple roses.

7 Flip the stencils over and position as mirror images below the previously stencilled motifs. Stencil the roses in camel and the fleurs-de-lys in red.

8 Add in the highlights as before, using camel emulsion on the fleurs-de-lys and purple emulsion on the camel roses.

9 Using a fine lining brush and camel paint, paint a narrow line where the red and purple paints meet. If you do not have the confidence to do this freehand, position two rows of masking tape on the wall, leaving a small gap in between. When the line is dry, remove the tape.

OPPOSITE: Create a medieval dining room with these decorative stencils and add gilt accessories, heavy fabrics and a profusion of candles to complete the look.

CLASSICAL URN PANELS

A traditional Wedgwood blue colour scheme is ideal for this design of elegant urns set within a coach line frame. For a simpler effect, stencil the frame and omit the urns.

You will need

- low-tack masking tape
- scissors
- flat paintbrush
- emulsion (latex) paints in mid-blue and pale blue
- ceramic tile
- stencil brush
- piece of card (stock)
- tracing paper and pen
- stencil card
- craft knife and self-healing cutting mat
- metal ruler
- spray mount
- soft pencil

1 Using masking tape, mask off a rectangle at least 45cm/18in wide. Mask off another rectangle 1.5cm/⅝in inside the first rectangle to create a frame for the urn to sit within.

2 Cut four pieces of masking tape 6mm/¼in wide. Stick the tapes diagonally across the corners of the frame. This will create a three-dimensional effect when stencilled.

3 Using a flat paintbrush, spread a thin coat of mid-blue paint on to a ceramic tile. Dab at the paint with a stencil brush and stencil two adjacent sides of the frame. Protect the diagonal ends of the unpainted sides with a piece of card (stock).

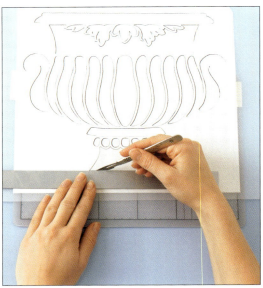

4 Blend the mid-blue and pale blue paint together and stencil the other sides of the frame. Leave to dry completely then peel off the tapes to reveal the neat, straight edges of the frame.

5 Trace the templates at the back of the book. Tape a piece of stencil card to the tracing. Using a craft knife and cutting mat cut out the stencils, cutting straight lines against a metal ruler.

6 Using spray mount, stick one urn stencil within the frame. Paint a thin coat of mid-blue paint on to the tile. Dab at the paint with the stencil brush and stencil the urn. Leave to dry.

7 Blend mid-blue and pale blue paint together and then shade the centre of the urn to highlight the urn and create its rounded appearance. Leave to dry and remove the stencil.

RENAISSANCE HALLWAY

Turn your hallway into a dramatic entrance with ornate stencils and rich lustrous colours. Combine them with gold accessories, velvets and braids to complete the theatrical and luxurious setting. This design would also be ideal for creating an intimate atmosphere in a dining room, perfect for candlelit dinners.

You will need

- ruler
- spirit level
- pencil
- masking tape
- emulsion (latex) paints in pale slate-blue, terracotta and pale peach
- large household sponge
- stencil brushes
- stencil card
- craft knife and self-healing cutting mat
- stencil paints in dark grey-blue, terracotta, emerald and turquoise

1 Using a ruler and spirit level, divide the wall in half horizontally with a pencil line, then draw a second line 15cm/6in above the first. Stick a line of masking tape just below this top line. Dilute one part slate-blue emulsion (latex) paint with one part water and colour the top half of the wall using a household sponge.

2 Stick masking tape just above the bottom pencil line. Dilute one part terracotta emulsion paint with one part water and sponge over the lower half of the wall.

3 Sponge lightly over the terracotta paint with slate-blue emulsion (latex) paint to add a textural effect. Remove the strips of masking tape once you have covered the whole of the wall.

4 Colour the centre band with diluted peach emulsion, using a stencil brush. Trace the templates at the back of the book and cut out the stencils from stencil card using a craft knife and cutting mat.

5 Stencil the wall motifs at roughly regular intervals over the upper part of the wall, using dark grey-blue stencil paint, keeping the brush upright and moving it in a circular motion. Rotate the stencil with every alternate motif to give movement to the design.

6 Starting at the right-hand side of the peach band, stencil the border motif with terracotta stencil paint. Add details in emerald and turquoise. Continue along the wall, positioning the stencil beside the previous motif so that the spaces are equal, creating a balanced effect.

FOLK ART WALL

This combination of border patterns and larger single motifs is typical of the stencil designs used by the itinerant painters who worked in the American colonies in the early 19th century. There was little anxiety about whether patterns turned the corners accurately, it was the harmonious colour schemes that made the result so successful.

You will need

♦ acetate sheet
♦ craft knife and self-healing cutting mat
♦ spray mount
♦ stencil paint in brick red and dull green
♦ two stencil brushes
♦ plumbline

ABOVE: This door was painted but you could easily stencil heart motifs instead.

1 Enlarge the templates at the back of the book on a photocopier. Cut out from acetate sheet using a craft knife and cutting mat. Spray the border stencil lightly with spray mount and align it with either the picture or the dado (chair) rail.

2 Begin stencilling the border design, using a separate stencil brush for each colour.

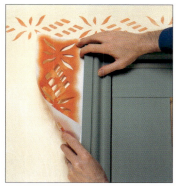

3 If your stencil is an acetate sheet you will be able to see where the second stencil meets the first; if you are using stencil card place it above the first and lift the bottom corner to check that it is in position.

4 Turn the stencil to make the border panels, using a plumbline from the ceiling in order to check the borders are aligned. Repeat this process to frame the room with as many stencilled panels as you need.

5 Using dull green paint, stencil the willow trees in the centre of the panels, one above the other, keeping the stencil brush upright and moving it in a circular motion. The tree looks best with a bit of space all around it.

PENNSYLVANIA DUTCH TULIPS

This American folk art inspired idea uses the rich colours and simple motifs beloved by the German and Dutch immigrants to Pennsylvania. Create the effect of all-over handpainted wallpaper or, for a beginner's project, take a single motif and use it to decorate a cabinet, a chest of drawers or the top of a wooden chest.

You will need

- dark ochre emulsion (latex) paint
- large and small decorator's paintbrushes
- woodwash in indigo blue and mulberry
- tracing paper
- stencil card
- craft knife and self-healing cutting mat
- ruler
- pencil
- masking tape
- stencil brushes
- stencil paints in red, light green, dark green and pale brown
- clean cotton rag
- artist's brush

1 Dilute one part ochre emulsion (latex) paint with one part water. Using a large decorator's paintbrush, cover the top half of the wall. Use vertical brushstrokes for an even texture.

2 Paint the lower half of the wall, underneath the dado (chair) rail if there is one, with indigo blue woodwash. Finish with a curving line using a dry brush to suggest woodgrain.

3 Using a small decorator's paintbrush, paint the dado rail or a strip at dado-rail height in mulberry woodwash.

4 Trace the tulip and heart template from the back of the book. Cut the stencils from stencil card using a craft knife and cutting mat. Mark the centre of each edge of the stencil. Measure the wall and divide it into equal sections, so that the repeats will fall at about 20cm/8in intervals. Mark the positions lightly in pencil, so they can be erased later.

5 Tape the first stencil in position using low-tack masking tape. Dip a medium stencil brush into red stencil paint. Rub the brush on a white tile, saucer or rag until it is almost dry before stencilling in the tulips. Leave to dry.

6 Paint the leaves in light green stencil paint with darker green shading. Paint the stems in dark green using a fine stencil brush. Leave to dry.

8 Stencil a single heart between the two baskets of tulips using a very little red stencil paint.

7 Lightly stencil the tulip basket in pale brown stencil paint using a chunky stencil brush and a small amount of paint.

RIGHT: Decorate a matching key cupboard or storage box following the same method and using just one motif in the centre. You could alter the colour of the tulips if you so wish.

OPPOSITE: These vibrant colours will instantly lift a dull hallway, bringing a touch of spring into your home with the use of a charming floral theme.

PAISLEY PATTERN WALL

The paisley or pine motif originated in India, where it has been used in painted, woven and embroidered decoration for centuries. This interpretation in soft earthy tones could be used for a living or dining room in either a traditional or contemporary setting.

1 Paint the wall with one or two coats of pale terracotta emulsion (latex) paint, depending on the density of colour you require. Leave to dry.

2 Cut a rectangle of paper 30 x 40cm/ 12 x 16in. With a soft pencil, lightly pencil a grid across the wall drawing along the sides of the paper.

3 Enlarge the template at the back of the book on a photocopier. Transfer on to stencil card using carbon paper. Cut out using a craft knife and cutting mat, and transfer the registration marks. Draw a central cross on each, dividing it into quarters, then cut a notch at the end of each line. Spray the outline stencil with spray mount and line it up on the wall, matching the notches to the pencilled grid. Tape it down and draw in the registration marks.

OPPOSITE: The colours used in this enduring motif can be adapted to suit a room of your choice such as a study or hallway.

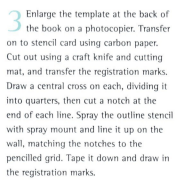

4 Using a large stencil brush, fill in the outline with cream paint, using a heavy stippling. Leave to dry.

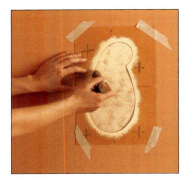

5 Fill in the remaining space with more paisley shapes, placing one in every other space in a half-drop or brick arrangement.

6 Using the registration marks and grid as a guide, tape the second stencil in place over the paisley outline once the paint has dried.

7 Using a smaller stencil brush and turquoise acrylic paint, stipple all over the design. Work in light strokes across the background shape.

8 Add a light stippling of terracotta paint over the central part of each motif.

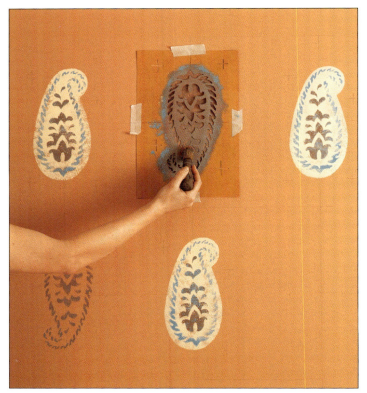

9 Fill in the rest of the paisley motifs in the same way. Any variation in colour will add interest and authenticity to the design.

10 Lightly paint a terracotta detail stencil in each remaining space, positioning the paisley the other way up. Erase all the pencil marks. If the wall is in an area where it will receive a lot of wear and tear, spray with two coats of matt (flat) varnish to protect the stencils.

LEAFY FIREPLACE SURROUND

This row of stylized leaves turns a plain fireplace into a bold design statement and adds an element of pattern and colour to an otherwise plain wall. Adapt the size and number of the motifs to suit the width of your mantelpiece.

You will need

- carbon paper
- sharp pencil
- stencil card
- craft knife and self-healing cutting mat
- ruler
- soft pencil
- set square (triangle)
- stencil brush
- dark green stencil paint
- eraser

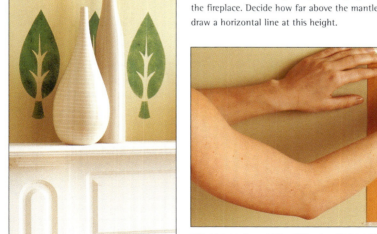

1 Enlarge the template at the back of the book and trace it on to stencil card. Using a craft knife and cutting mat cut it out, leaving a 3cm/1¼in border at each side edge and a 1cm/½in border along the bottom. Draw in a vertical line along the centre of the leaf. Using soft pencil, lightly draw a vertical line to mark the centre of the fireplace. Decide how far above the mantelpiece you wish the border to be and draw a horizontal line at this height.

2 Line up the middle of the stencil along the centre point with the bottom edge on the horizontal line.

3 Stipple in the first leaf using a large stencil brush. Apply the paint in a slightly uneven way to give texture to the motif: stipple two coats, if necessary, to create the desired effect.

4 To space the leaves regularly, position the stencil so that the right-hand edge of the card almost touches the left-hand edge of the previous leaf.

5 Continue stencilling a row of leaves towards the left-hand end of the mantlepiece, then work towards the right-hand edge in the same way. Make sure that the motifs are all spaced evenly and that the design is symmetrical.

6 Mark the position of the final leaf on the left by drawing a guideline downwards from the outside edge of the last stencil. Decide how far down you wish the leaf to be – this will be roughly half the height of the leaf, depending on the shape of the fireplace.

7 Stencil in the leaf. Repeat at the right-hand end, making sure that the two final leaves are at the same height. Erase the pencil mark. For a more subtle look you could paint the leaves in a more pastel shade of green, or use an autumnal deep red or brown for a warmer effect.

OPPOSITE: *The fresh green leaves make a good contrast against the soft green background wall.*

ELEGANT ROSE TREE

Create a dramatic effect on a wall with this beautiful and elegant rose tree. Full-bloom roses, buds and leaves are stencilled along the painted branches. The tree can be worked as large or small as you wish. The background wall was painted in soft pink emulsion (latex) but you can adapt this colour if you so wish.

You will need

- tracing paper and pen
- masking tape
- stencil card
- craft knife and self-healing cutting mat
- soft pencil
- medium artist's brush
- acrylic paints in brown, dusky pink and purple
- eraser
- ceramic tile
- flat paintbrush
- stencil brush

1 Trace the rose, leaves and bud templates from the back of the book. Tape to the stencil card and cut out using a craft knife and cutting mat. Use a soft pencil to very lightly draw a trunk and branches for the rose tree on the wall.

2 ▼ Using a medium artist's brush, paint the trunk along the pencil lines with brown acrylic paint.

OPPOSITE: A dusky pink background tones well with the warm colours of the tree.

3 Tape the rose stencil to the wall at the top of the trunk. If the rose covers the pencil lines, gently rub them away with an eraser. Apply a thin coat of dusky pink paint to a ceramic tile with a flat paintbrush. Dab at the paint with a stencil brush and stencil the rose, holding the stencil brush upright and moving it in a circular motion.

4 Stencil the leaves a few times around the rose using brown acrylic paint and a small stencil brush.

5 The rose, leaves and bud stencils are worked outwards along the branches from the first rose. As you work, erase any pencil lines that will be covered by the stencils. Blend dusky pink and purple paint together on the tile for the buds.

6 Continue stencilling the roses, leaves and buds along the branches. Apply some leaves singly, masking the surrounding leaves on the stencil with card to protect them from any splashes of paint.

7 Apply the stencils to the outer reaches of the branches and continue the stencilling.

8 Stencil leaves or buds at the ends of the branches using card to protect the roses.

9 Stencil single leaves in any of the gaps, masking the surrounding leaves as before. Using the medium artist's brush, carefully paint in the branches, radiating outwards from the trunk.

10 Add a few stems to the leaves with brown paint using the medium artist's brush. Stand back from the tree to see if there are any obvious gaps that could be filled with a bud or leaves and then stencil them in place.

JAPANESE ORANGE BLOSSOM WALL

Inspired by delicate Japanese silk hangings, this blossom and bamboo design is made up from two versatile stencils, which can be adapted and rearranged in an endless variety of ways to fill any space, from a small recess to an entire wall.

You will need

♦ masking tape
♦ large sheet of acetate
♦ sheet of glass
♦ heat knife
♦ spray mount
♦ stencil brushes
♦ acrylic paints in pale jade, dark green, light brown, apricot and pink

1 Enlarge the templates at the back of the book and make up the acetate. Spray the back of the bamboo stencil lightly with spray mount and tape in place. Lightly stipple the whole motif in pale jade paint.

2 Add a little dark green paint to the jade acrylic paint and mix the colours thoroughly. Stipple the ends of the leaves with a light, tapping action to give depth to the shape and a three-dimensional look.

3 Using a fine brush and a small amound of paint stencil a light brown layer over the green stems. Do the same on each stem across the design.

4 Stencil one or more additional branch designs around the first, using the same colours. You can use parts of the stencil to fill in smaller areas.

5 Fix the blossom stencil in position and stipple in the stems with jade green paint. Add a darker colour along the edges as before.

6 Using a soft brush, stencil in the flowers and buds using apricot paint. Be careful not to overload the brush to maintain a delicate effect.

7 Add soft pink shading to the outer edges of the blossom flowers and the buds to give them a three-dimensional look.

8 Choose part of the bamboo stencil to add further foliage to the motifs and stipple in the design as before, using the same colours.

9 Single flowers or small sprigs can be added using parts of the blossom motif. Mask off the parts of the stencil that are not being used with tape, if necessary.

10 Using the dark green paint and the third stencil, add the stamens to the blossom flowers. Vary the angle of the stencil for each group of flowers.

STAR BATHROOM

This misty blue colour scheme is ideal for a bathroom or staircase because the lower part of the wall is varnished to provide a practical wipe-clean surface. The tinted varnish deepens the colour and gives it a sheen that contrasts well with the chalky distemper (tempera) paint above. The star is a traditional quilting motif.

You will need

- tracing paper and pen
- scissors
- spray mount
- stencil card
- craft knife and self-healing cutting mat
- soft blue distemper (tempera) paint or chalk-based paint
- large decorator's paintbrushes
- straightedge
- spirit level
- soft pencil
- clear satin water-based varnish and brush
- Prussian blue artist's acrylic paint

1 Trace the star template from the back of the book and cut out. Lightly spray the back with spray mount and stick to the stencil card.

2 Cut out the star using a craft knife and cutting mat. Cut inwards from the points towards the centre so that the points stay crisp.

3 Taking a corner first, carefully peel away the paper template on the top to reveal the stencil underneath.

4 Dilute the paint, if necessary, according to the manufacturer's instructions. Brush it onto the wall with sweeping, random strokes to give a colourwashed effect.

5 Using a straightedge and spirit level, draw a pencil line across the wall at the height you want to end the darker varnished surface.

6 Tint the satin water-based varnish with a squeeze of Prussian blue acrylic paint. Using a separate decorator's brush, apply this on the lower part of the wall up to the marked line.

7 Spray the back of the stencil with spray mount and position at one end of the wall, 5cm/2in above the marked line. Stencil with the tinted varnish, using a broad sweep of the brush. Repeat along the wall, spacing the stars evenly.

BATHROOM FRIEZE

reate a mosaic border on a tiled splashback using ceramic paints, available from art and craft shops. The mosaic design works well as a frieze because the narrow silver bands match up to create continuous lines flowing across the tiles.

1 Trace the template at the back of the book. Tape the tracing to a piece of stencil card. Using a craft knife and cutting mat, cut out the stencils along the solid outer lines. You will need two stencils – the mosaics and the silver bands.

2 Spray the back of the mosaic stencil with spray mount. Stick it to a tile, matching the outer edges and smoothing the stencil outwards from the centre. Stick masking tape around the outer edges to protect the surrounding area from paint.

3 Using a flat paintbrush, spread a thin coat of blue paint on to a spare tile. Dab at the paint with a stencil brush and stencil the mosaics holding the stencil brush perpendicular to the tiles and moving it in a circular motion. Leave to dry then remove the stencil.

4 Spray the back of the silver bands stencil with spray mount. Stick it to the tile, matching the outer edges. Mask off the surrounding area at the ends of the bands with masking tape. Stencil the bands with silver paint. Leave to dry. Repeat on the remaining tiles.

MAKING SANDCASTLES

Evocative of childhood summers spent on the beach, sandcastles are simple, colourful shapes to stencil. Perfect for a child's room or for a bathroom, they will bring a touch of humour to your walls. Instead of stencilling the flags you can glue on paper flags for added interest.

You will need

- emulsion (latex) paints in blue and white
- decorator's paintbrush
- household sponge
- acetate sheet
- craft knife and self-healing cutting mat
- tape measure
- soft pencil
- masking tape
- stencil paints in yellow, black and other colours of your choice
- stencil brushes
- fine artist's paint brush
- coloured paper (optional)
- PVA (white) glue (optional)

1 Paint below the dado (chair) rail height in blue emulsion (latex) paint. When dry, lightly rub on white emulsion with a sponge. Trace the templates at the back of the book. Cut the stencils from an acetate sheet using a craft knife and cutting mat.

2 Measure the wall to calculate how many sandcastles you can fit on and make very light marks with a soft pencil at regular intervals. Hold the stencil above the dado rail and secure the corners with low-tack masking tape.

3 Using the yellow stencil paint and a thick stencil brush, stencil in the first sandcastle. Repeat for the other sandcastles.

OPPOSITE: Vary the colours of the central stars and the flags but work within a chosen colour palette.

4 Stencil each flag in a different colour of your choice.

5 When the paint has dried, stencil a star on each sandcastle in a contrasting colour of paint.

6 Using a fine artist's paintbrush and black stencil paint, carefully paint in the flagpoles.

7 Continue stencilling the sandcastles along the wall, using your pencil marks to position them.

8 As an alternative to stencilling the flags, cut triangles of coloured paper and glue them to the wall with PVA (white) glue, then paint in the flagpoles.

FLAG STENCILS

This strong graphic design will add colour and fun to a child's room or a study. The easiest way to make a stencil is to photocopy a simple motif on to acetate sheet. Here, two complementary flag motifs are combined. Use the stencils as a border at picture or dado (chair) rail height, randomly around the room, over a chimney breast, or in straight lines to make a feature of, for example, an alcove on one wall.

You will need

- acetate sheet
- craft knife and self-healing cutting mat
- masking tape
- emulsion (latex) paint in black and several bright colours
- stencil brush or small decorator's paintbrush

OPPOSITE: *Bold and primary colours have been used here and work well on a plain white background. You could soften the effect by using pastels if you wish.*

1 Photocopy the designs from the back of the book at various sizes until you are happy with the size. Photocopy them directly on to the acetate sheet.

2 Cut out the stencils using a craft knife and cutting mat.

3 Tape the stencils to the wall using masking tape, alternating the flags and the direction they are facing. Stencil a bold outline in black.

4 Use a medium stencil brush to apply the colour inside the outlines, or paint it freehand for a looser, more childlike effect.

CHILD'S SEASIDE ROOM

This pretty frieze shows a jaunty crab, a starfish and a scallop shell riding on the crest of a wave stencilled along a practical peg rail. A small co-ordinating mirror bordered with little fishes and a wave completes the effect. Use sea-inspired colours such as blue, aquamarine or pale coral as here or choose your own colour palette.

You will need

- tracing paper and pen
- masking tape
- stencil card
- craft knife and self-healing cutting mat
- small decorator's paintbrush
- wooden peg rail
- pale blue emulsion (latex) paint
- flat paintbrush
- acrylic paints in aquamarine, turquoise, dark coral and pale coral
- ceramic tile
- stencil brush
- spirit level
- soft pencil
- eraser
- wooden framed mirror
- fine-grade abrasive paper (optional)
- damp rag (optional)
- sheet of paper

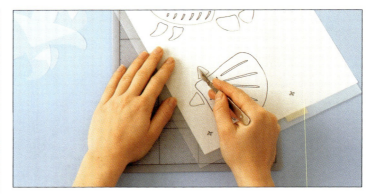

1 Trace the templates at the back of the book. Tape a piece of stencil card to the tracings. Using a craft knife and cutting mat, cut out the stencils. You will need two stencils for the frieze – the starfish, crab and shell, and the details.

2 Remove the pegs from the peg rail. Paint the peg rail with pale blue emulsion (latex) paint. Leave to dry. Tape the waves stencil to the top of the peg rail at one end. Using a flat paintbrush, spread a thin coat of aquamarine and turquoise acrylic paints on to a ceramic tile. Dab at the paints with a stencil brush and stencil the wave, blending the colours together at random.

3 Leave to dry completely then remove the stencil. Move the stencil along the peg rail, matching the valley of the waves so the stencil appears to "flow" seamlessly, and continue stencilling.

4 Use the stencil brush to paint the ends and lower edge of the peg rail to match the waves using a flat paintbrush blending the colours together at random as before. Fix the pegs in place. Paint the pegs with dark coral paint.

5 Using a spirit level, lightly mark the position of the peg rail on the wall with a soft pencil. Tape the starfish, crab and shell stencil to the wall above the peg rail position. Stencil the cut-outs with dark coral paint and leave to dry.

6 Stencil the centre of the starfish, crab and shell with pale coral acrylic paint.

7 Lightly shade the edges of the crab stencil with aquamarine acrylic paint. Leave to dry completely then carefully remove the stencil.

8 Tape the stencils of the details to the wall, matching up the registration marks. Stencil the details with turquoise paint. Leave them to dry then erase the pencil marks. Fix the peg rail to the wall matching the top edge of the peg rail to the drawn pencil line.

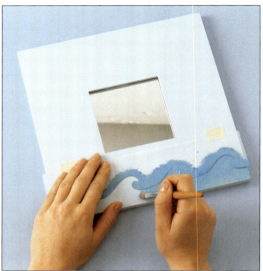

9 If your wooden mirror frame is varnished or already painted, sand it first with fine-grade abrasive paper then wipe it clean with a damp rag. Slip pieces of paper under the edges framing the mirror to protect it from any splashes of paint. Paint the frame with pale blue emulsion paint. Leave to dry.

10 Tape the waves stencil across the bottom of the frame. Using the flat paintbrush, spread a thin coat of aquamarine and turquoise paint on the ceramic tile. Dab at the paints with the stencil brush and stencil the wave, blending the colours together on the frame. Use the stencil brush to paint the lower edges of the frame to match the waves.

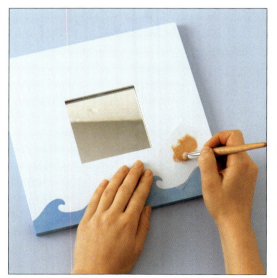

11 Tape the fish stencil to the frame above the waves. Stencil the fish with dark coral paint. Leave to dry.

12 Lightly shade the fish with aquamarine paint. Stencil more fish at random on the frame.

ANIMAL BEDROOM

S mall children like the security of enclosed sleeping spaces and older children relish the privacy, especially if their room is shared with a brother or sister. The panels can be attached to the bed base or simply rested in a corner so that they enclose the space but cannot be pushed over. The animal stencils can also be used on the walls.

1 The shorter pieces of chipboard (particle board) are used for the head and foot of the bed. Screw the batten (furring strip) to butt up to one 1.2m/2ft edge of the head and foot pieces. Place the long piece of chipboard up against the batten on the headboard, at right angles, and screw in place. Repeat with the foot, to make a three-sided surround for the bed. The bed surround will now be reasonably stable, but it is advisable to position the long side against a wall. Paint the surround with pale grey emulsion (latex) paint.

2 To stencil the bed linen, enlarge the templates from the back of the book on a photocopier. Coat the backs lightly with spray mount and stick them on to stencil card.

3 Cut out the stencils using a craft knife and self-healing cutting mat.

4 Wash and iron the sheet and pillowcase. Place some paper inside the pillowcase to protect the back. Position the first stencil, holding it in place with masking tape.

5 Spread each of the fabric paints on to a plate. Using a stencil brush, dab the first colour on to the pillowcase. Apply the paint sparingly because the colour is best when built up gradually.

6 Position the next stencil, being very careful not to smudge the first one, and then stencil the second animal in another colour.

7 Position a third stencil and apply the final colour. Continue alternating the stencils and colours. Decorate the top of the sheet in the same way.

8 To make the "window", enlarge the crocodile template at the back of the book in sections so that you end up with a large pattern. Tape the sections together.

9 Rub the back of the pattern outline with a soft pencil.

10 Place the pattern face up on the chipboard and draw over the outline with a hard pencil. Drill a hole at any point on the outline as the insertion point for the jigsaw (saber saw) blade.

11 Cut out the crocodile shape, working slowly and holding the blade vertically so that it cuts at its own speed without being dragged through the chipboard.

12 Rub down all the edges of the cut-out crocodile shape using fine-grade abrasive paper to smooth the edges and remove any burrs.

13 Stencil a frieze of animals around the bed screen, using the fabric paints or matching stencil paints.

OPPOSITE: *You can use the animal stencils to decorate walls, borders and friezes, bed linen and wash bags to create a co-ordinated room scheme.*

BRIGHT TRANSPORT BORDER

Any small child keen on cars, vans and trucks would love to have these cute and colourful vehicles making their way around the bedroom walls. Complete the theme by stencilling a favourite car on a co-ordinating laundry bag.

You will need
◆ tracing paper and pen
◆ 12mm/¹/₂in wide masking tape
◆ stencil card
◆ craft knife and self-healing cutting mat
◆ metal ruler
◆ spirit level
◆ flat paintbrush
◆ acrylic paints in grey, blue, lilac, lime green, pink and yellow
◆ ceramic tile
◆ stencil brush
◆ soft pencil
◆ eraser
◆ plastic bag
◆ ready-made fabric bag
◆ fabric marking pen
◆ fabric paints in pink, blue and yellow
◆ iron

1 Trace the templates at the back of the book. Tape a piece of stencil card to the tracings. Using a craft knife and cutting mat cut out the stencils, cutting straight lines against a metal ruler. You will need three stencils for each vehicle – the wheels, the body and the hub caps.

2 Stick a length of low-tack masking tape across the wall to designate the road, using a spirit level to check that it is straight. When positioning the road, remember to allow space above for the cars and trucks.

3 Stick lengths of tape immediately above and below the first tape. Peel off the first tape. Do not discard it but cut it into approximate 4cm/1¹/₂in lengths. Stick the pieces vertically across the road 8cm/3¹/₄in apart to create a broken line. Alternatively, leave the line unbroken if you prefer.

4 Using a flat paintbrush, spread a thin coat of grey paint on to a ceramic tile. Dab at the paint with a stencil brush and stencil the road. Leave the paint to dry then carefully pull off all the masking tape.

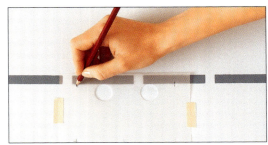

5 Tape the wheels stencil to the wall, placing the lower registration marks on the upper edge of the road. Mark the top registration marks and the top strut of the lower registration marks with a soft pencil.

6 Spread a thin coat of blue acrylic paint on the ceramic tile. Dab at the paint with the stencil brush and stencil the wheels. Leave to dry. Remove the stencil then tape the vehicle body stencil in place, matching the registration marks. Stencil the vehicle body using lilac paint.

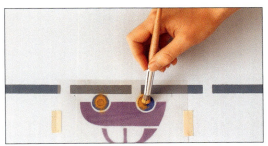

7 Leave to dry completely. Remove the stencil then tape the hub cap stencil in place, matching up with the registration marks. Stencil the hub caps with yellow acrylic paint. Leave to dry then remove the stencil. The first vehicle is now complete.

8 Move the stencils along the wall, matching the right-hand registration marks of the previous vehicle with the left-hand registration marks of the next. Stencil the vehicles in different colours and avoid having the same type of vehicles end to end. Leave to dry, remove the stencils then gently erase the registration marks.

9 Slide a plastic bag inside the fabric bag to prevent paint seeping through to the back. Tape the wheels stencil of one of the vehicles to the bag 6cm/2¹/₂in above the lower edge. Mark the registration marks with a fabric marking pen. Using the flat paintbrush spread a thin coat of pink fabric paint on to the tile. Dab at the paint with the stencil brush and stencil the wheels. Leave to dry.

10 Remove the stencil then tape the vehicle body stencil in place, matching the registration marks. Stencil the vehicle using blue fabric paint. Leave to dry. Remove the stencil then tape the hub cap stencil in place, matching the registration marks. Stencil the hub caps with yellow fabric paint. Leave to dry then remove the stencil. Pull the plastic bag partly out to protect the work surface under the handles of the bag.

11 Stick masking tape along each edge of one handle, leaving a 1cm/¹⁄₂in gap, and tape over the ends of the handle. Lay a section of the handle out flat, then stencil along the masked line with yellow fabric paint.

12 Leave to dry completely then lay the next section flat and continue stencilling. Peel off the tape when the paint has dried. Repeat to stencil the other handle in the same way. Iron the bag on the wrong side to fix (set) the paint, following the manufacturer's instructions.

RIGHT: Use the stencils of the cars, vans and trucks to decorate items in a child's room such as walls, borders and bags to create a co-ordinated scheme.

VICTORIAN WINDOW

This idea originated from the etched-glass windows of the Victorian era. The paint needs to be sprayed very lightly, so practise on some picture frame glass first to judge the effect. The stencil design is provided at the back of the book, but you could easily design your own. Look at examples of lace panels to get some inspiration.

OPPOSITE: This simple, but effective, method can be used in bathrooms or closets.

1 Measure the window panes, and mark the halfway points with masking tape. Trace the stencil design at the back of the book and cut out from stencil card using a craft knife and cutting mat.

2 Tape the main stencil pattern in position. Then use brown wrapping paper to mask off the surrounding area, at least 50cm/20in deep on all sides. (The spray spreads more than you think.)

3 Follow the paint manufacturer's instructions and shake the can for as long as needed, since this affects the fineness of the spray. Spray from a distance of at least 30cm/12in.

4 Depending on the dimensions of the window panes, there may be strips along the sides of the main panel that also need stencilling. This pattern has a border to fit around the edge.

ART NOUVEAU TILES

These elegant and highly stylized designs are inspired by the work of Scottish artist Charles Rennie Mackintosh and the Glasgow School of Art at the turn of the 20th century.

1 Enlarge the designs at the back of the book on a photocopier to fit your tiles. Cut two pieces of stencil card to the size of the tiles and transfer one design to each. Cut away the centre of each design using a craft knife and cutting mat. Coat the back of the stencils with spray mount. Place the stem stencil on a tile. Using a dry artist's brush, apply dark green paint to the stems and light green to the leaves.

2 Allow the paint to dry completely, then use a clean, dry brush to add a little deep red paint to pick out the thorns on the stem. You might also like to try reversing the stem stencil on some of the tiles, which will make the overall effect more symmetrical.

3 Mix deep red with white ceramic paint to make a dusky pink shade. Using this colour and a dry paintbrush, stencil the rose motif on to another tile. Leave the paint to dry completely.

4 Add deep red around the edges of the petals to emphasize the rose shape and give it depth.

BELOW: This design could be adapted to create a stylized border.

5 Using a fine artist's brush, add a few green dots in the centre of the rose. Leave to dry, then seal the surface of the tiles with two coats of varnish, allowing them to dry between coats.

MEDALLION STENCILLED FLOOR

In America, floor stencilling began in imitation of expensive Oriental rugs. Some early Pennsylvania Dutch houses used oak flooring, but more usually floorboards were of pine painted with many layers of oil paint to prevent the wood from splintering, and then stencilled with intricate colourful borders and repeat patterns.

OPPOSITE: This design could be used to create a simple border pattern on the floor.

1 Prepare the surface by washing with sugar soap or all-purpose cleaner. When dry, paint with green emulsion (latex) paint. If you like a worn-looking surface thin the emulsion half and half with water and wipe it on with a rag. The paint will stay in the grain and give a patchy effect. Leave to dry.

2 Measure the floor space to judge how many medallions will fit easily between each corner. Enlarge the template at the back of the book and cut out of acetate or card using a craft knife and cutting mat. Spray lightly with spray mount. Begin by stencilling a medallion in each corner then one midway between the two. Continue stencilling alternate sides of the central medallion, spacing by eye until you reach the corner motif.

3 Stencil one row of medallions all around the room first, to act as a guide when positioning the other rows. The grid of large medallions can be broken up by using the centre of the motif between each block of four. Use masking tape to isolate the centre and make a smaller stencil to fill in the gaps. Finally paint the floor surface with two or three coats of varnish.

GREEK KEY FLOOR BORDER

Classic patterns have a timeless air, which makes them suitable for a formal room scheme. This geometric pattern is derived from the border on an Ancient Greek vase. It consists of two simple motifs, which can be stencilled in straight lines or around corners.

You will need

- medium-grade abrasive paper
- large decorator's paintbrush
- white floor paint
- masking tape
- stencil card
- craft knife and self-healing cutting mat
- set square (triangle)
- piece of card (stock)
- stencil brush
- black acrylic paint
- matt (flat) varnish and brush

OPPOSITE: Bold shapes and strong geometric patterns work well on painted white or light-coloured floorboards.

1 Prepare the floor by sanding down the boards, then painting them with white floor paint. If the floor has already been painted, wash it down with a soft cloth to remove any dust, grease and marks. If you wish, you can also sand it lightly to key the surface.

2 Enlarge the templates at the back of the book on a photocopier to the size required and tape on to stencil card. Cut out and trim the border to 1cm/^{1}/$_2$in all round. Starting from one corner of the room, position the stencil in the centre of a floorboard.

3 Tape the stencil in position. While you are stencilling, hold a piece of card (stock) over the edge of the stencil to protect the floor from surplus paint or splashes.

4 Load the stencil brush very lightly with black paint and block in the design, using two coats if necessary for a dense look. When dry, lift the stencil and remove the tape.

5 Line up the stencil so that one short edge lies against the painted design and one long edge lies against the masking tape. Tape the two long edges in place, avoiding any already painted areas, then fill in the stencil as before.

6 Continue stencilling to the end of the wall. Start the next side of the floor border by lining up the stencil at right angles to the first motif. Use a set square (triangle) as you work to ensure the border is straight.

7 Repeat on the other two sides using the set square to make sure that each corner is at a right angle. Leave to dry then apply three coats of clear, heavy-duty matt (flat) varnish to seal the floor and protect it from hard wear.

FURNITURE AND STORAGE

Stencilling is a quick and effective way to revive an old piece of furniture or flea market find, or to add decoration to a plain flat-pack chest of drawers or table. Take the time to sand and prime the wood before you start for the best results, and don't be put off by working on a larger scale: start off with a smaller item such as a key cabinet and then progress to tables, chairs and shelving.

ABOVE: Old-fashioned style trains and carriages are popular themes for children's rooms and storage.

LEFT: Smarten up a simple kitchen chair with delicate Scandinavian-style stencilling.

BRONZE CHAIR

This handsome gilded design was inspired by the high-quality "Hitchcock" chairs popular in America in the 19th century, named after the man who mass-produced them. The brilliance of the colour comes from real bronze powder (or gold powder, which is more expensive), and the effect is quite different to bronze or gold paint, or bronze or gold leaf. The original makers used the finest velvet to apply the powder, moulding the shapes of fruit and flowers by varying the amount of powder.

You will need

- kitchen chair with broad rails and turned legs (or plain pine rocking chair)
- fine-grade abrasive paper
- clean cotton rag
- black emulsion (latex) paint
- small decorator's paintbrush
- spray mount
- stencil card
- craft knife and self-healing cutting mat
- water-based gold size
- plate
- stencil brush
- bronze or gold powder
- square of lint or velvet
- fine artist's brush
- antiquing varnish (or clear satin varnish) and brush

1 Rub down any existing paintwork with abrasive paper.

2 Dust off the surface with a clean cotton rag.

3 Paint the chair with black emulsion (latex) paint.

OPPOSITE: The stencil for this chair is very intricate and will take time to cut out.

4 Photocopy the stencil pattern at the back of the book, enlarging it to fit your chair back. Spray the back of the pattern with spray mount and stick it on to stencil card. Cut out the small shapes using a craft knife and cutting mat.

5 Complete cutting out the pattern, then cut away the extra card so that the stencil fits your chair back. Lay the stencil in position on the chair back.

6 Place a small amount of size on a plate. Using a stencil brush, stipple the size through the shapes. Use the size sparingly, but fill in each shape.

7 When the size is just tacky (see manufacturer's instructions), dust on bronze or gold powder. Work it into the size by applying it with a piece of lint or velvet.

8 Leave the bronze or gold powder for 1–2 hours to set. Gently wipe away any excess with a small square of lint or soft velvet.

9 Highlight details on the rest of the chair. Apply size with a fine artist's brush, then add the bronze or gold powder. If desired, you can soften the gold effect with a coat of antiquing varnish, which will also protect the stencilling. Clear satin varnish will give protection without dulling the gold.

SCANDINAVIAN CHAIR

These motifs can be adjusted to fit any style of wooden chair, which can be decorated as simply or lavishly as you wish. Here, white paint is applied to a blue chair but other combinations such as red paint on a white chair would also look good.

1 Trace the templates at the back of the book. Place a piece of carbon paper face down on to a sheet of stencil card. Tape the tracings on top. Redraw the templates with a sharp pencil to transfer the design. Using a sharp-bladed craft knife and cutting mat cut out the stencils, cutting straight lines against a metal ruler.

2 Tape the large star flower stencil centrally on to the chair seat. Using a flat paintbrush, spread a thin coat of white paint on to a ceramic tile. Dab at the paint with a stencil brush and stencil the flower motif. Leave to dry completely. Apply a second coat of paint for a stronger image then remove the stencil.

3 Tape the tulip stencil upright to the centre of the upper rail of the chair. Lightly stencil the motif with the white acrylic paint. Leave to dry then remove the stencil.

4 Stencil the tulip again at each end of the rail. Stencil a medium star flower between the tulips. If your chair does not have enough space for a medium star flower, stencil one of the smaller images instead.

5 Tape the strip stencil to one upright of the back on the chair, placing the single diamond at the centre. Shorten the stencil to fit if necessary. Stencil the upright. Leave it to dry completely then swivel the stencil, matching the single diamond position to stencil the other half of the upright.

6 Repeat this process on the other chair upright. Stencil the front and sides of the legs in the same way. Shorten the stencil or repeat the images to fit the length of your chair legs.

7 Tape the strip stencil to the lower rail, placing the small star flower at the centre. Shorten the stencil to fit if necessary. Stencil the rail.

8 Stencil the small star flower in the centre of the front seat support. Stencil any other parts of the chair using the entire strip stencil or just a section of it.

PAINTED DRAWERS

Jazz up plain drawers with bright paintbox colours and simple daisy stencils. The stencils could also be used to decorate larger pieces of furniture such as a chest of drawers for a child's room, a small wardrobe, or kitchen units. Sample pots of emulsion (latex) paint are ideal to use on small projects such as this.

You will need

- set of wooden drawers
- fine-grade abrasive paper
- emulsion (latex) paints in various bright colours
- medium and small decorator's paintbrushes
- screwdriver
- acetate sheet
- craft knife and self-healing cutting mat
- stencil brushes
- matt (flat) acrylic varnish
- wood glue (optional)

1 Remove the drawers and sand down the frame and drawers to remove any rough areas or patches of old paint.

2 Paint the drawer frame with emulsion (latex) paint. Leave to dry, then apply a second coat of paint.

3 Unscrew the drawer knobs and paint each drawer in a different-coloured emulsion paint. Leave to dry and apply a second coat. Trace the flower template at the back of the book and cut a stencil from acetate sheet using a craft knife and cutting mat.

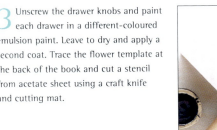

OPPOSITE: If you use more muted colours such as pale green or cream, you can create a much subtler effect.

◆ 115 ◆

▶

4 When the drawers are dry, position the flower stencil in the centre of a drawer and, using a stencil brush and paint in a contrasting colour, stencil on the flower. Leave to dry.

5 Stencil a daisy flower in the centre of each drawer, using a different colour paint for each one.

6 Paint the drawer knobs with two coats of paint, leaving them to dry between coats. Leave to dry.

7 Screw or glue a painted knob to the centre of each drawer. Varnish the drawers with matt acrylic varnish. Leave to dry before reassembling.

TRAIN TOY BOX

This chugging train stencil will fit a child's toy box and is perfect for a young boy who loves steam engines. Simply add or decrease the number of wagons to suit your requirements. You could add more wagons to extend the train around the entire box.

1 Stick a length of masking tape around the toy box immediately below the intended position of the rails. Stick another length of tape 5mm/¼in above the first. Keep the tape parallel with the base of the toy box.

2 Using a flat paintbrush, spread a thin coat of grey paint on to a ceramic tile. Dab at the paint with a stencil brush and stencil the rails. Leave the paint to dry then carefully pull off the tape.

3 Trace the toy box and clouds templates at the back of the book. Tape a piece of acetate to the tracings. Using a craft knife and cutting mat cut out the stencils, cutting straight lines against a metal ruler. You will need two toy box stencils – the train engine, wagons and smoke, then the wheels and the details. Also cut out the registration marks to help guide your positioning.

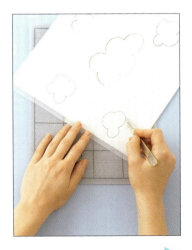

4 Tape the engine, wagons and smoke stencil to the front of the box, placing the lower registration marks on the upper edge of the rails. Mark the top registration marks and the top strut of the lower registration marks with a soft pencil. Using the flat paintbrush, spread a thin coat of red paint on to the tile. Dab at the paint with a stencil brush and stencil the engine. Leave to dry.

5 Using the flat paintbrush, spread a thin coat of aquamarine and pink paint on to the tile. Stencil the wagons with the aquamarine and pink paint. Spread grey and white paint on to the tile. Dab at one paint then the other and stencil the steam to create a mottled effect. Leave to dry completely then remove the stencil.

6 Tape the wheels and details stencil in place, matching the registration marks. Stencil the chimneys using yellow paint. Stencil the wheels and couplings with blue paint. Stencil the coal with black paint. Hold the stencil brush upright when stencilling and move the brush in a circular motion. Leave to dry. Remove the stencil.

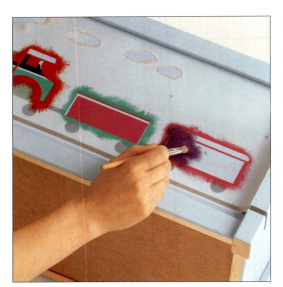

7 Move the wagon stencil along the box, matching the right-hand registration marks of the previous wagon with the left-hand registration marks of the next. Stencil the wheels and couplings with blue paint. Leave to dry. Replace the stencil with a wagon stencil, matching the registration marks. Stencil the wagon with purple paint.

8 Leave to dry then erase the registration marks. Tape the clouds stencil centrally to the lid of the box. Use the flat paintbrush to spread a thin coat of white paint on to the tile. Stencil the clouds with the white paint. Leave to dry. To make the toy box hardwearing paint it with two or three coats of clear matt (flat) varnish.

HAWAIIAN HIBISCUS CABINET

Transform a plain wooden cabinet with this flamboyant floral stencil. Enlarge the template on a photocopier to fit your cupboard door.

1 If necessary, fill any screwholes in the cabinet with wood filler. Leave to dry, then sand lightly with abrasive paper. Paint the cabinet with apricot emulsion (latex) paint. Leave to dry, then sand lightly with abrasive paper. Wipe with a damp rag. Apply a second coat of paint.

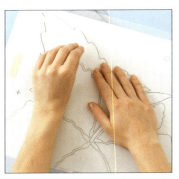

2 Enlarge the template at the back of the book on a photocopier. Tape a piece of acetate to the photocopy with masking tape. Resting on a cutting mat, cut out the stencils with a craft knife. You will need three stencils – the petals, the stigma and leaves, and the stamens and spots.

3 Stick the petals stencil to the door with spray mount. Mark the registration marks with a soft pencil. Using a flat paintbrush, spread a thin coat of pink paint on to a ceramic tile. Dab at the paint with a stencil brush and stencil the petals.

4 Leave to dry. Shade the petals at the centre of the flower with apricot acrylic paint. Leave to dry then remove the stencil.

5 Stick the stigma and leaves stencil in place with spray mount, matching the registration marks. Stencil the stigma with apricot paint.

6 Stencil the leaves with lime green paint. Leave to dry.

7 Shade the leaves along their centres and around the petals with mid-green paint to darken the areas and give a slight three-dimensional effect.

8 Leave to dry then remove the stencil. Stick the stamens and spots stencil to the door with spray mount, matching the registration marks. Mix a little lime green and yellow paint and use to stencil the stamens.

9 Stencil the spots with the mixed lime green and yellow paint. Leave to dry.

10 Shade the edges of the spots with apricot paint. Remove the stencil and erase the registration marks.

11 Position part of the spots stencil on the side of the cabinet. Tape in place and stencil the spots with the mixed lime green and yellow paint. Leave to dry. Move the stencil along to stencil another part of the side if necessary. Repeat on the other side of the cabinet and on the top if that will be visible.

12 Set the cabinet aside to dry overnight then remove the stencil. Apply two coats of clear matt varnish, lightly sanding the cabinet between coats. This will protect the cabinet from wear and tear.

OPPOSITE: *Any large single flower can be used to decorate a cabinet.*

CELTIC KNOT BOX

Intertwined, maze-like designs like this circular motif appeared on Irish carvings and manuscripts as early as the fifth century AD. The knot is made up of four quarters, repeated individually in the corners of the box.

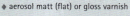

1 Sand down the box to key the surface and, if necessary, fill in any holes or deep scratches with wood filler.

2 Paint the box with a coat of white wood primer to prepare the surface. Porous wood may need two coats.

3 Paint the box with one or two layers of pale gold paint.

4 To give interest to the pale yellow
surface of the box, colour wash it
with dark gold paint. Dilute the paint
with four parts of water and apply with
broad strokes using a decorator's brush.

5 Trace the template at the back of the book. Tape it on to stencil card and cut
out, using a craft knife and cutting mat. Mark the quarter sections on the stencil.
Using a soft pencil, lightly pencil in two lines to divide the box top into quarters.
Spray the stencil with spray mount, then line it up along the pencil lines and fill in
with green paint.

6 Stencil in a quarter section of the
knot in each corner of the box. Line
it up so that the centre division of the
stencil lies at the edge of the lid and
mask off carefully with tape.

7 Stencil the bottom of each side of
the box in the same way using
sections of the main motif that will fit
neatly into the right-angled corners. Mask
off the surrounding area as necessary.

8 Once the paint is quite dry, sand the
box lightly to give it a distressed
finish. Spray with one or more coats of
craft varnish to protect the surface with
a matt (flat) or gloss finish.

DAISY STOOL

G ive a simple wooden stool a new lease of life with pretty folk art motifs. The fine
stripes around the legs are achieved by stencilling between strips of masking tape.

1 Trace the templates at the back of
the book. Tape a piece of acetate
to the tracings. Using a craft knife and
cutting mat, cut out the stencils. You
will need two stencils for each seat
flower – the circle and leaves, then the
flower centre, petals, stalk and leaf veins.
Remember to cut out the registration
marks.

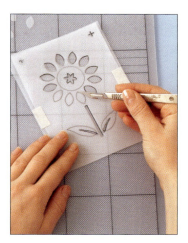

2 Measure the seat and divide it into
quarters with a soft pencil. Tape
the circle and leaves stencils of the seat
flowers inside two of the quarters. Mark
the registration marks in pencil. Using
a flat paintbrush, spread a thin coat of
beige paint on to a ceramic tile. Lightly
dab at the paint with a stencil brush
and stencil the circles and leaves holding
the stencil brush upright and moving it
in a circular motion. Leave to dry then
repeat in the other quarters.

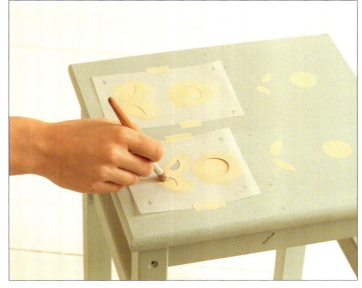

3 When the paint is dry tape the flower centre, petals, stalk and leaf veins stencils in place, matching the registration marks. Stencil the cut-outs with dark green paint. Leave to dry then repeat on the other flowers. Leave to dry then erase the pencil marks.

4 Position the small flower stencil centrally on a top strut of the stool. Carefully stencil the flower with dark green paint, protecting the surrounding area from paint with a piece of card (stock). Repeat the stencil centrally on the other top struts.

5 Tape the pair of leaves of one seat flower stencil centrally to a lower strut. Stencil the leaves with dark green paint. Leave to dry. Remove the stencil and tape the leaf veins stencil in place. Tape over the stem cut-out. Stencil the leaf veins with beige paint. Repeat on the other struts.

6 Stick three lengths of low-tack masking tape around one stool leg, leaving a 5mm/¼in gap between each tape to create stripes around the bottom of the leg.

7 Stencil the stripes with dark green paint. Repeat on the other legs. Peel off the tape when the paint has dried. Give the stool two coats of varnish to finish.

TEA TABLE

A fun approach to stencilling using a simple reverse technique that doesn't involve cutting any stencils, this trompe l'oeil table top is quick and easy to do and can transform an old table into a cheerful centrepiece. The paper doilies give a pretty, lacy effect, complemented by the blue-and-white polka dot "tablecloth".

You will need

- medium and fine-grade abrasive paper
- electric sanding machine (optional)
- small wooden table
- medium decorator's paintbrush
- white wood primer
- spray mount
- four round paper doilies
- light blue acrylic paint
- large stencil brush
- packet of 1cm/½in adhesive dots
- piece of paper
- craft knife
- matt (flat) varnish and brush

1 Sand down the table top, sides and legs to key the surface ready for the new paint. Use medium then fine-grade abrasive paper to give a smooth finish. If you have an electric sanding machine, this will speed up the preparation.

2 Paint the table top with a coat of white primer and leave to dry completely. If you prefer a more subtle paint finish with some of the underlying colour showing through, make this a very light coat.

3 Spray the wrong side of the first doily lightly with spray mount and position it along the centre of one side of the table. Smooth it down gently with the flat of your hand, then fix the other three doilies in place spacing them at regular intervals.

OPPOSITE: *You can vary the pattern of the stencilled doilies to create an individual place setting if you wish.*

4 Using a very small amount of blue paint and a dry stencil brush, block in a circle of colour around the doilies, filling in all the spaces and covering the edge completely.

5 When the paint is dry, carefully pull back and discard the doilies. Stencil the other three "mats" in the same way taking care not to overload the brush with paint.

6 Stick the adhesive dots randomly over the remaining white paint, spacing them at roughly equal intervals across the surface of the table top.

7 Using a stippling action and a dry stencil brush, paint over the rest of the table, filling in the space between the stencils with an even layer of colour.

8 Leave to dry completely. Gently lift off each adhesive dot in turn using the sharp point of a craft knife, being careful not to dig it into the wood so you do not scratch the surface of the paint.

9 Paint the rest of the table with blue paint, paying attention to any moulded areas around the top edge and on the legs. When dry, apply two coats of matt (flat) varnish to make the table top hardwearing.

AFRICAN BEDSIDE CHEST

Warm rustic colours and a bold graphic design have transformed a utilitarian modern chest of drawers into a more interesting piece. The African motifs are stencilled across a band of subtle colour, which is applied with a natural sponge.

1 Moisten the sponge. Using a flat paintbrush, spread a thin coat of yellow ochre paint on to a ceramic tile. Dab at the paint with the sponge.

2 Dab the paint in a 12cm/4^1/$_2$in wide band on the top of the chest approximately 4cm/1^1/$_2$in from the front and back edges. Leave to dry.

3 Trace the templates at the back of the book enlarging or reducing them as necessary using a photocopier. Tape a piece of acetate to the tracings. Using a craft knife and self-healing cutting mat, cut out the stencils. Cut the straight lines freehand for a natural effect.

4 Stick the top stencil to the top of the chest at the front with spray mount. Using the flat paintbrush, spread a thin coat of terracotta paint on to the tile. Dab at the paint with a stencil brush and stencil the top of the chest. Move the stencil to the back of the top of the chest and repeat.

5 Using a flat paintbrush, spread a thin coat of yellow ochre acrylic paint on to the ceramic tile. Dab at the paint with a natural sponge. Dab the paint across a drawer front. Leave to dry completely.

6 Stick the zigzag stencil to one half of a drawer front with spray mount. Stencil the zigzags with terracotta paint. Leave to dry then remove the stencil.

7 Stick the rotating lines stencil to the other half of the drawer front with spray mount and stencil with terracotta paint. Leave to dry then remove the stencil. Paint with two or three coats of matt (flat) varnish to protect the chest.

STRIPED TABLE AND CHAIRS

Pencils, paintbrushes and colourful stripes will provide inspiration for the young artist in your family on this charming set of child-sized furniture.

You will need

- 12mm/¹/₂in wide masking tape
- small wooden table and chairs, painted cream
- set square (triangle)
- craft knife and self-healing cutting mat
- metal ruler
- flat paintbrush
- acrylic paints in pale blue, apricot, aquamarine, lilac and grey
- ceramic tile
- stencil brush
- piece of card (stock)
- tracing paper and pen
- acetate sheet
- soft pencil
- eraser
- clear varnish and brush
- fine glass paper
- a damp rag

1 Using masking tape, mask off a 30 x 20cm/12 x 8in rectangle on the centre of the table. Make sure that all the corners are right angles using a set square (triangle) and adjust the tapes if necessary.

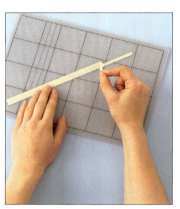

2 Apply lengths of masking tape in rows across the rectangle to make stripes of various widths. Cut some lengths 5mm/¹/₄in wide. To do this, stick the tape to a cutting mat and use a craft knife to cut the tape lengthwise in half, cutting against a metal ruler. Peel the tapes off the mat.

3 Using a flat paintbrush, spread the pale blue, apricot, aquamarine and lilac paints on to a ceramic tile. Dab at the paint with a stencil brush and stencil the stripes in different colours. To stop the paint straying over the 6mm/¹/₄in wide tape, hold a piece of card over the next stripes. Leave the paint to dry then carefully pull off the tapes.

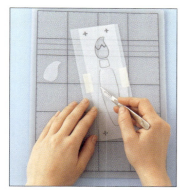

4 Trace the pencil templates at the back of the book. Tape a piece of stencil card to the tracings. Using the craft knife and cutting mat cut out the stencils, cutting straight lines against a metal ruler. You will need two pencil stencils – the wood, then the pencil and lead. You will need two paintbrush stencils – the handle and bristles, then the metal band and paint.

5 Lay the pencil stencils together on the table, matching the registration marks along two adjacent sides of the stripes. Tape the pencil wood stencil in place. Mark the registration marks with a soft pencil. Using a flat paintbrush, spread apricot paint on to a ceramic tile. Dab at the paint with a stencil brush. Stencil the pencil woods with apricot paint. Leave to dry.

6 Move the stencil to the other sides of the stripes, matching up the registration marks. Stencil the pencil woods with apricot acrylic paint as before. Leave to dry completely then remove the stencil.

7 With masking tape, secure the pencil and lead stencil to the table, matching up the registration marks exactly. Stencil the pencils and leads using lilac, aquamarine and pale blue acrylic paint. Protect the next pencil from any stray paint with a piece of card when stencilling the leads and ends of the pencils. Leave it to dry completely then move the stencil to the other side of the stripes and continue working.

8 Apply masking tape in rows across the chair seat, making some of the lengths of tape 5mm/¼in wide as before. Mask off the bottom of the chair back and around the edges of the seat.

9 Stencil the seat in coloured stripes to match the table using blue, purple, apricot and an aquamarine paint. Leave the paint to dry completely then peel off the tapes.

10 Tape the paint-brush handle and bristles stencil to the top rail of the chair. Mark the registration marks. Stencil the bristles using apricot paint and stencil the handle.

11 Tape the band and paint stencil to the top rail, matching the registration marks. Stencil the band with grey paint. Stencil the paint in a different colour. Repeat on the other rail but turn the stencil so the paintbrush is pointing in the other direction and then use different colours for the handle and paint.

12 Paint any rungs on the chair to co-ordinate with the stripes. Leave to dry then erase the registration marks. Apply two coats of clear varnish, sanding the furniture and wiping it with a damp rag between coats. This will help protect the table and chairs from wear and tear.

FLOWER POWER CHAIR

Recalling the bright floral patterns of the sixties, this colourful chair will cheer up any kitchen, little girl's bedroom, or bathroom. Only the seat is decorated, giving the impression that it is covered in a vintage patterned fabric.

1 Sand down the chair seat with medium then fine-grade abrasive paper to prepare the surface for painting, paying special attention to any chips or scratches. Sand the legs, struts and back of the chair in the same way. You may need to repair any deep holes with wood filler.

2 Paint the whole chair with white primer. Leave to dry. Trace the templates at the back of the book and tape them on to stencil card. Cut out, using a craft knife and cutting mat. Trim the edges, leaving a small margin around the motifs, so that the stencil can be positioned close to the struts.

3 Stencil the first flower in blue, using a blocking technique and a fine dry brush. Stencil a sprinkling of blue flowers across the seat, spacing them regularly and altering the angle of each one. Make sure that you have enough space between them to fit in the pink flowers and the tiny green flowers. If you wish, you can mark the positions in with pencil before you start stencilling, to be sure that the spacing is correct.

4 Fill in some of the spaces either side of the blue stencilled flowers with pink acrylic paint, using the same stencil cut out.

5 Using the same paint colours, stencil a few part flowers to overlap the edges of the seat.

6 Add yellow dots in the centre of the large flowers with the small round stencil, dabbing the brush lightly to give a slight texture.

7 Using the small flower stencil, add a few small green flowers in the remaining spaces. Leave to dry completely then protect the seat with two or three coats of matt (flat) varnish. Paint the back and legs of the chair with white wood paint. If your chair has a large flat area across the top edge or wide struts, you could add more flowers to the back. Stencilling and painting four or six different chairs in this way would give you an attractive mismatching set for a modern kitchen or dining room.

RIGHT: Enliven an old kitchen chair by using bright, fresh colours and motifs.

FABRICS

Stencilling is one of the oldest methods of textile printing (it was used in Japan over a thousand years ago) and the only technique for transferring patterns that can easily be done at home. Use it to decorate fabrics from sheer organza to plush velvet, with repeating, scattered or all-over designs, and then make your unique materials up into one-off soft furnishings: cushions, blinds, curtains, tablecloths and floorcloths.

ABOVE: A simple seashell motif is perfect for a summer beach bag.

LEFT: Graphic rose print cushions add elegance to a light, modern living room or conservatory.

ORGANZA CUSHION

If you always thought stencilling had a simple country look, then think again. This beautiful organza cushion with gold stencilling takes the craft into the luxury class. Use the sharpest dressmaking pins when handling organza to avoid marking the fabric.

1 Copy the border template at the back of the book on to dressmaker's graph paper and cut out. In addition, cut out a 52cm/21in square and a 52 x 40cm/21 x 16in rectangle from graph paper.

2 Pin the square and rectangle to the main colour organza. Cut two 52cm/21in squares, and two rectangles measuring 52 x 40cm/21 x 16in from main fabric. Cut four border pieces from the contrasting fabric.

3 Cut a piece of stencil card 18 x 52cm/7 x 21in. Trace the template and transfer to the card, 8cm/3¼in from the bottom edge and with 6cm/2½in to spare at each end. Cut out the stencil using a craft knife and a self-healing cutting mat.

4 Spray the back of the stencil with spray mount and position along the edge of the main organza fabric square. Cut two 45-degree mitres from stencil card, spray with adhesive and press in place. Mask off the surrounding areas with paper.

5 Spray with gold paint. Leave to dry and spray again. Remove the masking paper and stencil. Place the stencil along the next edge, put the mitres in place and continue as before. Stencil the remaining two sides. Hem one long edge of each fabric rectangle by folding over 1cm/$\frac{1}{2}$in, then 1.5cm/$\frac{5}{8}$in. Pin, tack (baste) and machine stitch the hem, then press.

6 Lay the stencilled fabric square face down and the second square on top. Lay the two rectangles on top of these squares, overlapping the stitched edges so that the raw edges line up with the square pieces. Pin, tack and machine stitch 1cm/$\frac{1}{2}$in from the raw edge. Trim the seam allowance to 5mm/$\frac{1}{4}$in. Then, pin, tack and stitch the border pieces together at the mitred corners 1cm/$\frac{1}{2}$in from the raw edges. Trim the corners and turn the material the right way out. Press the fabric with a protective cloth. Continue until the border pieces make a ring.

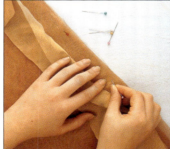

7 Using a protective cloth, press one of the raw edges under by 1cm/$\frac{1}{2}$in. Lay the pressed edge of the border fabric along the edge of the main fabric square and pin, tack and stitch in place.

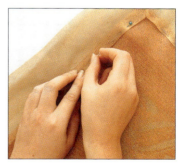

8 Turn the cushion over and pull the border over. Turn under the border's raw edge by 1cm/$\frac{1}{2}$in and pin in place along the front of the cushion. Them tack and stitch in place. Press and insert the cushion pad.

FIFTIES ROSE CUSHIONS

Reminiscent of the stylized designs of the 1950s, these rose print cushions would look at home in a classic or contemporary setting. Use your imagination to create more variations on the theme and alter the number of roses on each cushion.

1 Wash the fabric to remove any dressing and press to remove any creases before cutting out the panels. Place the first panel on a pad of newspaper to absorb paint, then check the position of the stencil by placing it over the square.

2 Cut out the stalk and four flower head stencils from acetate using a heat knife or an ordinary craft knife. Spray the reverse of the large rose background stencil with spray mount, then position it towards the top left corner. Block it in with coral paint, using a dry stencil brush.

3 Leave the paint to dry completely, then line up the large petal stencil over the background. Fill it in with a small amount of aubergine paint to complete the rose.

4 Spray the back of the stalk stencil and place it diagonally across the fabric. Fill it in with dark green fabric paint, again loading the brush with the minimum amount to prevent seepage.

5 The design on the second cushion cover consists of one large and two small roses. Stencil in the rose backgrounds first using coral paint, positioning them so that they point towards the centre of the cushion.

6 Using aubergine paint, add the second layer (the petal stencil) to each of the roses. Line the stencils up by eye so that they fit within the area already painted, and secure in place with spray mount.

7 Stencil in the stalks, allowing the lower part of each one to overlap the edge of the fabric. Leave to dry, then iron both covers on the back to fix (set) the paint, following the instructions supplied by the manufacturer.

8 To make up each cushion cover, stitch a narrow seam along one long edge of the two back panels. With right sides facing and the three raw edges lined up, place one at each side of the front panel so that the seams overlap. Pin and tack (baste) in place, then machine stitch 1cm/$\frac{1}{2}$in from the outside edge. Clip the surplus fabric from the corners and ease the corners into shape with the point of a pencil. Turn through and press using a cloth to protect the stencilled side of the cover, then insert the square cushion pad through the opening.

RIGHT: Vary the number of roses on each of the cushions to make them different.

DRAGONFLY CURTAIN

Beautiful, fragile dragonflies hover on this simple and eyecatching, delicate muslin (cheesecloth) curtain. The wing tips of the dragonflies are shaded in a contrasting colour and the insects are stencilled singly and in groups of three.

You will need

- tracing paper and pen
- masking tape
- acetate
- craft knife and self-healing cutting mat
- sheer curtain
- iron
- plastic carrier bag
- ceramic tile
- flat paintbrush
- stencil brush
- fabric paints in lilac and aquamarine

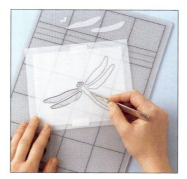

1 Trace the template at the back of the book. Attach a piece of acetate to the tracing with masking tape. Cut out the stencil using a craft knife and self-healing cutting mat, cutting carefully around the acute curved edges.

2 Iron the curtain to remove creases. Lay a section of the curtain out flat on a plastic carrier bag, to protect the work surface. Tape the stencil smoothly to the fabric with masking tape. Stencil the dragonfly with lilac fabric paint. Leave to dry.

3 Stencil the tips of the dragonfly wings with aquamarine paint. Leave to dry then remove the stencil.

4 Move the stencil to the next position, close to the first dragonfly but not touching it. Tape it in place and stencil as before.

5 When the paint is dry, move the stencil again so that the dragonflies are positioned to "hover" in a group of three. Stencil the third dragonfly.

6 Move the stencil and place it at random on the curtain. Stencil a single dragonfly. Continue stencilling dragonflies all over the curtain in groups of three and singly.

7 Leave the paint to dry overnight then iron the curtain on the wrong side to fix (set) the paint, following the manufacturer's instructions.

RAINFOREST CURTAINS

Both the positive and negative parts of this stencil are used to create a sophisticated pattern from a single, almost abstract motif. Light streaming through the unlined cotton enhances the hothouse look of this design.

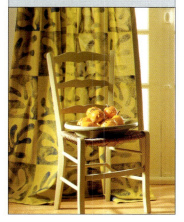

1 Cut the cotton fabric to required size for the curtains, allowing 5cm/2in seam allowances at the sides and lower edge and 2cm/³⁄₄in at the top. Press under, pin and machine-stitch 2.5cm/1in double hems down each side, then repeat the process for the hem at the bottom of the curtain.

2 Calculate the number of tabs you will need, spacing them about 20cm/8in apart. Cut a rectangle of fabric for each tab, using the template at the back of the book. Fold each rectangle in half lengthways and stitch, with a 1cm/¹⁄₂in seam allowance. Open out the seam allowance and pin and stitch across one end of the tab so that the seam lies at the centre.

3 Turn each tab to the right side and press. Pin the raw ends of the material to the right side of each curtain, spacing the tabs evenly along the top. For the facing, cut a 7.5cm/3in strip of fabric the width of the curtain plus 4cm/1¹⁄₂in for seam allowances. Pin the strip to the curtain with right sides together and then machine-stitch the top edge.

4 Fold the facing to the wrong side, fold in the seam allowances at each end and along the raw edge and then pin in place.

5 Machine-stitch the facing close to the folded edge.

6 Fold the tabs over on to the front side of the curtain and then hand-stitch one of the buttons to hold each tab in place.

7 Enlarge the stencil template at the back of the book on a photocopier to your desired size. Cut a square of acetate sheet the size of the design and fasten it to the design with tabs of masking tape. Cut out using a craft knife and cutting mat. Retain the cut-out part of the stencil for the negative images.

8 Using tailor's chalk, mark the curtains into squares the same size as the stencil. Protect the work surface. Using spray mount, attach the stencil in place in the first marked square. Apply fabric paint with the stencil brush to create a mottled effect. Leave the stencil in place. To make the negative image, mask off the areas around the square with tape.

9 Use spray mount to fix the cut-out motif in the centre, then apply green fabric paint all around it. Remove the stencil and move it to the next marked square. Repeat this pattern all over the curtain. Leave to dry completely then iron the curtain on the wrong side to fix (set) the paint following the manufacturer's instructions.

SPRIGGED CURTAIN

This repeating pattern is easy to achieve if you iron the curtain fabric to mark a grid before you start to stencil. Alternatively, the leaf motif could be stencilled randomly across the fabric for a more informal look. Wash and iron the fabric before you start.

You will need

- tracing paper and pen
- stencil card
- craft knife and self-healing cutting mat
- cotton voile to fit window
- iron
- newspaper
- masking tape
- spray mount
- fabric paints in green, blue, brown and pink
- stencil brushes
- sewing machine
- matching sewing thread
- curtain wire

1 Enlarge the template at the back of the book on a photocopier so that it is 17cm/6¹/₂in high. Transfer the outline to stencil card and cut out using a craft knife and cutting mat. Fold the fabric into 20cm/8in vertical pleats and 25cm/10in horizontal pleats, then iron lightly to leave a grid pattern. Cover the work surface with newspaper and tape the fabric down so that it is fairly taut.

2 Spray the back of the stencil with spray mount and place it in the first rectangle. Mix (combine) the fabric paints to achieve subtle shades. Stencil the leaves in green, adding blue at the edges for depth. Stencil the stem in brown and the berries in a brownish pink. Repeat in alternate rectangles.

3 Turn the stencil upside down and, using pink fabric paint, stencil the top leaf in the centre of the plain rectangles. Add a darker shade at the tip and mark the stalk in brown. Iron the curtain on the wrong side to fix (set) the paints according to the manufacturer's instructions. Hem the sides and lower edge of the curtain. Make a 2.5cm/1in channel at the top and then insert the curtain wire.

BELOW: Use soft shades of green and pink to create a light, elegant look to this small curtain.

ZODIAC CAFÉ CURTAIN

Use gold fabric paints to dramatize a plain muslin (cheesecloth) curtain. Paint the shapes at random on the curtain, but try to plan your design so that they all appear frequently. Add variety by blending the two shades of gold on some of the designs.

You will need

- tracing paper and pen
- stencil card
- craft knife and self-healing cutting mat
- kitchen paper
- newspaper
- white muslin (cheesecloth),
  to fit window
- iron
- masking tape
- spray mount
- fabric paints in light and dark gold
- stencil brushes
- sewing machine
- matching thread
- curtain clips and metal rings

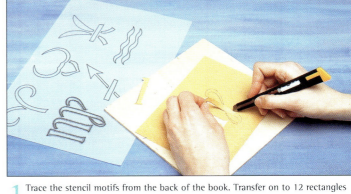

1 Trace the stencil motifs from the back of the book. Transfer on to 12 rectangles of stencil card and cut out using a craft knife and cutting mat. Practise your stencilling technique on some spare fabric. Don't overload your brush and wipe off any excess paint on kitchen paper before you begin.

2 Cover your work table with newspaper. Iron the muslin, then tape one corner to the table with masking tape, keeping it flat. Coat the back of each stencil lightly with spray mount before positioning it on the fabric. Stencil with the light gold fabric paint, then stencil over the edges of the motif with dark gold to give depth. Leave to dry, then gently peel the stencil off.

3 Cover the rest of the fabric with the zodiac motifs, repositioning it on the work table as necessary and stencilling one section at a time. Leave to dry then iron the curtain on the wrong side to fix (set) the paints according to the manufacturer's instructions. Hem the edges and attach the curtain clips to the upper edge of the material.

BELOW: *You can change the colours of the zodiac symbols to suit your existing colour scheme if you wish.*

CITRUS ROLLER BLIND

The stylized, almost abstract, oranges and lemons on this stencilled blind (shade) give it a fifties feel. It would look great in a kitchen decorated with strong, fresh colours.

You will need

◆ tracing paper and pen
◆ stencil card
◆ craft knife and self-healing
  cutting mat
◆ plain white cotton fabric, to fit window
◆ newspaper
◆ masking tape
◆ acrylic gouache paints in orange, yellow,
  lime green, black and red
◆ stencil brushes
◆ fabric stiffener spray
◆ large decorator's paintbrush
◆ roller blind (shade) kit

1 Enlarge the template at the back of the book on a photocopier so that the repeat design will fit across the width of your blind (shade) and trace it. Transfer it three times on to stencil card. Using a craft knife and cutting mat, cut out only the areas you will need for each stencil: (1) the lemons, oranges and red spots; (2) the leaves; (3) the black details.

2 Lay out the white cotton fabric on the work surface, covered with newspaper, and secure with masking tape. Using gouache paints, carefully stencil the oranges and lemons motif all over the fabric. Keep the stencil brush as dry as possible, blotting off excess paint, and clean the stencil if paint starts to bleed under the edges.

3 Leave the orange and lemon motifs to dry, then proceed with the remaining colours. Stencil the leaves next, then the red spots (using the first stencil) and finally the black details. Leave to dry then spray the fabric with fabric stiffener following the manufacturer's instructions and hang on a washing line to dry, keeping it straight. Make up the blind using the blind kit.

GARDEN SHADOWS BLIND

Recreate the effect of a bright summer's day in the garden for the gloomiest of dull winter mornings. The beautiful patterns are formed as shafts of sunlight cast shadows from clematis and jasmine climbing plants on to a white wall.

You will need

- closely woven white cotton fabric such as ticking, 30cm/12in deeper and 15cm/6in wider than the window
- iron
- newspaper
- large sheet of acetate
- sheet of glass
- heat knife
- spray mount
- silver fabric paint
- stencil brush
- fabric stiffener spray
- tape measure
- ruler and pencil
- set square
- roller blind (shade) kit
- hacksaw
- abrasive paper (optional)

1 Wash and iron the fabric then place it on a pad of newspaper. Cut out the templates at the back of the book from acetate. Starting at the top centre edge, fix the clematis stencil in place with a light spray of adhesive. Stencil it in with silver fabric paint.

2 Moving down the fabric, stencil a second spray of clematis so that it appears to be joined on to the first. Add another long clematis spray in the same way, just to one side. Use only a small amount of paint at a time to prevent seepage, and build up two or three thin layers of paint to give solid colour.

3 Stencil in a spray of jasmine on the other side, starting it again at the top edge. This will give a denser look to the top part of the design, with the other tendrils trailing down from a leafy branch.

4 Continue stencilling until the fabric is covered, keeping the bottom part less densely patterned with just a few stems trailing down towards the edge.

5 Leave the fabric to dry completely. Fix (set) the paint according to the manufacturer's instructions using a hot iron and coat it with fabric stiffener, again following the manufacturer's instructions supplied.

6 Check the width of the finished blind (shade) once again against the actual window space, then trim the two side edges to this measurement. Mark in the cutting lines with a set square and ruler so that they are straight.

7 Using a hacksaw, cut the wooden batten (furring strip) so that it is 1cm/$\frac{1}{2}$in shorter than the finished width of the blind. Sand the ends to neaten, if necessary.

8 Following the directions given with the blind kit, press and stitch a channel along the lower edge. Insert the batten into the channel.

9 Cut the wooden roller to size and attach the metal fittings as directed. Fix the top edge of the blind to the adhesive tape supplied on the roller. Add the tacks if necessary to secure it in place.

10 Knot the acorn on to the cord, then thread the other end through the oval metal plate as shown in the instructions. Screw it in place at the centre back of the batten, then fix the blind to the window.

MOSAIC TABLECLOTH

Create a mosaic-effect border reminiscent of the colours and patterns of Moroccan tiles for a kitchen tablecloth. Just one simple stencil and a vibrant co-ordinating blue and aqua colour combination are used to effect. Hem the tablecloth fabric with smart mitred corners, for a professional finish to your work.

You will need

◆ cream cotton fabric, to fit the table
◆ iron
◆ scissors
◆ dressmaking pins
◆ needle and matching thread
◆ tracing paper and pen
◆ acetate sheet
◆ newspaper
◆ masking tape
◆ craft knife and self-healing cutting mat
◆ stencil brushes
◆ fabric paints in dark blue, light blue and light aqua

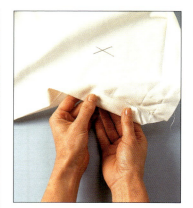

1 Press under a 2.5cm/1in wide double hem along all four edges of the cotton fabric square. Open out the fold at each corner and cut diagonally across with scissors to reduce the bulk at the corners.

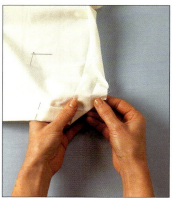

2 At each corner in turn, refold the complete hem on one edge. Fold the corner of the other edge of the fabric in at right angles to meet the inside crease.

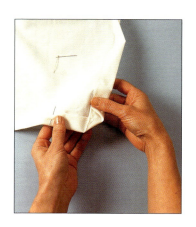

3 Refold the hem to form a neat mitred edge.

4 Pin the mitred corner into place and then repeat with the other three corners. Stitch the hem close to the inside folded edge.

5 Trace the template at the back of the book. Attach it to a piece of acetate sheet with masking tape. Carefully cut out the stencil using a craft knife and self-healing cutting mat.

6 Cover the work surface with newspaper. Place the stencil in position on the edge of the tablecloth and secure with small strips of masking tape.

7 Using a stencil brush, take up a small amount of dark blue fabric paint and carefully apply to the outer border of the stencil, dabbing lightly.

8 Apply light blue paint to the inner sections, leaving the central motif clear.

9 Apply light aqua paint to the central star motif. Remove the stencil and place it in the next position along the edge of the tablecloth. Repeat this pattern until the mosaic border is complete. Stencil the central star motif randomly over the centre of the tablecloth. Leave to dry then iron on the wrong side to fix (set) the paints, following the manufacturer's instructions.

ROSE TABLECLOTH

Two stencils are arranged here to decorate a square tablecloth; the same motifs could be used in many different combinations and sizes. Use two or three shades with each stencil shape to give a rounded, three-dimensional look to the roses, leaves and branches.

You will need

◆ tracing paper and pen
◆ stencil card or acetate
◆ craft knife and self-healing cutting mat
◆ 76cm/30in square of heavy white cotton fabric
◆ iron
◆ newspaper
◆ spray mount
◆ fabric paints in dark pink, pale pink, yellow, dark green, light green and warm brown
◆ stencil brushes
◆ vanishing fabric marker
◆ long ruler and T-square
◆ sewing machine
◆ white sewing thread

1 Enlarge the rose template at the back of the book on a photocopier so that it measures 15cm/6in across. Enlarge the branch template so that it is 30cm/12in long. Transfer both on to stencil card or acetate and carefully cut out using a craft knife and self-healing cutting mat.

2 Cover the work surface with newspaper. Fold the fabric in half each way, to find the centre. Press lightly along the creases. Spray the back of the rose stencil with spray mount and place it in the middle of the cloth. Stencil the rose, starting with dark pink paint in the corner petals and around the outer edge of the inner petals.

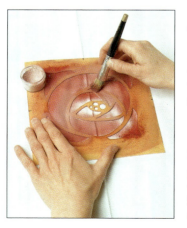

3 Fill in the rest of the petals with pale pink and colour the centre dots in yellow. Keep the brush upright and use a small circling motion to transfer the paint. Be careful not to overload the bristles. Peel off the stencil and allow the paint to dry.

4 Work a branch motif on each side of the rose, using the crease as a placement guide, to form a cross. Spray the back of the card with adhesive, as before. Stencil yellow paint in the centre of each leaf. ▶

5 Blend dark and light green paint and finish painting the leaves.

6 Work a small amount of brown fabric paint around the base of the leaves and the outside edge of the branches. Stencil a rose at the end of each branch. With a vanishing fabric marker, and using the ruler and T-square to get a perfectly accurate square, draw a line about 15cm/6in from each edge so that it is on the same level as the outer edge of the roses. Stencil a rose in each corner and then work a branch between the roses.

7 Leave the paint to dry then iron the tablecloth on the wrong side to fix (set) according to the manufacturer's instructions. To finish the tablecloth, turn under, press and stitch a narrow double hem along the outside edge.

BELOW: *If your tablecloth is larger than 76cm/30in, add in more rows of this stencilled rose pattern to fit the size of your chosen cloth.*

SUMMER QUILT COVER

A combination of stencilling and sponging is used to decorate this ready-made duvet cover. Choose light colours for the stripes so that the stencilling will show up.

You will need

- newspaper
- pale-coloured duvet cover, pre-washed
- dressmaking pins
- iron
- tracing paper and pen
- acetate or stencil card
- magic marker
- craft knife and self-healing cutting mat
- tailor's chalk
- string
- fabric paints in pink, green and yellow
- large household sponge
- spray mount
- small sponges or stencil brushes
- sewing machine

1 Cover the work surface with newspaper. Protect the back of the duvet cover from paint bleeding through by unpicking the sides of the cover and opening it out into a large rectangle. Roll up the underside of the cover and pin it so that it is out of the way. Lay out the upper side of the duvet with the area to be painted ironed flat.

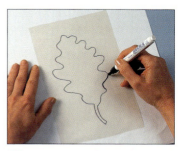

2 Enlarge the templates at the back of the book on a photocopier, to suit your design. Trace on to stencil card and cut out using a craft knife and a self-healing cutting mat.

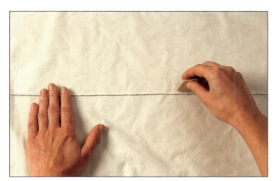

3 Using tailor's chalk, mark stripes across the duvet. First mark the position of the stripes at the edge of the duvet, making them deep enough for the stencils to fit. Then mark the midpoint on each stripe. Using a piece of string stretched across the duvet and pinned at each side, rule these lines across.

4 Dilute the fabric paint with water to the consistency of ink. Using the large household sponge, fill in the stripes of colour. Do not worry if the edges are a little rough, because this will make the final effect look more interesting. Leave each section of paint to dry before moving on to the next.

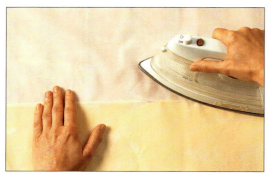

5 When the whole area is painted and completely dry, iron the fabric on the reverse to fix (set) the paint according to the manufacturer's instructions.

6 Spray the reverse of a stencil with spray mount. Place it on the midpoint of a stripe and apply colours using a small sponge or stencil brush.

7 Continue to stencil, keeping the motifs evenly spaced. After removing each stencil from the fabric, wipe away the excess paint to keep the colours clean.

8 Try blending colours together to give the finished stencil a textured appearance.

9 When the stencilling has been completed and the paint is thoroughly dry, iron again on the wrong side to fix (set) the paints according to the manufacturer's instructions.

10 Pin and stitch the side seams of the duvet cover. The fabric may seem stiff at first but washing it should solve this.

FEATHER THROW

The fringed border of this beautiful throw is created by simply pulling away the woven threads along each edge. Choose a fabric with a square, rather than a twill, weave that can easily be unravelled. Linen or heavy cotton would be ideal.

1 Wash the fabric to remove any chemical residue and press it well. Cut it into a perfect 1.3m/50in square by snipping between the threads to get a straight line along each edge.

2 To make the fringed edging, carefully unravel the fabric, one thread at a time, for a distance of 4cm/1½in along each side.

3 Enlarge the template at the back of the book on a photocopier and transfer it on to the stencil card using carbon paper. Cut it out, using a sharp craft knife and self-healing cutting mat. Spray the back lightly with spray mount and place it on the first corner. Mix a small amount of white and brown fabric paint in a saucer and stipple the feather with a dry brush.

4 Repeat the motif at roughly regular intervals across the fabric, altering the angle of the stencil so that the feathers are positioned randomly. Mix two shades of brown paint to make some of them light and others slightly darker, giving variety to the pattern.

5 Following the manufacturer's instructions, fix (set) the paint by ironing it with a hot steam iron and pressing cloth.

RIGHT: This throw is made from an upholstery-weight fabric, which gives it a rather heavy look, ideal to go across the arm of a chair or back of a sofa. Stencilling on to organza or a metallic voile would make a much more ethereal version to drape over a romantically dressed bed or to hang at a window.

LOVE PILLOWS

Make sure the message gets across by stencilling the word "love" on your pillows in both English and French. The typeface used is Gill Sans Bold, enlarged here to 42.5cm/17in long. Always pre-wash and iron the pillowcase fabric first to remove any glazes that could block the colour absorption of the paint.

1 Enlarge the templates at the back of the book to the required size on a photocopier. Coat the backs of the photocopies with spray mount and stick them to the stencil card.

2 Cut out the letters using a craft knife and cutting mat. The O, A and R need ties to retain the internal letter features, so draw in "bridges" before you cut out the letters.

3 Place a sheet of thick card (stock) inside the pillowcase, so that the paint colour does not bleed through to the other side.

4 Stencil the letters. Leave to dry then remove the card and iron the pillow cases on the reverse side to set the paint following the manufacturer's instructions.

GIRL'S BED CANOPY AND CUSHION

This must be the ultimate design for a very feminine bedroom. The muslin (cheesecloth) canopy is stencilled with fairies and hearts and tied with heart-stencilled ribbons.

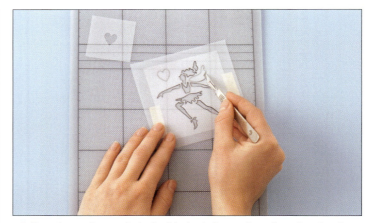

1 Trace the templates at the back of the book. Tape a piece of stencil card to the tracings. Using a craft knife and cutting mat, cut out one fairy stencil and one heart stencil.

2 Iron the muslin (cheesecloth) canopy to remove creases. Lay a section out flat on a plastic bag, to stop paint seeping through to your work surface. Tape the fairy stencil to the fabric and stencil with pale pink fabric paint.

3 Move the stencil to another position on the fabric and turn it at a different angle. Tape in place and stencil the fairy again.

4 Tape the heart stencil to the canopy. Stencil the heart then continue stencilling the fairy at random all over the front and sides of the canopy, adding the heart in any gaps.

5 Cut one 1m/1yd length of ribbon for a drawstring for the top of the canopy and four 48cm/19in lengths for the ties. Stencil hearts at random on the ribbons using bright pink paint.

6 Leave the paint to dry overnight then iron the canopy and ribbons on the wrong side to fix (set) the paint, following the manufacturer's instructions. Thread the drawstring through the channel at the top of the canopy with a bodkin and adjust the ends of the drawstring to extend equally from the channel. With a hot iron, press under 1.5cm/⁵⁄₈in at one end of each tie.

7 Pin and tack (baste) the pressed end of one ribbon to the canopy where it can be fastened around the opening edges. Pin and tack a corresponding ribbon underneath in the same position. Stitch close to the pressed edge then 1cm/¹⁄₂in from the first stitching. Repeat to attach the remaining ties. Trim all the ribbon ends diagonally.

8 Cut a 34 x 31cm/13$\frac{1}{2}$ x 12$\frac{1}{4}$in rectangle of mid-pink cotton fabric for the cushion front. With the long edges as the horizontal edges of the cushion, stencil three fairies across the centre using bright pink paint.The outer fairies should be at least 4cm/1$\frac{1}{2}$in within the short edges.

9 Stencil five hearts above and below the fairies using bright pink paint positioning the hearts at different jaunty angles. The hearts should be at least 4cm/1$\frac{1}{2}$in within the long edges. Leave to dry overnight then iron on the wrong side to fix the paint according to the manufacturer's instructions.

10 Cut two 31 x 10cm/12$\frac{1}{2}$ x 4in rectangles of chenille fabric for the borders, and a 48 x 31cm/19 x 12$\frac{1}{2}$in rectangle for the back. With right sides facing, pin the borders to the side edges of the front. Machine stitch, leaving a 1.5cm/$\frac{5}{8}$in seam allowance. Press the seams toward the borders.

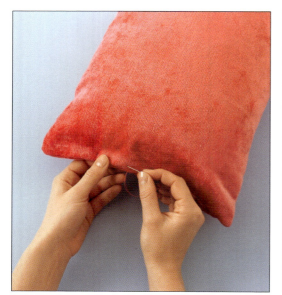

11 With right sides facing, pin the front and back together. Stitch, leaving a 1.5cm/$\frac{5}{8}$in seam allowance and a 20cm/ 8in gap to turn through. Clip the corners. Turn the cushion right side out and fill with toy filling. Slip-stitch the gap closed.

12 Stitch marabou trim along the front seams by handsewing with a double length of thread through the central core of the trim.

SEASHELL BEACH BAG

Crisp cream and navy give this smart beach bag a nautical look. Much of the charm of the stencilling lies in combining colours to give a three-dimensional look to the seashell shapes, so it's worth practising on spare fabric or lining paper first.

1 Wash and iron the cream fabric then cut in two lengthways. Trace the stencil from the back of the book or enlarge it on a photocopier. Transfer the outline to stencil card and cut out using a craft knife and cutting mat. Coat the back lightly with spray mount, and stencil five shells on each piece of fabric, using two or three colours. Leave to dry then iron on the reverse side to fix (set) the paint according to the manufacturer's instructions.

2 With the fabric right sides together, stitch a blue strip to the top edge of each cream piece, leaving a 1cm/½in seam allowance. Press the seam upward. Pin the rectangles right sides together, and stitch around the main bag. Press under the seam allowances on the open sides of the blue fabric, and topstitch in orange sewing thread. Fold in half lengthways. Machine-stitch parallel to the topstitch.

3 Cut the cord in half, and bind the ends with masking tape. Thread both pieces through the bag. Remove the tape, and bind the ends with blue thread, 5cm/2in from the ends. Fringe and comb the cord to make tassels. Trim neatly.

OPPOSITE: The choice of navy blue and red gives this beach bag a nautical look.

GINGERBREAD APRON

This apron wraps right around the waist so will protect clothing from the stickiest of fingers. The gingerbread pattern is so appealing there will be no question about young chefs wanting to put it on before creating their culinary masterpieces.

You will need

- cream cotton fabric, height the distance from the child's collar to the knee and width the child's waist measurement
- iron
- pencil
- scissors
- sewing needle and thread
- sewing machine
- cream thread
- tracing paper and pen or carbon paper and sharp pencil
- masking tape
- stencil card
- craft knife and self-healing cutting mat
- newspaper
- stencil brush
- fabric paints in ochre, brown, black and red
- fine artist's paintbrush
- 1m/30in of 2.5cm/1in-wide cream or white ribbon or tape

1 Wash and press the fabric. Fold it in half widthways and mark the child's waist position at the side edges. Mark a point 7.5cm/3in from the fold at the top edge and draw a curve between these two points. Cut along this curve, through both layers of fabric. Check the size against the child and alter if necessary. Neaten the cut edges with a 1cm/½in seam. Tack (baste) then machine stitch.

2 Fold the apron in half widthways again and press along the crease, then press a turning about 12cm/4½in from the bottom edge. These creases will act as a guide for positioning the stencil.

3 Trace the template at the back of the book and tape it on to stencil card. Using a craft knife and cutting mat, cut it out. Place the fabric on a layer of newspaper. Position the stencil in the centre of the apron so that the feet touch the horizontal crease. Using a dry brush, stipple it in with a light layer of ochre paint.

4 Add a stippling of brown paint around the edges of the stencil to give a more three-dimensional look to the gingerbread figure. Any irregularities in the surface will add to the cookie-like texture, so the paint does not have to be too smooth or densely applied.

5 Stencil in another two gingerbread figures at either side, varying the density of colour in each one to give them an individual appearance. Keep their feet along the crease so that they stand in a straight row. Measure the distance between their hands before positioning the stencil to make sure they are evenly spaced.

6 Using a fine artist's paintbrush, paint in two black "currant" circles for the eyes and a red semicircular "cherry slice" mouth to complete the face on the gingerbread men. Each one can have their own individual expression if you wish. Paint three "currant" buttons down their bodies. Leave to dry completely, then iron the apron on the reverse to fix (set) the paint, following the manufacturer's instructions.

7 Cut two 30cm/12in lengths of ribbon and trim one end of each into a fishtail shape. Stitch the other ends in position at the waist. Stitch the remaining ribbon in a loop at the neck.

SEVENTIES FLOWER CANVASES

Stencilling doesn't have to have a folk art theme as this set of bold canvases shows. Adapt the colours to suit your own room scheme and choose from a range of different-sized canvases, available from good art suppliers.

You will need

- three artist's canvases
- acrylic primer (optional)
- medium decorator's paintbrush
- acrylic paints in turquoise, orange and pink
- tracing paper and pen or carbon paper and sharp pencil
- masking tape
- stencil card
- craft knife and self-healing cutting mat
- stencil brushes
- fine artist's paintbrush

1 Most shop-bought canvases are already primed, but if you are reusing an old canvas or have made your own, paint all three with a layer of acrylic primer. Leave to dry completely.

2 Paint the first canvas with a base coat of turquoise paint. Trace the templates at the back of the book and tape them on to stencil card. Using a craft knife and cutting mat, cut them out. You can make the stamen stencils from either card or acetate.

3 Using orange paint, stencil a large flower on to the coloured background, with a thick brush. Apply the paint in two thin layers and use the blocking technique (see Stencilling Basics section) to give a dense colour. Make sure no acrylic primer shows through.

4 Start on the second canvas while the first one is drying. Stencil a large turquoise flower on to the top surface, applying two thin layers of paint and using the blocking technique to give a dense colour.

5 You will also need to colour in the areas where the petals overlap the edges. Hold the stencil against the side and draw in the outline with a pencil to complete the petal shape. Fill in with matching paint, using a fine brush.

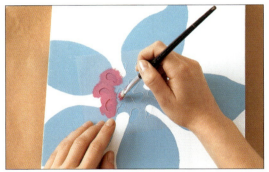

6 Stencil a small white flower to overlap the orange flower on the turquoise canvas.

7 Using bright pink paint, stencil in the stamens over the centre of the large flower.

8 Add the stamens to the two flowers on the small canvas. If you wish, you can make a third painting to go with these two, using the canvas that appears at the bottom left of the finished picture as a guide to colour and layout. The variations on this theme are endless. Choose colours to match any colour scheme, arrange nine squares in three rows of three, or make just one enormous canvas for real visual impact.

OPPOSITE: Limit your choice of paint colours to three and allow the white of the artist's primer to show through.

AMISH FLOORCLOTH

Floorcloths were very popular in America during the 18th century, using painted sailcloth canvas to imitate chequered marble floors or the geometric designs of oriental carpets. The pattern for this floorcloth is adapted from an Amish quilt and the colours are also Amish-inspired, but you can use any combination.

1 Turn the canvas over. If you want to secure it, staple it down. Apply three coats of primer or emulsion (latex) paint, rubbing lightly with abrasive paper between coats.

2 Using a ruler and pencil, draw a border 4cm/1$\frac{1}{2}$in wide around the edge, mitring the corners. Apply strong fabric adhesive to the border and fold it flat, using the back of a spoon to apply pressure and smooth any bumps.

3 Mark out the design from the back of the book except for the stars. Paint the framework following the colour scheme illustrated.

4 Cut three simple geometric stencils following the design at the back of the book from acetate sheet or stencil card using a sharp craft knife and self-healing cutting mat.

5 Stencil the red and blue stars in the centre of the large squares. Give the back of the stencil a light coat of spray mount to keep it in place as you paint. Use the paint sparingly on a dry brush but try to get a flat colour finish.

6 When the stars are dry add the purple and light blue triangles. Lightly spray the back of the stencil with adhesive and place it over the star, aligning the white space with the stencil cut-out.

7 The corner boxes are done in alternate colours. Begin by painting half of them using dusky pink acrylic or stencil paint and a medium-to-large stencil brush.

8 Finish the colour scheme for the floorcloth by painting the rest of the corner boxes with light emerald green acrylic or stencil paint.

9 Apply one coat of varnish tinted with a squeeze of raw umber and raw sienna acrylic paint to mellow the colour. Leave to dry then apply two coats of clear varnish, allowing adequate drying time between them.

STARS AND STRIPES FLOORCLOTH

Varnished floorcloths were introduced by the early American settlers, who recycled the canvas sails that had carried them to the New World. Make this bright floorcloth to cover most of the room or just as a small mat – artist's suppliers sell canvas in a wide range of sizes. It is available pre-primed or you can prime it yourself. Each coat of varnish you apply will add years to the floorcloth's life.

You will need

- natural-coloured artist's canvas, size as required
- ruler and pencil
- craft knife and self-healing cutting mat
- 5cm/2in double-sided carpet tape
- white acrylic primer (optional)
- medium decorator's brush
- masking tape
- acrylic paint in scarlet, cobalt blue and white
- tracing paper
- stencil card
- stencil brush
- clear or antique tinted matt (flat) polyurethane varnish and brush

1 Draw a 10cm/4in border on all four sides of the back of the canvas. Using a craft knife and cutting mat, cut across the corners as shown.

2 Stick double-sided carpet tape along the border line. Peel off the backing tape, then fold over the raw edge of the artist's canvas.

3 If the canvas is unprimed, apply two coats of white acrylic primer. Leave to dry.

4 Mark vertical stripes 7.5cm/3in wide down the canvas. Outline alternating stripes with masking tape.

5 Paint alternating stripes on the canvas with scarlet acrylic paint and a medium decorator's brush.

6 Leave to dry completely, then carefully peel off the low-tack masking tape.

7 Trace the star template at the back of the book. Cut out from stencil card using a craft knife and cutting mat.

8 Place the stencil on a white stripe, about 5cm/2in from one end of the canvas. Using a stencil brush, apply blue paint sparingly, working inwards from the points of the star. Wipe the back of the stencil to avoid smudging. Space the stars about 10cm/4in apart along all the white stripes.

9 Repeat with white acrylic paint stencilled on the red stripes, positioning the white stars to fall halfway between the blue stars.

10 Apply at least three coats of varnish, leaving to dry between coats. Use an antique tinted varnish if you wish to mellow the bright colours.

OPPOSITE: *You can alter the colour of the stripes and the star motif to suit your preferences or your choice of flag.*

HOME ACCESSORIES

Here is a selection of wonderful ideas that you can make for your own home or to give as a gift to mark a birthday or other special occasion. Picture frames, candles, vases and trays are indispensable items, which everybody needs to have, but they become exclusive accessories when embellished with stencilled designs. Etching fluid and gold leaf techniques add an air of exclusivity and are also interesting to do.

ABOVE: Cream church candles look stylish and fresh with the addition of a simple stencilled star motif.

LEFT: Glass etching spray is a simple method of creating the illusion of etched glass.

GILDED LAMPSHADE

A simple parchment lampshade makes an ideal base for gilding. The heraldic stencilled design on a shellac base coat gives the shade an antique appearance. Use a low-wattage bulb with this shade to avoid tarnishing.

You will need

- plain parchment lampshade
- stencil brushes
- amber shellac varnish
- tracing paper and pen
- stencil card or acetate
- craft knife and self-healing cutting mat
- masking tape
- gold stencil paint

1 Using a large round stencil brush, stipple an even but blotchy coat of amber shellac varnish over the surface of the lampshade. Leave to dry for 30 minutes to 1 hour.

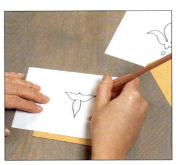

2 Trace the templates from the back of the book and transfer to stencil card or acetate.

3 Cut out the stencils using a craft knife and cutting mat.

4 Mark the positions for the stencils around the lampshade. Secure the first stencil at the bottom of the shade with masking tape. Stir the gold paint well, then stipple through the stencil. Do not load the brush with too much paint or it will bleed. Remove the stencil carefully before repositioning it.

5 When you have completed the bottom row, secure the second stencil at the top of the shade. Stencil the top row in the same way as before. Leave the shade to dry for at least 1 hour.

OPPOSITE: *You could try using silver, bronze or pewter stencil paint on this lampshade.*

ELIZABETHAN LAMPSHADE

Here, an Elizabethan border design is applied to a lampshade using a combination of sponge and stencil techniques. The pattern would also look sumptuous using deep blue or red with gold. For a larger lampshade, enlarge the template on a photocopier.

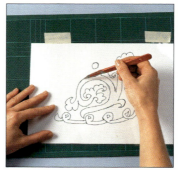

1 Trace the template at the back of the book on to the acetate sheet. Cut out using a craft knife and cutting mat or a heat knife.

2 Lay the design on a sheet of white paper and, using a stencil brush, apply undiluted black paint to the paper around the acetate. Keep the brush upright and dab, rather than brush, the paint on.

3 Apply the base colours of gold and white to the lampshade using a sponge. Take up only a small amount of paint each time, so that the texture of the sponge is transferred to the shade. Leave to dry.

4 Using strips of low-tack masking tape, attach the stencil to the lampshade. Use small curls of tape on the underside of the stencil to attach parts that do not lay flat.

5 Using the stencil brush, apply small amounts of black paint to the lampshade, gradually building up the density of colour. Remove the stencil and allow the paint to dry. To speed up the drying process, you can use a hairdryer.

6 Tape the stencil to the next position and apply paint as before until the whole lampshade has been patterned. Leave to dry.

7 Retape the stencil to the lampshade, taking care to position the stencil over the previous work. Use a small piece of sponge to apply gold highlights.

GOLD LEAF PICTURE FRAME

This picture frame has been decorated using a simple square stencil, which has been embellished with gold leaf. Applying leaf metals is a technique that should not be rushed.

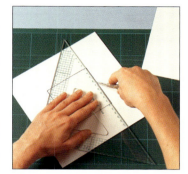

1 Using a craft knife and a self-healing cutting mat, cut two pieces of card (stock) to the size that you wish your frame to be. Cut a central window in one piece. The frame illustrated here has a total area of 21 x 21cm/8$^1/_2$ x 8$^1/_2$in with a central window of 9 x 9cm/3$^1/_2$ x 3$^1/_2$in.

2 Cut out a piece of canvas, linen or heavy silk 2cm/$^3/_4$in larger all around than the picture frame.

3 Apply spray mount to the frame and place it in the centre of the fabric, wrong side up. Rub your hand over the card to form a secure bond.

4 Using a vanishing fabric pen or pencil, draw two diagonals across the window. Measure and cut out a 5cm/ 2in square in the centre of the frame.

5 Apply strips of double-sided tape all round the reverse edges of the frame. Pull the extra fabric back and stick it down. Cut a mitre in each corner and stitch.

6 To keep the back of the frame neat and tidy, apply masking tape over the raw edges of the fabric.

7 Using a craft knife, cut a piece of stencil card or acetate film to a rectangle the same size as one side of the frame, corner to corner (21 x 6cm/8$\frac{1}{2}$ x 2$\frac{1}{2}$in for the frame illustrated). Mark out equally spaced squares along the length (4cm/1$\frac{1}{2}$in squares with a 1cm/$\frac{1}{2}$in division), and cut out.

8 Using masking tape, attach the stencil to one side of the front of the frame. Fill in the squares with colour using a stencil brush or sponge. Leave to dry then remove the stencil and tape it to the next side, matching the corner squares. Continue until all four sides have been coloured.

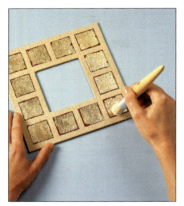

9 Carefully following the manufacturer's instructions, apply a small gold leaf square inside the stencilled one. Usually, this involves applying size and leaving for 15 minutes before applying the gold leaf with a soft brush. Leave for about 2 hours to set, then buff up the gold leaf and remove the unstuck pieces of gold.

10 Using heavy card and a sharp-bladed craft knife, cut out a right-angled triangle of the same height as the frame and 10cm/4in wide. Score along the longest side 1cm/$\frac{1}{2}$in from the edge and then use PVA (white) glue to stick it to the backing board cut out in step 1.

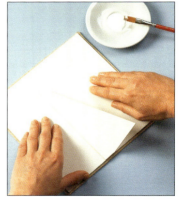

11 Apply PVA glue to the reverse of the backing board on three sides and stick it to the frame. The top is left open to slide in a picture. To protect the gold leaf and to prevent dust from collecting on the fabric, paint the front of the frame with one or two coats of clear varnish or lacquer.

FRAMED CHALKBOARD

Once you have had a chalkboard in the kitchen it becomes one of life's absolute essentials. Here the frame is made of an old plank sawn into four pieces – two long, two short glued together. Choose the size to suit your wall space. Cramp the frame while the glue sets or hold it together with string, twisting a pencil in the string to tighten it.

You will need

- frame made up as above
- tracing paper and pen
- spray mount
- stencil card
- craft knife and self-healing cutting mat
- emulsion (latex) paints in dull blue and red
- small decorator's paintbrush
- medium-grade abrasive paper
- spray mount
- stencil brush
- artist's acrylic paint in black
- antiquing varnish and brush
- hardboard, 2.5cm/1in larger all around than the inner frame measurement
- blackboard paint
- small hammer and panel pins (brads)
- (you will also need a piece of chalk!)

1 Trace the templates, or enlarge them on a photocopier. Spray the back lightly with spray mount and stick on to stencil card. Cut out the shapes using a craft knife and cutting mat.

2 Paint the frame with dull blue emulsion (latex) paint. Leave to dry completely.

3 Paint the inner and outer edges of the frame with red emulsion paint. Leave to dry.

4 Rub the paint with medium-grade abrasive paper to reveal the grain of the wood.

5 Spray the back of each stencil lightly with spray mount and position on the frame. Arrange the shapes as shown in the main picture.

6 Using a small stencil brush, lightly apply the red emulsion paint to the frame.

7 Darken the red paint slightly by mixing in a little black acrylic paint.

8 Using the stencil brush, rub the dark red paint deep into the grain in just a few places.

9 When dry, rub over with abrasive paper to remove any dark red paint from the surface.

10 Apply one or two coats of antiquing varnish. Leave the frame to dry.

OPPOSITE: *The best country accessories usually look worn and loved like this framed chalkboard.*

11 Paint the hardboard with two coats of blackboard paint. Leave to dry.

12 Attach the blackboard to the back of the frame, using panel pins (brads).

LEAFY PICTURE FRAMES

The stylish raised leaf patterns around these frames are simple to create using ordinary white interior filler instead of paint to fill in the stencilled leaf shapes. Keep the background colours soft and muted for an antique effect.

You will need

- 2 wooden frames
- dark green acrylic paint
- medium decorator's paintbrush
- fine-grade abrasive paper
- stencil card
- scissors
- ready-mixed interior filler
- stencil brush

1 Paint the frames dark green. When dry, gently rub them down with abrasive paper to create a subtle distressed effect.

2 Enlarge the templates at the back of the book to fit the frames. Transfer the designs to stencil card and cut them out using scissors.

3 Position a stencil on the first frame and stipple ready-mixed filler through the stencil. Reposition the stencil and continue all around the frame. Leave to dry.

4 Repeat with a different combination of motifs on the second frame. When the filler is completely hard, gently smooth over the leaves with abrasive paper.

OPPOSITE: You can also use textured gel combined with acrylic paint and stippled on to the frame to achieve a similar effect.

ART NOUVEAU HATBOX

An elegantly stencilled hatbox and matching shoe bag would be perfect for storing a bride's hat and shoes after the big day. Or, you could make a set for yourself and a set to give to someone special. And you needn't stop there: stencil a whole stack of matching hatboxes to use for stylish storage in a bedroom.

You will need

- round hatbox
- medium decorator's paintbrushes
- white undercoat
- pale green water-based woodwash
- tape measure
- pencil
- tracing paper and pen
- stencil card
- craft knife and self-healing cutting mat
- ruler
- spray mount
- stencil brushes
- stencil paints in dark green, royal blue and pale green

1 Paint the hatbox with two coats of white undercoat. Dilute one part pale green woodwash with one part water and apply two or three light washes to the hatbox, allowing them to dry between coats. Measure the circumference of the box and divide by six or eight. Lightly mark the measurements on the lid and side of the box with a pencil.

3 Continue to work around the box. Reposition the stencil on the leaves and add shadow to the points where the leaves join the stem, using royal blue paint and a clean brush.

LEFT: *Stencil a matching calico shoe bag to protect a treasured pair of shoes.*

OPPOSITE: *Line a hatbox with matching tissue paper.*

2 Trace the flower and heart templates at the back of the book and cut from stencil card. Rule a pencil line across the bottom of the stencil to help align it on the box. Spray with spray mount and position on the box. Using a stencil brush and dark green stencil paint, stencil the leaves and stem. Remove the stencil when dry, respray with spray mount and reposition.

4 Using the single heart stencil, add a pale green heart between each pair of leaves.

5 Stencil flowerheads around the rim of the lid in dark green, adding a royal blue shadow as before. Stencil the flower motif in the centre of the lid.

6 Add pale green heart motifs around the main motif, using a very small amount of paint for a delicate touch.

CITRUS FRUIT TRAY

This bamboo tray has been given a tropical look with juicy orange and lime stencils, perfect for summer drinks on a sunny day, or to use in a conservatory. You could also transform an old tray by painting over the existing surface.

You will need

- fine-grade abrasive paper
- tray
- tracing paper and pen or carbon paper and sharp pencil
- masking tape
- stencil card
- craft knife and self-healing cutting mat
- acrylic paints in pale orange, dark orange, pale green, dark green, dark brown and white
- stencil brush
- gloss or matt (flat) varnish and brush

1 Sand the tray lightly to remove any existing varnish. Trace the templates at the back of the book and tape on to stencil card. Using a craft knife and cutting mat cut them out, leaving a narrow margin round each motif.

2 Stipple a couple of pale orange circles using a small to medium-size stencil brush, as the background for the orange slices, protecting the surface of the rest of the tray with masking tape.

3 Fix the circle stencil back in place over the oranges and slot the segment stencil within it. Using dark orange, fill in the segments, adding some light and dark stippling to create texture within the shapes.

4 Stipple the lime and leaves in two shades of green. Give the fruit a more three-dimensional look by stippling light green in the centre and dark green around the outside edge. Stipple the stalk in dark brown.

5 Stencil the "rind" of the lime segments in dark green and the main part in light green. Add light white stippling across the "pips". Leave to dry completely then apply three coats of gloss or matt (flat) varnish.

GILDED CANDLES

Church candles look extra special adorned with simple gold stars and stripes. Always associated with Christmas, candles are popular all year round for their soft romantic lighting. Cutting the stencils may be fiddly but it is then a quick job to spray on the gold paint.

You will need

- acetate
- selection of candles
- marker pen
- tracing paper and pen
- craft knife and self-healing cutting mat
- spray mount
- masking tape
- metallic spray paint
- protective face mask

1 Wrap a piece of acetate around the candle. Mark and cut it to fit exactly. Do not overlap the edges. Cut it a few millimetres shorter than the candle.

2 Trace the star templates at the back of the book. Lay a piece of acetate over the stars and trace over them with a marker pen.

3 Cut out the stars using a craft knife and cutting mat.

4 Spray one side of the stencil with spray mount and wrap around the candle, centring it so that there is a small gap at either end. Secure the acetate join with masking tape. Mask the top of the candle, ensuring there are no gaps.

RIGHT: Create a range of attractive gilded patterns by varying the size of the stencilled stars and stripes used on the candles.

5 Spray a very fine mist of metallic spray paint over the candle, holding the can about 30cm/12in from the surface. If too much paint is applied, it will drip underneath the stencil. Keep checking that the stencil is well stuck down to avoid any fuzzy lines around the stars. Leave the paint to dry for a couple of minutes, then carefully remove the masking tape and acetate.

6 For a stars and stripes candle, cut strips of acetate and trace a line of stars along each strip. Cut out as before. Spray one side of the acetate strips with spray mount. Stick the strips on to the candle at equal spaces. Secure them with small pieces of tape at the join.

7 Mask off the top of the candle as before. Spray the candle with metallic paint and remove the masking tape and stencil when dry.

8 For a reverse stencil design, cut out individual star shapes from acetate. Apply spray mount to one side, stick on to the candle and mask off the top of the candle as before. Spray with metallic paint and carefully remove the acetate stars when the paint is dry.

CITRUS FRUIT BOWL

Stencilling offers a quick and easy method of decorating china and this lime motif is ideal for a fruit bowl. The simple shape of the lime can be drawn freehand.

You will need

- soft pencil
- tracing paper
- masking tape
- stencil card
- craft knife and self-healing cutting mat
- plain china bowl
- cleaning fluid
- clean cotton rag
- yellow chinagraph pencil
- water-based ceramic paints in citrus green, mid-green, dark green and yellow
- artist's paintbrushes
- acrylic varnish and brush (optional)

1 Draw a freehand lime shape on tracing paper. Using masking tape to hold the tracing paper in place, transfer the outline to a piece of stencil card. Cut all around the shape using a craft knife and cutting mat.

2 Clean the china bowl. Attach the stencil to the bowl using masking tape. Draw inside the stencil outline on to the bowl using a yellow chinagraph pencil. Repeat the lime motif all over the bowl.

3 Fill in all the lime shapes with citrus green paint using a fine artist's brush. Leave the paint to dry completely then add highlights to each of the fruits, using the mid-green paint. Leave the paint to dry.

4 Paint a stalk at the end of each lime shape in dark green paint. Leave to dry. Paint the background all over the outside of the bowl yellow, leaving a thin white outline around each of the lime shapes to help them stand out.

5 Apply a coat of acrylic varnish over the painted section, or bake the bowl in the oven following the paint manufacturer's instructions.

LEAF-ETCHED VASE

The delicate effect of etched glass is easy to imitate nowadays with a glass etching spray, which is now available from most good art and craft suppliers. For the best results, spray through a stencil cut from adhesive plastic.

You will need

- tracing paper and pen
- masking tape
- sticky-back plastic (contact paper)
- craft knife and self-healing cutting mat
- straight-sided vase at least
  23cm/9in tall
- object taller than the vase to support
  it while spraying
- glass etching spray
- scrap piece of plastic or paper

1 Trace the template at the back of the book. Using masking tape, tape the tracing face down on to the back of a piece of sticky-back plastic (contact paper). Draw over the design to transfer it. Cut out the stencil using a craft knife and cutting mat.

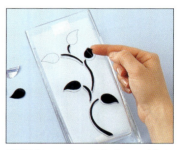

2 Make sure the vase is clean and free from grease. Trim the tracing to fit inside the vase. Tape the tracing inside the front of the vase. Peel the backing paper off the stencils and stick in position on the front of the vase matching the positions on the template.

3 Upturn the vase and slip it over a taller item so the vase rim does not rest on the work surface. Cover the surrounding area with a scrap piece of plastic or paper. Spray the vase with glass etching spray following the manufacturer's instructions.

4 Leave the vase to dry thoroughly and apply a second coat if necessary. Carefully peel off all the stencils. Do not clean the vase in a dishwasher but wash gently in warm soapy water.

STATIONERY AND PAPER

Stencilling on to paper is easy, quick and fun and any good art store or stationer should have a selection of handmade and textured papers to choose from. You can make lanterns, greetings cards, gift tags or wedding stationery, or stencil a whole sheet of paper to wrap up a present or cover a special book. Ready-made boxes can also be adorned with patterns to turn them into special storage containers for keepsakes and gifts.

ABOVE: Paper lanterns with various stencilled motifs can be used to decorate a room during a festive season.

LEFT: Handmade stencilled Christmas wrapping paper will add a special touch to any present.

TAURUS GIFT WRAP

Personalize a special birthday gift for a friend or loved one with gift wrap stencilled with their relevant star sign. Deep red and black have been used here to match the energetic, earthy character of the Taurean but you can choose colours to suit the person.

You will need

◆ thin card (stock) or paper and pencil
◆ acetate sheet
◆ black felt-tipped pen
◆ craft knife and self-healing cutting mat
◆ plain deep red gift wrap
◆ masking tape
◆ black acrylic paint
◆ stencil brush

1 Using the main photograph as a guide, draw the Taurus motif freehand on to card (stock) or paper.

2 Place the acetate over the template and trace the outline with a black felt-tipped pen. Cut out the stencil using a craft knife and cutting mat.

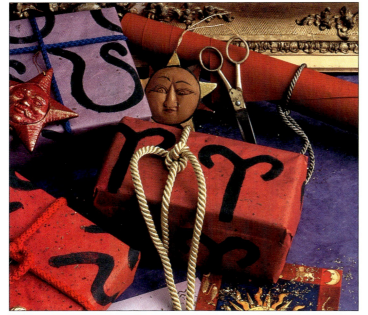

3 Decide on the positioning of the motifs on the gift wrap, marking lightly with a pencil if necessary. Position the stencil and use a little masking tape to hold it in place. Stipple the design with the stencil brush. Lift the stencil off carefully and repeat to cover the paper.

BUTTERFLY GIFT WRAP

Original hand-printed wrapping paper turns a present into something very special. Once you've tried stencilling you may never want to buy printed gift wrap again.

You will need

- tracing paper and pen
- acetate sheet
- black felt-tipped pen
- craft knife and self-healing cutting mat
- coloured paper
- masking paper
- stencil brush
- acrylic paints in red and black

1 Trace the butterfly template at the back of the book, enlarging it on a photocopier if necessary. Place a piece of acetate over it and draw the wings for the first stencil, using a felt-tipped pen. Use a second piece of acetate to make a stencil of the body and wing markings.

2 Cut out both stencils using a craft knife and cutting mat. Secure the first stencil lightly to the paper with masking tape and then stipple on the red paint. Do not overload the stencil brush. Reposition the acetate stencil and repeat to cover the paper.

3 When the red acrylic paint is completely dry, secure the second butterfly stencil in place with masking tape. Stipple on the black paint and then repeat to complete all the butterflies. You can try this in different colourways.

SEAWEED GIFT WRAP

Swirling seaweed shapes in shades of green and blue produce an underwater effect that makes a really unusual wrapping paper for someone who lives by the sea. Vary the paint colours according to the background paper you choose.

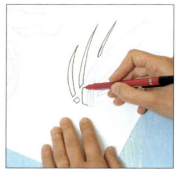

1 Trace the templates A, B and C from the back of the book, enlarging them on a photocopier if necessary. Go over the outline with the black pen. Lay the acetate on top and cut out the stencil using a craft knife and cutting mat.

2 Position the acetate stencil on the wrapping paper. Mix sap green acrylic paint with a little white paint. Using a stencil brush, stencil templates A and B side by side in rows across the paper, leaving space for a row of template C between them.

3 Using white paint, add highlights to the seaweed tips.

4 Mix blue paint with white and stencil C in rows, leaving a stencil space in between for the lighter blue seaweeds. Overlap some of the fronds slightly.

SNOWFLAKE GIFT WRAP

Create your own Christmas gift wrap and your friends and family will appreciate their presents even more than usual. This is one project where the finished effect is more important than accuracy and neatness, so it is quicker than you might think.

1 Trace the three templates at the back of the book and tape on to stencil card. Using a craft knife and cutting mat, cut each one out in a single piece. The cut-out shapes will be used to make a reverse stencil.

2 Load the stencil brush with white paint. Using the first stencil, block in a scattering of positive snowflakes across the sheet of wrapping paper. Leave enough space between them to fit in the other motifs, about six or seven shapes.

3 Fill in some of the spaces between them with positive stencils of the other two snowflake stencils, overlapping them if you wish.

4 To make reverse stencils of the three snowflakes, use a blocking action to work over the outlines and on to the surrounding background.

BUTTON GIFT WRAP AND GIFT TAGS

Stencil colourful button motifs at random on plain paper to make an unusual gift wrap, with cut-out buttons as co-ordinating gift tags.

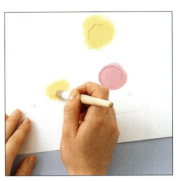

1 Trace the template at the back of the book. Tape a piece of stencil card to the tracings with masking tape. Cut out the stencils using a craft knife and cutting mat. You will need three stencils – the outer buttons and heart button, the inner buttons, and the buttonholes. Tape the outer button and heart button stencil to white paper with masking tape, then mark the registration marks lightly with a soft pencil.

2 Apply a thin coat of pink paint to a ceramic tile with the flat paintbrush. Dab at the paint with a stencil brush and stencil a button holding the stencil brush upright and moving it in a circular motion. Stencil all the buttons using pink, mustard, lilac and turquoise acrylic paint. Leave to dry completely.

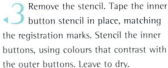

3 Remove the stencil. Tape the inner button stencil in place, matching the registration marks. Stencil the inner buttons, using colours that contrast with the outer buttons. Leave to dry.

4 Remove the stencil. Tape the button-hole stencil in place, matching the marks. Stencil the buttonholes using dark green paint. Remove the stencil and erase the marks. Tape the outer button stencil to the paper in a different position. Continue until the paper is covered. ▶

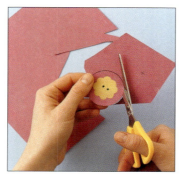
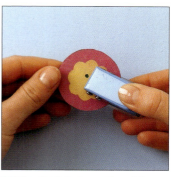

5 To make a button gift tag, draw a 5cm/2in diameter circle on coloured card. Tape the outer button stencil of the flower-shaped button in the centre. Mark the registration marks. Stencil the button. Leave to dry. Remove the stencil.

6 Tape the buttonhole stencil in place, matching up the registration marks. Stencil the buttonholes in dark green acrylic paint. Leave to dry completely then cut out the circle with sharp scissors.

7 Punch a hole at one edge of the tag using a hole punch. Tie up the parcel using co-ordinating coloured wool, thread or string and threading it through the button gift tag to secure in place.

BUTTERFLY GREETINGS CARDS

The simple outlines of these three butterflies can be used in various combinations to produce a range of very personal greetings cards or invitations. Here are just a few ideas of how they could be used – the possibilities are endless.

You will need

- selection of handmade paper, tracing paper and blank cards in pinks, lilacs and purples
- tracing paper and pen or carbon paper and sharp pencil
- masking tape
- stencil card
- craft knife and self-healing cutting mat
- acrylic paints in pink, purple and lilac
- stencil brush
- PVA (white) glue
- ruler

1 Trace the templates at the back of the book and tape on to stencil card. Cut out, using a craft knife and cutting mat. Stencil a single pink butterfly on to a small rectangle of textured handmade paper. Cut four angled slots in a purple card blank to mount it, one at each corner, and slip the paper in place under the slots.

3 Create a multi-layered image by stencilling four butterflies on to a piece of tracing paper. Stencil more butterflies on to the front of a darker card blank. Trim the trace to size and glue it to the front of the card.

4 If your paper does not have a deckle edge, tearing it against a ruler will give an attractive finish to the card. Mount the finished piece as in step 1 to make a larger version of the single butterfly card.

2 For a card with a three-dimensional look, stencil several overlapping butterflies on to a paper blank, each in a different colour. Cut out carefully around the edges of the wings with a craft knife. Ease the wings gently upwards so that the butterflies appear to be in flight but do not cut into the central bodies.

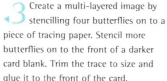

▶

WEDDING STATIONERY

Linked rings are a symbol of love because they have no end, so these elegantly entwined rings and hearts are ideal motifs for wedding stationery. Continue the theme and stencil them on invitations, place names and thank you cards.

You will need

- ◆ tracing paper and pen
- ◆ carbon paper
- ◆ stencil card
- ◆ masking tape
- ◆ sharp pencil
- ◆ craft knife and self-healing cutting mat
- ◆ white deckle-edged stationery
- ◆ flat paintbrush
- ◆ gold paint
- ◆ ceramic tile
- ◆ stencil brush

1 Trace the templates at the back of the book. Place a piece of carbon paper face down on to stencil card and tape the tracing on top. Redraw the template with a sharp pencil to transfer the design. Using a craft knife and cutting mat, cut out the stencil.

2 Tape the linked rings stencil to the top of a sheet of writing paper either in a corner or centrally. Using a flat paintbrush, spread a thin coat of gold paint on to a ceramic tile. Dab at the paint with a stencil brush and stencil the rings.

3 Stencil the linked hearts centrally on the back flap of an envelope. Leave the stationery to dry. The stencils can be used in various ways, the linked rings on the envelope or the linked hearts in a row as a border on an invitation or on writing paper for example.

HANDPRINTED BOOK COVERS

These small overall repeat prints are inspired by the individual woodcut patterns that once appeared on hand-bound books of the past. Stencil several sheets, using a different colourway for each volume or book title.

You will need

- ruler
- book
- pencil
- sheet of white paper
- tracing paper and pen or carbon paper and sharp pencil
- masking tape
- stencil card
- craft knife and self-healing cutting mat
- blue acrylic paint
- stencil brush
- scissors
- PVA (white) glue

1 Measure the width of the book from the edge of the back cover to the edge of the front cover (including the spine), and its height. Add on 10cm/4in to each measurement to allow for the folded turnings. Draw a horizontal rectangle on the paper to this size.

2 Trace the template at the back of the book and tape on to stencil card. Cut out, using a craft knife and cutting mat. Starting at the right side edge and using only a small amount of paint on the brush, stencil in the first block of pattern.

3 To continue the repeat, line up the right edge of the stencil with the completed print. Line up the pattern by eye, so that the painted areas can be seen within the cut-out shapes. Continue filling in blocks of pattern to fill in the entire rectangle. Use an extra piece of paper where necessary to protect the stencilled area. Leave the stencilled paper to dry completely.

OPPOSITE: Stencilled bookcovers can give a new lease of life to a book and look good on bookshelves.

4 Cut out the cover and wrap it around the book to find out where the spine fits. Cut slanting lines in to each edge of the spine and fold over the side and top and bottom edges.

5 Unfold the four edges, mitre the corners by turning them in at 45-degree angles. Refold the edges to check that the cover will fit when the book is closed, and adjust them if necessary.

6 Put the jacket back over the book and fold the edges back in place. Secure each corner with a light dab of glue. For a different look, stencil in white on a coloured background.

CONFETTI BOX

Make a pretty box ready for scattering confetti at a wedding and stencil it with a romantic pair of cupid's wings. You can put wedding keepsakes in it afterwards.

You will need

- pen
- bright blue card (stock)
- craft knife and self-healing cutting mat
- metal ruler
- scissors
- tracing paper
- carbon paper
- masking tape
- stencil card
- sharp pencil
- silver acrylic paint
- ceramic tile
- small flat decorator's paintbrush
- stencil brush
- double-sided adhesive tape

1 Referring to the templates at the back of the book, draw the box and lid on bright blue card (stock). Using a craft knife and cutting mat, cut out the box and lid plus an 11.7cm/4⅝in square for the base, cutting the straight edges against a metal ruler. Score the box and lid along the broken lines with the blade of a pair of scissors against the ruler.

2 Trace the lid template on to tracing paper with a pen, tracing the top of the lid and one side edge. Place a piece of carbon paper face down on a piece of stencil card. Tape the tracing on top with masking tape. Redraw the template with a sharp pencil to transfer the design. Remove the template. Cut out the wings and the border motif using a craft knife and cutting mat.

3 Tape the stencil to the lid with masking tape. Apply a thin coat of silver paint to a ceramic tile with the paintbrush. Dab at the paint with a stencil brush and stencil the wings.

4 Stencil the border motif. Leave the paint to dry then move the stencil around the lid to stencil the next side edge. Stencil all the side edges. Leave to dry.

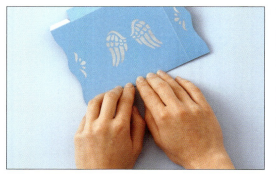

5 Apply double-sided tape to the end tab of the box on the right side. Apply double-sided tape to the base tabs of the box and the tabs of the lid on the wrong side. Fold the box and lid backwards along the scored lines.

6 Wrap the box around the base and stick the base tabs under the base folding the scored edges of the box around the corners of the base.

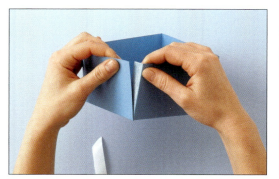

7 Stick the end tab inside the opposite end of the box. Run your fingers along the joins to secure the tabs in place.

8 Firmly stick the tabs on the lid under the adjacent ends of the side edges.

PASTEL PAPER LANTERNS

Suspend these pretty lanterns by their handles on colourful ribbons or omit the handles and slip them over a night-light. The candle glow will softly illuminate the translucent paper – perfect for a still evening in the garden. Never leave naked flames unattended.

You will need

- tracing paper and pen
- transfer paper
- stencil card
- masking tape
- sharp pencil
- craft knife and self-healing cutting mat
- metal ruler
- scissors
- translucent paper in mauve, pale blue and purple
- acrylic paint in lavender and grey
- ceramic tile
- small flat decorator's paintbrush
- stencil brush
- double-sided adhesive tape

1 Trace the template at the back of the book. Place a piece of transfer paper face down on a piece of stencil card. Tape the tracing on top with masking tape. Redraw the template with a sharp pencil to transfer the design. Cut out the stencil using a craft knife and cutting mat.

2 Using the craft knife and cutting mat, cut a 23 x 13cm/9 x 5in rectangle of mauve translucent paper for the lantern. Tape the stencil centrally on top. Apply a thin coat of lavender paint to a ceramic tile. Dab at the paint with a stencil brush and stencil the feather holding the stencil brush upright, moving it in a circular motion.

3 Leave to dry then blend the grey and lavender paint together. Stencil in the tips of the feather.

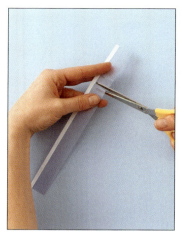

4 Cut strips of double-sided tape 5mm/¹/₄in wide. Apply one strip to one short edge of the lantern. Peel off the backing tape. Overlap the short ends and stick them together.

5 Using the craft knife and cutting mat, cut a 23.5 x 2.5cm/9¹/₄ x 1in strip of pale blue translucent paper. Apply a strip of 5mm/¹/₄in wide double-sided tape to one long edge. Cut a fringe 2mm/¹/₁₂in wide to the tape.

6 Peel off the backing part of the double-sided tape and stick down the fringe around the top of the lantern keeping the upper edges level and overlapping the ends of the fringe at the back.

7 Cut a 22 x 1.5cm/8³/₄ x ⁵/₈in strip of purple paper for the handle. Centre the feather and stick the ends of the handle inside the top of the lantern at each side with double-sided tape.

RIGHT: These translucent pastel paper lanterns will add a special touch to any festive party. They can be hung both inside and outdoors.

SHOE BOX

Flat-pack boxes are easy to decorate before assembly. These glamorous high-heeled stencilled shoes will transform a utilitarian cardboard box into a storage container worthy of your favourite footwear. It's a great idea for storing seasonal shoes.

You will need

- tracing paper and pen or carbon paper and sharp pencil
- masking tape
- stencil card
- craft knife and self-healing cutting mat
- flat-pack storage box
- acrylic paints in silver, turquoise and dark green
- stencil brush

1 Trace the templates at the back of the book and tape on to stencil card. Cut out using a craft knife and cutting mat. Decide where the first shoe is to go. Using silver paint and a dry brush, stipple in the drop shadow using the bottom half of the stencil.

2 Position the stencil slightly upwards and to the left of the shadow so that the bottom part of the shadow is covered. Fill in the entire shoe using a small stencil brush and turquoise paint. Use two layers if necessary to cover up all the silver paint.

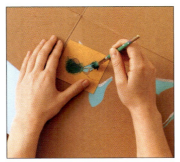

3 Continue stencilling shoes at intervals over the box and lid, varying the angles and alternating between the three different stencils. Add a dark green bow to the front of some of the shoes.

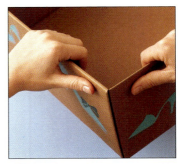

4 When the paint is quite dry, assemble the box, following the instructions supplied by the manufacturer. Line the box with matching tissue paper as a luxurious finishing touch, and to protect your shoes.

STAMPING

STAMPING STYLES

Although stamping has a shorter life history than stencilling, its application is as broad. Stamps are available in a myriad of designs and sizes, all of which can be used to create any amount of pattern on a surface. Used singly over a wall in a specified grid and with minimal colouring they add formality to a room. Carefully positioned and unobtrusively added, they can create an eye-catching detail that helps blend all the design elements and colours of the room together. Match appropriate motifs to styles.

PRACTICAL STAMPING

Printing blocks can be made and carved from almost any material and historically metal, mud, wood, hide and stones have all been used, but it was the development of rubber by Charles Goodyear in the mid 19th century that led to the development of the first stable printing block. By the late 19th century stationers were selling rubber stamps for formal and official administrative purposes. It was not until the late 20th century that manufacturers exploited the technology to produce fun and graphic images for art and craft purposes. At the same time new fast-drying inks and paints were being developed, along with embossing and heat-set glitter powders, expanding mediums and a myriad of gels and glazes that could be exploited by anyone with the know-how at relatively cheap cost, to create unique and individual pieces of art.

Rubber stamping became a craze that attracted creative people

BELOW: A formal and restful room scheme has been created using just one stamp and two paint colours.

who couldn't necessarily draw, but who now had the means to make and decorate highly individual greetings cards and giftwrap. The interior decorating industry saw the potential of rubber stamps too. Large scale motifs could be bought and used with appropriate paint to decorate walls, floors, tiles and fabric at a fraction of the cost of redecorating a room with wallpaper and carpets. The appeal quickly caught the public's imagination, but nowadays, rubber stamps are used to complement and embellish current interior design styling.

FORMAL STYLE

The beauty of stamps is that they are relatively small-scale items, which makes them easy to work with. Formal schemes can be created by using traditional motifs, which provide an instant look, or by using contemporary motifs positioned according to a carefully

ABOVE LEFT: The bold colours and mosaic-like pattern of this Mexican dining room are perfect for a space that has minimal furniture. Here the walls demand to be the main focus of attention in the room.

ABOVE RIGHT: The soft tones of country style are easy to live with.

set out pattern. Grids, borderlines, diagonals, frames around doorways and windows all need to be accurately positioned, or the formality will be lost. A carefully chosen colour palette will add restraint to the design.

COUNTRY STYLE

Perhaps the style most usually associated with stamping is country. Feminine and floral, the accent is usually on soft and warm colours, small-scale motifs and a more random approach to design. Country style is a more forgiving style to work with, and is easier for a beginner to create. Walls are often sponged or rag-rolled first

with pale layers of paint that each show through the top coat, and the stamp is the finishing touch.

MEDITERRANEAN STYLE

Think of the Mediterranean and images conjured up are of white-washed walls, with faded, sun-softened colours, old furniture that has stood the test of time and a room that is comfortable to be in; or you might think of bright and bold tones, azure blues and jade greens intense in their application and suggesting the heat of summer. A riot of colour, complementary and unrestrained is not for the faint-hearted, but makes for an attractive background on which to add appropriate stamps of mosaics, or a border of intricate pattern.

Whatever style appeals, there will be myriad stamps that co-ordinate and that can be used to extend and develop a design theme.

STAMPING
BASICS

The stamp decorating idea comes from the rubber office stamp and it uses the same principle – all the equipment you will need is a stamp and some colour. Commercial stamps are readily available, but included in this book is practical advice on how to create your own stamps from wood or sponge, rubber or linoleum – almost any material that will hold colour and release it. Stamps can be used with an ink pad, but a small foam roller gives a better effect: just coat the stamp with ink or ordinary household paint – this makes stamping a fairly inexpensive option. Follow the tips on application techniques and paint effects to achieve the look best suited to your home.

ABOVE: Simple home-made or ready-made stamps, printed at different angles, make a lovely alternative to machine-printed wallpaper.

LEFT: Making a stamp from wooden block is an art form in itself. Time spent perfecting the design will ensure good results.

CREATING STAMPS

There is a huge range of ready-made stamps to choose from in craft and decorating shops, but it is also very satisfying to make your own unique stamps. The following pages show you how to make several kinds of stamps, using different materials. These are often suitable for different surfaces and uses. For example, flexible foam stamps make printing on to a curved glass surface a much easier proposition, and you can also create large shapes. Wood and lino stamps are more difficult to cut, but you may want to graduate to these once you have gained experience and confidence. A good way to begin is with the humble potato-cut. Once you have started creating your own stamps, you won't want to stop!

WOOD AND LINOLEUM STAMPS

Stamped prints were first made with carved wooden blocks. Indian textiles are still produced by hand in this way and it has recently become possible to buy traditional carved printing blocks. Designs are cut in outline and the backgrounds are scooped out to leave the pattern shapes standing proud of the surface. Ink is applied, either by dipping the block or rolling colour on to the surface. The design is stamped and appears in reverse. The craft of making wooden printing blocks takes time to learn: you need special tools that are razor sharp, and an understanding about cutting with or against the grain. Practise on a bonded wood like marine plywood, which is relatively easy to carve.

Linoleum blocks are available from art and craft suppliers and usually come ready mounted in a range of sizes. Lino is a natural material made from ground cork and linseed oil on a webbed string backing. It is cut in the same way as wood, but has a less resistant texture and no grain to contend with, so is simple to cut.

To make a lino stamp you will need to trace a design and reverse the tracing before transferring it to the lino; this way you will print the design the right way around. Fill in all the background areas with a permanent marker pen: these are the parts to be scooped out, leaving the design proud of the surface. You will need at least three tools – a craft knife, a V-shaped gouge and a scoop. All the tools should be kept as sharp as possible to make cutting easier and safer. Lino is easiest to cut when slightly warm, so place the block on a radiator for ten minutes before cutting. Hold down the block with your spare hand behind your cutting hand, then if the tool slips you will not hurt yourself.

FOAM STAMPS

Different types of foam are characterized by their density. The main types used for stamp-making in this book are: high-density foam, such as upholstery foam; medium-density sponge, such as a kitchen sponge; and low-density sponge, such as a bath sponge. The different densities of foam are each suited to a particular kind of project; on the whole, medium- or low-density sponges are best for bold solid shapes, and high-density foam for fine details. Polystyrene foam (Styrofoam) can also be used but must be mounted on to hardboard. When the glue has dried, the polystyrene can be cut through to the board and the background can be lifted, leaving the design as a stamp.

ABOVE: Create the effect of wood blocks (top) with handmade linocuts (bottom).

ABOVE: Home-made stamps cut from high- and medium-density foam.

RUBBER STAMPS

Rubber stamps have come out of the office and playroom and emerged as remarkable interior decorating tools. Shops have sprung up dealing exclusively in an incredible range of stamp designs and the mail-order selections are astounding. The advantage of these pre-cut stamps is that you are instantly ready to transform fabric, furniture, even walls – and there can be no quicker way to add pattern to a surface. However, rubber stamps are most suited to small projects that require fine detail.

There are two methods of creating your own rubber stamp.

The first is to design on paper and then have a rubber-stamp company make one for you. This is worth doing if you intend to make good use of the stamp, and not just use it for a small, one-off project. Custom-made stamps are quite expensive to produce, so unless money is no object you may like to consider a second option. You can also make stamps by carving your design into an ordinary eraser. Many erasers are now made of a plastic compound instead of actual rubber, but the surface is smooth and easy to cut into. The best motifs to use on these eraser stamps are small geometric shapes, which can be used to build up patterns or border designs.

To make a sponge stamp, first trace your chosen design then lightly spray the back of the pattern with adhesive, which will make it tacky but removable. Stick the pattern on to the foam and use a sharp craft knife to cut around the shape. Remove any background by cutting across to meet the outlines. If you are using medium- or low-density foam, part it after the initial outline cut, then cut right through to the other side. High-density foam can be cut into and carved out in finer detail. It is also less absorbent, so you get a smoother, less textured print. If you are stamping over a large area, you will find the stamp easier to use if you mount the foam on to a hardboard base and use wood glue to attach a small wooden door knob to the back. This will then act as a convenient handle for you to hold.

RIGHT: Commercial rubber stamps are available in designs to suit all tastes.

JACOBEAN POLYSTYRENE FLOWER

Polystyrene (Styrofoam) is easy to cut and gives good, clean edges. Always mount the polystyrene on to a piece of hardboard backing before you begin to draw and cut your design. When the glue has dried the polystyrene can be cut through to the board, leaving the design as a stamp.

You will need

- sheet of polystyrene foam (Styrofoam), approximately 1cm/¹⁄₂in thick
- piece of hardboard, the same size as the polystyrene
- wood glue or PVA (white) glue
- felt-tipped pen
- craft knife

1 Stick the sheet of polystyrene (Styrofoam) and hardboard backing together with wood glue or PVA (white) glue.

2 Without waiting for the glue to set, draw the design using a felt-tipped pen. Remember that the pattern will reverse when printed.

3 Cut around the outline of the design using a craft knife. If this is done before the glue has set, these pieces will pull away easily.

4 Cut the edging details, removing unwanted pieces of polystyrene as you go.

5 Make shallow, angular cuts to scoop out the pattern details of the flower design. Use a new craft knife blade for this so that the cuts are sharp and you do not accidentally lift adjoining particles of polystyrene that have been only partially separated.

GEOMETRIC BORDER DESIGN

This border stamp is made from high-density foam. A good quality upholstery foam is recommended.

The piece used here was sold by a camping supply store for use as a portable, compact mattress. The

high-density foam is not very absorbent so creates a smoother, less textured print.

1 Stick the foam on to the hardboard by applying wood glue or PVA (white) glue to the rough side.

2 Without waiting for the glue to set, draw a geometric pattern on to the foam using a felt-tipped pen and ruler. Use a craft knife to outline the sections to be cut away, then lift them out. If the glue is still tacky, this will be much easier to do.

3 Finally, using wood glue or PVA glue, stick the wooden block in the middle of the stamp back, to act as a handle. Allow to dry thoroughly.

SQUIGGLE FOAM STAMP

Foam comes in all shapes, sizes and densities. Make a visit to a specialist foam dealer, as

inspiration for new ideas often springs from the discovery of new materials. Here is an idea for

making a bold stamp in an original way which does not require any drawing or cutting.

1 Lay out a length of masking tape, sticky side up. Twist the foam into a squiggle shape, pressing it on to the middle section of the tape.

2 Apply wood glue or PVA (white) glue to the untaped side of the foam and turn it face-down on to the hardboard. Fold the tape ends under the hardboard to hold the foam in place while the glue sets. When the glue is dry, peel off the masking tape.

FLORAL LINOCUT

Cutting linoleum is a simple technique to master. Linoleum blocks are available in a range of sizes from art and craft suppliers. You will be delighted with the intricacy of the motifs you can create using this medium. Remember to warm your linoleum ten minutes before cutting.

You will need

♦ tracing paper
♦ pencil
♦ sheet of carbon paper
♦ linoleum block
♦ masking tape
♦ craft knife
♦ lino-cutting tools: a V-shaped gouge and a U-shaped scoop

1 Make a tracing of your chosen motif, the same size as the linoleum block. Slip a sheet of carbon paper (chalky side down) between the tracing and the linoleum, then tape the edges with masking tape.

2 Draw over the lines of the motif with a sharp pencil. The tracing will appear on the linoleum block.

3 Remove the paper and cut around the outline with a craft knife. Cut any fine detail or straight lines by making shallow, angular cuts from each side, then scoop out the V-shaped sections.

4 Cut out the rest of the pattern using the lino tools – the U-shaped scoop for removing large areas of background, and the V-shaped gouge for cutting the finer curves and pattern details. Hold the lino down firmly, with your spare hand placed behind your cutting hand to avoid accidents.

POTATO PRINT SUNBURST

Most of us learn the technique of using potatoes for printing as very young schoolchildren. Potato prints are quick and simple to do but look amazingly effective, and they are an inexpensive way to achieve bright, bold results. This enjoyable technique should not be overlooked by adults.

You will need
◆ medium-sized raw potato
◆ sharp kitchen knife
◆ fine felt-tipped pen
◆ craft knife

1 Use a sharp kitchen knife to make a single cut right through the potato. This will give you a smooth surface to work with.

2 Draw the sunburst motif on to the potato with a fine felt-tipped pen. Remember that motifs reverse when stamped, although with the sunburst motif used here it will make no difference.

3 Use a craft knife to cut the outline, then under-cut and scoop out the background. Potato stamps will not last longer than a few hours before they deteriorate, so keep a tracing of your motif if your project cannot be completed in one go. The design can then be re-cut using a fresh potato.

APPLICATION TECHNIQUES

In the world of stamping, the coating of a stamp with colour is always known as inking, regardless of the substance applied. There are no hard and fast rules about what can or cannot be used – any substance that coats a stamp and is then released on to a surface when stamped, will be suitable. Stamp inkpads are available from art and craft suppliers or specialist stamp stores, and come in a wide range of shapes, sizes and colours. Some contain permanent ink and others are water-based and washable. Paints can be applied with brushes or rollers, or spread on to a flat surface and the stamp dipped into them. Experiment with different paints and inks and always test the stamp on scrap paper first before starting a project.

Using a brush

This is a way of applying thick water-based paint such as emulsion (latex) or artist's acrylic. One big advantage here is that you can use several colours on one stamp in a very controlled way. This would not be possible if you were inverting the stamp on to an inkpad.

Using a roller

Place a blob of paint on one side of a flat plate and run a small rubber roller through it several times until it is covered evenly with colour. Run the roller over the rubber stamp to transfer the paint. Make a test print on scrap paper first, as this method sometimes overloads the stamp with paint.

Using an inkpad

Simply press the rubber stamp lightly on to the surface of the stamp inkpad. Check that the stamp is evenly coated, then make your print. It is difficult to overload the stamp using this method.

Using a sponge

Spread an even coating of paint on to a flat plate and simply dip the sponge stamp into it. Check that the stamp is evenly coated, then make a test print on scrap paper to gauge the effect. Sponge is more absorbent than rubber, so you will need to use more paint.

Using miniature inkpads

These small inkpads come in a range of brilliant colours and metallics. Just wipe them across the rubber stamp. As with brush application you can use more than one colour at a time, but take care to avoid colours mixing on the stamp pads.

Using a glaze

You can apply a translucent colour glaze using a stamp or potato cut. Make up some wallpaper paste and tint it with liquid watercolour paint or water-based ink. Dip the stamp in the mixture and print. The paste dries to a clear sheen with a hint of colour.

PAINT EFFECTS

The same rubber stamp can be made to print with several different characteristics, depending on the colours and inks that you choose to use. The sun stamp below illustrates this very well. It has been used to create cool and warm effects, using a glittering glaze and brush-applied paints.

Metallic print

This metallic print was made with equal parts PVA (white) glue and water, to half of metallic powder. This mixture was applied to the stamp with a rubber roller. When dry, the glittering powder is held in a transparent glaze.

Two-colour print

The same sun stamp was coated with two different coloured paints, applied with a brush. When paint is applied in this way, it is possible to separate areas of colour, which is impossible when using an inkpad.

Light effects

This effect uses the almost powdery appearance of a medium-density sponge stamp lightly applied to a colourwashed wall. Emulsion (latex) paint was mixed half and half with prepared wallpaper paste, which gives a gelatinous quality when wet and a transparent glaze once dry.

OVERPRINTING EFFECTS

Once you have cut a complicated design like the one below, you can experiment with building up the pattern by adding colour and overprinting. This design can be printed one way, then turned around to print in the other direction. The second print fills in the triangle shapes that were left blank. This works particularly well for the central pattern. Care must be taken not to re-ink the border lines, because they are less effective when printed with more than one colour.

1 The first print was made in light yellow emulsion (latex) paint on to a light blue colourwashed wall.

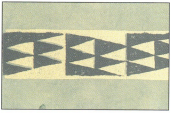

2 The stamp was cleaned and re-inked with dark blue-grey paint, avoiding the thin border. The print was made with the stamp turned around to face the other direction, but lined up to fit exactly on top of the first print.

3 Other colours were applied to selected areas of the stamp, including a separate colour for each of the border lines.

SPECIAL-EFFECT PAINT MIXTURES

There are many different kinds of paint available these days and they are often sold in huge self-service warehouses. Sometimes it is impossible to find any specialist assistance for your particular project. In this book we have tried to narrow down the paint options by suggesting either acrylic artist's colour, watercolour (available in small jars as a ready-mixed liquid from art and craft suppliers) or emulsion (latex) paint. This should not mean, however, that all paint finishes look the same; there are a number of very simple ways to vary the intensity and texture of these paints, using wallpaper paste or PVA (white) glue. The step-by-step photographs below explain the different methods and effects that can be achieved.

WATERCOLOUR PAINT AND WALLPAPER PASTE

This mixture is only suitable for surfaces that do not need wiping clean, so use it for paper and card but not for walls.

You will need
◆ wallpaper paste and water
◆ plate
◆ paintbrush
◆ ready-mixed liquid watercolour paint
◆ scrap paper

1 Mix the wallpaper paste to a slightly thinner consistency than usual. It will thicken after five minutes, when you will be able to thin it by adding more water. It should have a sloppy consistency.

2 Add a drop of ready-mixed liquid watercolour paint. The colour is intense and a small amount goes a long way. Add and stir in as many more drops as you need, testing the paint on a sheet of scrap paper to judge the brightness. The wallpaper paste gives the mixture the thickness that is needed for stamping – watercolour paint on its own would not be suitable.

EMULSION PAINT AND WALLPAPER PASTE

This mixture adds another dimension to the usual texture of emulsion (latex) paint. It is suitable for all household decorating, and the wallpaper paste makes it particularly suited to sponge stamping. The advantage of this mixture is that it is washable when dry, so it is suitable for all household decorating work. When dry, the wallpaper paste is transparent and adds an attractive glazed texture to the emulsion paint. Its gelatinous quality works well with sponge stamps.

You will need

♦ wallpaper paste and water
♦ plate
♦ paintbrush
♦ emulsion (latex) paint
♦ small wooden block
♦ foam stamp
♦ bowl of water
♦ kitchen paper
♦ scrap paper

1 Mix the wallpaper paste with the required amount of water according to the manufacturer's instructions. Make a glaze using one part emulsion (latex) paint to two parts wallpaper paste. Mix together well.

2 When you have achieved the desired colour and consistency, prop up one side of the plate with a small wooden block, or something similar. The plate should feel stable and remain in this position to provide an even coating of paint for stamping.

3 Soak the foam stamp in a bowl of water. All foam works a lot better for stamping if it is damp rather than dry as it will absorb and release the paint mixture more readily. Lift the stamp out of the water and squeeze out the excess moisture into a sheet of kitchen paper.

4 Scoop up some of the paint and use it to coat the raised side of the plate with a thin layer of colour. Dip the foam stamp into this.

5 First, make a test print on to a sheet of scrap paper to ensure that the stamp is not overloaded with paint. This photograph shows the effect of the final fish stamp printed on a light blue colourwashed background.

SURFACE FINISHES

When you print with stamps, the shape of the design remains constant but there are many different finishes that can be achieved. The factors affecting these are the surface that you stamp on to as well as the material used to make up the stamp, and the substance that you stamp with. All of these can vary enormously. To illustrate some of the possible effects that you can achieve, we have printed motifs with emulsion (latex) paint and then experimented with simple different finishes.

ALTERING EFFECTS

Once the pattern has been stamped on the wall (or on a wooden surface), there are various ways that you can alter its regular appearance. You can make the original print appear softer or darker using the following simple techniques. All you need is some abrasive paper (sandpaper) or tinted varnish.

1 This is the basic design. A foam rubber stamp was pressed into blue emulsion (latex) paint and printed on an emulsion-painted wall.

2 The print was allowed to dry and then it was lightly rubbed back using fine-grade abrasive paper (sandpaper).

3 This stamp has been darkened with a coat of tinted antiquing varnish. As well as protecting the surface, it deepens the colour and adds a slight sheen.

DEPTH EFFECTS

Varnish can be used over your designs to add depth to the colour and protect the wall surface. These prints, made with a polystyrene (Styrofoam) stamp, demonstrate the changes made by coats of varnish. Tinted varnish comes in many shades, and enriches the colour with each application.

1 This is the basic stamped pattern in grey emulsion (latex) paint on a light buttermilk-coloured background.

2 This is the surface after one coat of tinted varnish was applied. It has deepened the yellow considerably.

3 A second coat of the same varnish was applied and the colour has turned deep pine-yellow.

WOOD APPLICATION

You can use most types of paint on wood, although some will need sealing with a protective coat of varnish. New wood needs to be sealed with a coat of shellac – this stops resin leaking through the grain. Below are some examples of rubber, sponge and potato prints made on wood with a variety of media. Woodstains, varnishes and paints have different properties and create different effects depending on the stamp used. The wood grain gives extra texture and interest to the stamped design.

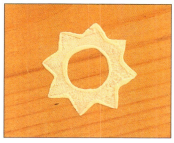

This example shows emulsion paint applied with a rubber stamp.

This print was made with emulsion paint applied with a sponge stamp.

This is an example of emulsion (latex) paint applied with a potato-cut.

This shows an example of woodstain applied with a rubber stamp.

This print was made with woodstain applied with a sponge stamp.

This is the effect of woodstain applied with a potato-cut.

This is an example of tinted varnish applied with a rubber stamp.

This print was made with tinted varnish applied with a potato-cut.

This shows an example of red ink applied with a potato-cut.

FABRIC APPLICATION

There are several types of fabric ink suitable for stamp printing – the two main types are those used to stamp directly on to fabric and those which are stamped on to paper first and then heat-transferred. The inks used in these samples are all stamped directly, but you can see transfer printing in the Trailblazer Scarf project in this book. Although the prints shown below have all been made with fabric printing ink, different methods of application have been used. Some stamps are more successful than others, but all produce their own distinctive effects. Experiment with different fabrics and inks from the wide range available, and see the colour transformation take place.

This multi-coloured print was made by inking a high-density foam stamp in two different colours.

These prints were made with wine bottle corks with bored holes. Corks make very effective stamps.

This print shows an example of a fish made by inking a high-density foam stamp in a single colour.

This high-density foam stamp was inked in blue with a halo of red dots.

This fleur-de-lys print was made with a high-density foam stamp and red fabric ink for a crisp, intense finish.

These red and blue potato-cut circles were inked with two colours to create an irregular pattern.

This print is an example made with a ready-made rubber stamp.

This print effect was made by using a sponge stamp.

This shows an example of a print made with a potato-cut.

CERAMIC AND GLASS APPLICATION

Different surfaces bring out the different qualities of paint. The kind of stamp used will also have a big influence on the final result. To illustrate the different effects that can be achieved, we have used motifs cut from rubber, foam and potato, with a variety of inks, paints and stains. Some choices may seem unusual, like woodstain on terracotta, but experimentation can produce unexpected successes!

The print on this flowerpot was made with emulsion (latex) paint using a sponge.

This print was made with woodstain applied with a sponge.

The print on this pot was made with tinted varnish using a rubber stamp.

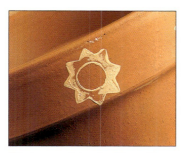

This shows a print made with emulsion paint applied with a rubber stamp.

This print was made with woodstain applied with a potato-cut.

This is an example of a print made with tinted varnish applied with a potato-cut.

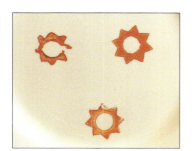

These prints were made on a ceramic plate with acrylic enamel paint, applied with a potato-cut (top left), a sponge (top right), and a rubber stamp (bottom).

These glass prints were made with acrylic enamel paint thinned with clear acrylic varnish, using a sponge (top left), rubber stamp (top right) and potato-cut (bottom).

These prints were applied to glass with a coil of foam dipped into emulsion paint. The emulsion was left to dry, then covered with a protective coat of clear varnish.

TILE APPLICATION

These are just a small selection of the different effects that can be achieved by stamp printing on to tiles. Remember to clean the tiles thoroughly before decorating. We recommend that you always use acrylic enamel paints and, wherever possible, decorate them before you put them on a wall because this gives you the chance to add to their resilience by baking them in the oven. Always follow the manufacturer's instructions for times and temperatures, and ensure your tiles can withstand this treatment. You can create borders, overall patterns or individual highlights.

These little circles were made by dipping bored wine bottle corks into red and blue paint, and printing in rows.

These larger circles were made using a potato-cut. The transparent effect comes from the potato starch mixing in with the paint.

This print shows an example made with a shaped, medium-density sponge. The textured effect is due to the density of the sponge.

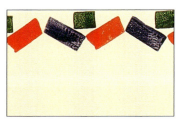

This pattern was made using small rubber stamps cut from an eraser. A zigzag pattern like this makes a good border.

This heart was cut from medium-density sponge. The textured effect is opaque but "powdery".

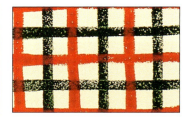

This pattern was made by dipping straight strips of high-density foam into red and blue paint. The thickness of the strips can be varied to produce a tartan pattern.

A small square of foam was used to print this chequerboard effect. This pattern is quite time-consuming, but very effective.

This high-density foam stamp was coloured with a brush to make a three-colour print. These make good highlights mixed in with single-colour prints.

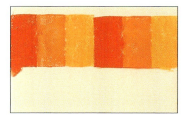

This border was made with a medium-density foam block, printed in different colours. The edges must be aligned accurately for best effect.

DESIGNING WITH STAMPS

To design the pattern of your stamps, you need to find a compromise between printing totally at random and measuring precisely to achieve a machine-printed regularity. To do this, you can use the stamp block itself to give you a means of measuring your pattern, or try strips of paper, squares of card or a length of string to act as a plumbline. Experiment by using a stamp pad on scrap paper to plan your design but always wash and dry the stamp before proceeding to print the main event.

Using paper cut-outs

The easiest way to plan your design is to stamp as many pattern elements as you need on to scrap paper. Cut them out with scissors and use them to arrange the position of your finished stamped prints.

Creating a repeat pattern

Use a strip of paper as a measuring device for repeat patterns. Cut the strip the length of one row of the pattern. Use the stamp block to mark where each print will go, with equal spaces in between. You could mark up a vertical strip, too. Position the horizontal strip against this as you print.

Using a paper spacing device

This method is very simple. Decide on the distance between prints and cut a strip of paper to that size. Each time you stamp, place the strip against the edge of the previous print and line up the edge of the block with the other side of the strip. Use a longer strip to measure the distance required.

Creating an irregular pattern

If your design doesn't fit into a regular grid, plan the pattern first on paper. Cut out paper shapes to represent the spaces and use these to position the finished pattern. Alternatively, raise a motif above the previous one by stamping above a strip of card positioned on the baseline.

Devising a larger design

Use the stamps in groups to make up a larger design. Try stamping four together in a block, or partially overlapping an edge so that only a section of the stamp is shown. Use the stamps upside down, back to back and rotated in different ways. Experiment on scrap paper first.

Using a plumbline

Attach a plumbline at ceiling height to hang down the wall. Hold a card (stock) square behind the plumbline so that the string cuts through two opposite corners. Mark all four points, then move the card square down. Continue in this way to make a grid for stamping a regular pattern.

WALLS AND SURFACES

Decorating walls and surfaces should not be a high-anxiety activity; it should be enjoyable to do and rewarding to view. Stamping is not only both of these, but also the quickest and easiest way to put a pattern on a wall. There are many different looks that you can achieve with stamps, depending upon the materials you use. Pre-cut rubber stamps produce a fine, sophisticated and subtle effect, while home-made foam stamps are often simple and bold. Both kinds of stamps give varying results according to how much pressure you use: regular pressure produces identical motifs; irregular pressure produces a more hand-painted look.

ABOVE: A single stamp, applied using varying amounts of paint, gives an exclusive hand-blocked effect.

LEFT: Small-scale stamps can be used to create large-scale projects by repeating motifs and altering the angles at which they are used.

TUSCAN FRIEZE

Three stamps are used in this project to transform a dull space into a wall frieze that you will want to preserve forever. The finished wall will bring a touch of Tuscany into your home, even when the sky is a gloomy grey outside. The wall is divided at dado height with a strong burgundy red below and a warm cream above to visually lower the ceiling. The vine leaf pattern has been stamped on to a grid of pencil marks that is simple to measure out using a square of card (stock) and a plumbline. The lines are hand-painted using a wooden batten (furring strip) as a hand rest but you could also stick parallel strips of masking tape around the walls and fill in the stripes between.

1 Measure the height of a dado (chair) rail and draw a line around the wall with a ruler and pencil. Paint the wall above the line cream and the area below burgundy. Mix roughly equal amounts of wallpaper paste, burgundy and terracotta paint on a plate.

2 Run the roller through the mixture until it is evenly coated and ink the grape stamp. Align the strip of card (stock) with the top of the burgundy section. Rest the base of the stamp block on the card to stamp a row of grapes.

3 Ink the tendril stamp and stamp a tendril at the top of each bunch of grapes. Allow some of the prints to be paler than others as the paint wears off the stamp block, to give a deliberately faded and patchy effect.

4 Mix a little cream paint into some white. With the lining brush, apply highlights to the grapes and the tendrils. Let the brushstrokes vary in direction and weight to add to the hand-painted look. Support your painting hand with your free hand.

5 Hold the batten (furring strip) just below the top edge of the burgundy section and rest your painting hand on it. Slide your hand along the batten to paint a smooth, thin line in off-white. Practise this movement first and try to relax your hand to avoid jerky lines. A slight waviness to the line will not spoil the effect. Try to avoid having to paint over the line, as a single, fresh brushstroke looks better.

6 Attach a plumbline above dado height, just in from one corner and so that it hangs down to the skirting (base) board. Place the card square against the wall so that the string cuts through the top and bottom corners. Mark all the corner points in pencil.

7 Move the card down so that the top corner rests on the lowest pencil mark. Complete one column of the grid in this way, then move the plumbline across and continue until the lower wall is completely covered with a grid of pencil marks.

8 Mix a small amount of black paint into the burgundy to deepen the colour. Spread some dark burgundy paint on to a plate and run the roller through it until it is evenly coated. Ink the leaf stamp and make a print on one of the pencil marks.

9 Position the stamp just above or just below the pencil mark each time to create a regular pattern over the whole lower wall.

10 Move the batten about 2.5cm/1in from the cream dado line and use the square-tipped artist's paintbrush to paint a second, broader line. Keep the line as fresh as possible; visible brushstrokes are preferable to solid, flat colour. Apply a coat of varnish to the lower wall to seal and protect the paint.

RIGHT: The grape motifs are printed with two stamps, one for the grapes and one for the tendrils. These are then highlighted by hand using a lining brush to create a hand-painted look. This technique can be applied to give extra depth and interest to other stamped designs.

FLORAL SPRIG

This all-over country floral motif is made with three sponge stamps. The background colour is creamy yellow and the sprigs echo the colours used on and below the dado (chair) rail. The sprigs change direction with every alternate print, giving the pattern its dynamic energy. Vary the intensity of the colour by applying less pressure on some prints, as well as making several prints before recharging your sponge. The most time-consuming part of the project will be marking out an accurate grid of pencil marks across the whole wall surface, but once that is in place the stamped pattern will grow very quickly. This pattern will suit a large or small room equally well.

You will need

- tracing paper
- pencil
- spray adhesive
- low-density sponge, such as a bath sponge
- felt-tipped pen
- craft knife
- plumbline
- card (stock), 14 x 14cm/5$\frac{1}{2}$ x 5$\frac{1}{2}$in
- emulsion (latex) paint in brick-red and dusky blue
- plates

1 Trace, transfer and cut out the pattern shapes from the template section. Lightly spray the shapes with adhesive and place on the sponge. Use a craft knife to cut out the shapes.

2 Attach a plumbline at ceiling height to drop down to dado (chair) rail height. Place the card (stock) square on the diagonal, with the plumbline running through the centre. Mark all the corners on the wall in pencil. Move the square up and continue to use this system to mark a grid on the wall.

3 Spread the brick-red and dusky blue paint on to separate plates. Make the first print on to scrap paper to make sure that the stamp is not overloaded. Using the pencil marks as your guide, stamp blue stem shapes. Change the direction of the curve from left to right with each alternate print.

4 Use the same blue paint to stamp
the leaf shape on to the base of
each stem, alternating the direction
of each print as you did with the stem.

5 Dip the flower-shaped sponge
into the brick-red paint. Make an
initial print on scrap paper to make
sure the stamp is not overloaded. Stamp
the flower shapes on to the tops of the
stems. Vary the pressure used, to give
different densities of colour.

*ABOVE: Home-made sponge stamps, using low-density sponge such as a bath sponge,
give a delicate, soft effect. This lovely design is an ideal example of how changing the
direction of the prints brings vitality and energy – the flowers really look as if they are
moving in the breeze.*

SPINNING SUN MOTIF

This rich combination of spicy red-brown and earthy yellow seems to infuse the room with warmth and colour. The spinning sun motif has a timeless quality. The pattern is a lot of fun to paint, because once you've marked out the grid it grows very quickly, and using a single colour makes for very easy stamping. Colourwash the wall with yellow-ochre emulsion (latex) paint, diluted half and half with water. Use random brushstrokes, working within arm's reach. The finish should look patchy rather than even – like dappled sunlight. Paint the lower section a deep terracotta.

You will need

- tape measure
- spirit level
- pencil
- paintbrush
- emulsion (latex) paint in terracotta and yellow-ochre
- clear satin varnish
- tracing paper
- craft knife
- adhesive spray
- high-density foam rubber, such as upholstery foam
- plate
- plumbline
- card (stock), 15 x 13cm/6 x 5in

1 Divide the wall at dado (chair) rail height, using a tape measure, spirit level and pencil. Paint terracotta below the line and yellow-ochre above. Apply a coat of clear satin varnish to the terracotta. Trace, transfer and cut out the pattern shapes from the template section. Lightly spray with adhesive and place them on the foam rubber. Cut around the designs with a craft knife.

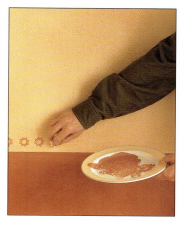

2 Spread an even coating of terracotta paint on to a plate and press the smaller stamp into it. Make a test print on scrap paper to make sure that the stamp is not overloaded with paint, then stamp a row above the dado rail height. Attach a plumbline at ceiling height, and mark out a grid using the card (stock) and a pencil, as described in the Sunstar Wall project.

3 Press the larger stamp into the terracotta paint and test print on scrap paper. Following the grid of pencil marks, stamp the large sunwheels on to the wall.

4 Connect the sunwheels by stamping three small sunstars in a straight line between them, across the whole surface of the wall.

RIGHT: Use a plumbline such as a weighted piece of string to measure complex grid designs accurately.

SUNSTAR WALL

It is hard to believe that decorating can be this easy. Gone are the days of the perfectly even finish of flat colour – now we are more attuned to the comfort of patchy paintwork. If you have a minute and a piece of sponge to spare, that is all it takes to make the sunstar stamp. It could not be simpler. The wall was colourwashed with diluted coffee-coloured emulsion (latex) paint. Just mix the paint half and half with water, stir well and paint the wall using random sweeping strokes. Work within an arm's reach and blend any hard edges with a dryish brush before the paint dries.

You will need

- medium-density sponge, such as a kitchen sponge
- felt-tipped pen
- craft knife
- plumbline
- card (stock), 26 x 26cm/10 x 10in
- pencil
- wallpaper paste, for mixing
- cup
- plate
- emulsion (latex) paint in terracotta
- paintbrush

1 Draw a circle on the sponge using a felt-tipped pen and a round object as a template.

2 Draw the shape of the sunstar within the circle, referring to the pattern in the template section. The motif can be made to any size.

3 Cut out the circle with a craft knife. Cut around the shape, then part the sponge and cut all the way through.

4 Cut around the drawn pattern shape and discard the sponge scraps.

5 Attach a plumbline at ceiling height (this can be done with masking tape). Place the card (stock) square on the diagonal behind the line, so that it falls through two points. Mark all the corners on the wall in pencil, then move the square up, continuing to mark all the corners. Use this system, moving the line along the wall, until a grid of pencil marks covers the wall.

6 Mix a cup of wallpaper paste, place a blob on the plate alongside an equal amount of terracotta paint and blend the two together with a paintbrush. Press the sponge into the mixture and make a test print on a sheet of scrap paper. Then start stamping the wall, using the pencil marks as your guide. Mix the paste and paint together as you go, so that the density of the colour varies.

7 Continue stamping so that the sunstars form a regular pattern across the whole wall.

MEXICAN BORDER

Banish gloomy weather with vibrant sunshine-yellow and intense sky-blue. With the heat turned up, it will be time to add an ethnic touch by stamping an Aztec border along the walls. Use the patterns from the template section to cut basic geometric shapes from a medium-density sponge, like the ones used for washing dishes. Mix shades of green with purples, add an earthy red and then stamp on diamonds of fuschia-pink for its sheer brilliance. It's a bold statement. These days emulsion (latex) paint is available in a huge range of exciting colours. Try not to be tempted by muted colours for this border – it will lose much of its impact. Bright colours go well with natural materials, like straw hats, sisal matting, wicker baskets and clay pots.

You will need

- tape measure
- spirit level
- pencil
- emulsion (latex) paint in sunshine-yellow and deep sky-blue
- paint rollers and tray
- small amounts of emulsion paint in light blue-grey, purple, brick-red, fuschia-pink and dark green
- plates
- foam rubber strip
- medium-density sponge, such as a kitchen sponge, cut into the pattern shapes from the template section

1 Divide the wall at dado (chair) rail height using a tape measure, spirit level and pencil. Paint the upper part sunshine-yellow and the lower part deep sky-blue using the paint rollers. Then use the spirit level and pencil to draw a parallel line about 15cm/6in above the blue section.

2 Use a foam rubber strip to stamp a light blue-grey line directly above the blue section. Then use the same strip to stamp the top line of the border along the pencil line.

3 Spread an even coating of each of the frieze colours on to separate plates. Use the rectangular and triangular shapes alternately to print a purple row above the bottom line and below the top line. Stamp on to scrap paper first to make sure the stamp is not overloaded.

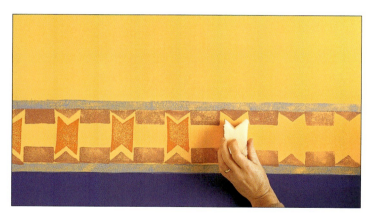

4 Stamp the largest shape in brick-red, lining it up to fit between the points of the top and bottom triangles. There should be approximately 1cm/1/2in of background colour showing between this brick-red shape and the triangles.

5 Stamp the diamond shapes in fuschia-pink between the central brick-red motifs. The points of the diamonds should touch the purple rectangular shapes.

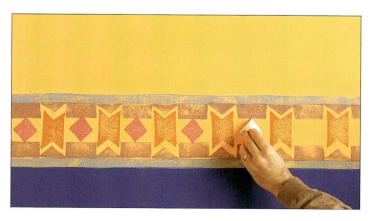

6 Finally add a zigzagged edge by overprinting dark green triangles along the light blue-grey lines.

BELOW: Bold geometric shapes and a vibrant mix of colours would transform a landing or a small space such as a dark hallway or a spare bedroom.

SCANDINAVIAN LIVING ROOM

Create a cool atmosphere with this sophisticated Gustavian-influenced wall stamping. This project is less instant than others featured in the book, but the elegance of the result justifies all the preparatory work. The stamps are cut from high-density foam rubber which is mounted on to blocks of composition board, and a small door knob is added for easy handling. Before any stamping can be done, a grid must be drawn across the wall using a plumbline and a card (stock) square. If you find the effect of the two blues too cool, you can add warmth by applying a coat of tinted varnish to the whole wall, including the woodwork. It has the effect of bathing the room in golden sunlight.

You will need

- wood glue or PVA (white) glue
- 2 pieces composition board, 8.5 x 8.5cm/ 3½ x 3½in
- 2 pieces high-density foam rubber, such as upholstery foam, 8.5 x 8.5cm/ 3½ x 3½in
- tracing paper
- pencil
- spray adhesive
- craft knife
- ruler
- 2 small wooden door knobs
- plumbline
- card (stock), 18 x 18cm/7 x 7in
- plate
- emulsion (latex) paint in dark blue

1 Apply glue to the composition board squares and stick the foam rubber on to them. Leave the glue to dry.

2 Trace and transfer the pattern shapes from the template section. Lightly spray with adhesive and place on the foam rubber blocks.

3 Cut around the edges of the designs and remove the paper pattern. Scoop out the background to leave the stamps free of the composition board.

4 Draw two intersecting lines across the back of each square of composition board and glue a wooden door knob in the centre to act as a handle.

5 Attach a plumbline at ceiling height to give a vertical guideline (this can be done with a piece of masking tape). Mark a point 8cm/3¼in above the dado (chair) rail and place one corner of the card (stock) square on it, lined up along the plumbline. Mark all the corners on the wall in pencil, then move the square up, continuing to mark the corners. Use this system to mark a grid of squares across the whole upper wall.

6 One of the stamps has a static motif and the other has a swirl. Use the static one first, dipping it into a plate coated with paint and making the first print on a sheet of scrap paper to make sure that the stamp is not overloaded. Then print up the wall, starting from the 8cm/3¼in mark.

7 Continue printing up the wall, working up the diagonal and following the grid of pencil marks.

8 Change to the swirl motif, and stamp this pattern in the spaces between the static motifs.

RIGHT: Traditional Scandinavian design has a timeless appeal. Blue and white is the classic combination, and always looks cool and serene. If you prefer, you can stamp the prints in a lighter shade of blue on a plain white wall. Continue the theme with white-painted furniture and simple checked fabrics.

♦ 284 ♦

TULIPS AND LEAVES

Corridors, entrance halls and landings are good for "sudden inspiration" decorating jobs, as there is very little furniture to be moved. Make the most of these spaces using warm colours and bold all-over patterns. Here the woodwork, table and chair are all painted a pale duck-egg blue, which is also used to stamp the leaf pattern on the semi-transparent blind. You can use fabric paint on the blind but it is not absolutely essential, as the blind is unlikely to be washed. A painted border in the same colour as the tulips adds a very smart finishing touch to the walls and small decorative objects such as the wall sconce can be stamped in similar shades.

You will need

- emulsion (latex) paint in terracotta, deep plum and grey-green
- large and small household paintbrushes
- plumbline
- card (stock), 25 x 25cm/10 x 10in
- pencil
- plates
- foam rollers
- tulip and leaf stamps
- ruler
- masking tape (optional)
- scrap paper
- black stamp pad
- scissors
- white, semi-transparent roller blind
- newspaper
- duck-egg blue emulsion paint or fabric paint
- iron (optional)

1 Paint the walls with terracotta emulsion (latex) paint and leave to dry. Attach the plumbline at ceiling height. Hold the card (stock) square against the wall so that the plumbline string cuts through the top and bottom corners of the square. Mark all four points in pencil. Continue moving the square and marking the points to form a grid all over the wall.

2 Spread some deep plum emulsion (latex) paint on to a plate and run a roller through it until it is evenly coated. Ink the tulip stamp and, holding it on the diagonal, make a print on each pencil mark. Position the stamp just above or just below the mark each time to create a regular pattern.

3 Change the angle of the stamp from right to left with each alternate print to give the pattern a hand-printed rather than a machine-printed look. Continue stamping tulips until the whole wall is covered.

4 Draw a line around the window a ruler's width away from the edge of the window frame. Stick masking tape along the line if you are not confident about painting a straight line.

5 Using the small paintbrush, paint a deep plum border between the edge of the window frame and the pencil line.

6 For the blind, use the stamp pad to print 16 leaves on scrap paper. Alternate two different stamps so that the leaves point in different directions. Cut out the patterns. Lay the blind on newspaper and arrange the leaves to plan the design, starting at the bottom edge.

7 Spread some duck-egg blue emulsion or fabric paint on to a plate and run a roller through it until it is evenly coated. Ink the stamp and remove one paper shape at a time to stamp a leaf in its place.

8 As you complete each row, move the paper patterns up to make the next row, keeping the spacing consistent. If you are using fabric paint, fix (set) it with a hot iron, following the manufacturer's instructions.

OPPOSITE: Printing motifs on the blind and accessories as well as the walls creates a completely unified decorative scheme. If you prefer a more nature-inspired effect, print the leaves on the blind in green ink.

STARS AND STRIPES

All too often, creative decorating is restricted to the larger rooms of a house, but the hall is the first thing everybody sees when they come through the front door. Why not use stamping to make a stunning first impression on your visitors? This colour scheme combines two earth colours with bright silver stars to give a slightly Moroccan feel. If you have an immovable carpet or tiles that don't suit these shades, then choose a colour from your existing floor covering to highlight the walls. Hallways seldom have windows to give natural light and the inclination is to use light, bright colours to prevent them from looking gloomy. A better idea is to go for intense, dramatic colours with good electric lighting – they will turn a corridor into a welcoming hallway.

You will need

- household sponge
- emulsion (latex) paint in light coffee and spicy brown
- plumbline
- reusable adhesive
- straight-edged card (stock), the width required for the stamps
- pencil
- paintbrush
- scissors
- silver acrylic paint
- plate
- foam roller
- starburst stamp

1 Use a household sponge to apply irregular patches of light coffee emulsion (latex) paint to the wall. Aim for a mottled effect. Leave to dry.

2 Attach a plumbline at ceiling height with reusable adhesive so that it hangs just away from the wall. Line up one straight edge of the card (stock) and use it as a guide to draw a straight line in pencil down the wall.

3 Move the card marker one width space along the wall, and continue to mark evenly spaced lines. This will create the striped pattern.

4 Paint the first stripe spicy brown. Try to keep within the pencil lines, but don't worry too much about slight mistakes as the wall should look hand-painted and not have the total regularity of machine-printed wallpaper.

5 Continue painting each alternate stripe, keeping within the pencil lines, but attempting to create a slightly irregular finish.

6 Cut the card spacer to the length required to use as a positional guide for the stars. Spread some silver paint on to the plate and run the roller through it until it is evenly coated. Ink the stamp and print a star in each of the spicy brown stripes along the wall, above and below the card spacer. Continue printing across the wall, then return to the first stripe and start printing again, one space below the lowest star.

7 Using the card spacer as before, print the first two rows of stars in the coffee-coloured stripes. Position these stars so they fall midway between the stars in the spicy brown stripe.

8 Continue this process to fill in the remaining silver stars all down the coffee-coloured stripes.

RIGHT: Painting stripes on the wall gives a bold background for the silver stamped stars. You could try this technique with other motifs, for example diamonds. The stripes do not need to be perfectly accurate as the whole effect of the wall is intended to look hand-done rather than like mass-produced wallpaper.

HEAVENLY CHERUBS

The cherubs are stamped in silhouette on this wall, framed in medallions of pale yellow on a dove-grey background. The yellow medallions are stencilled on to the grey background and the combination of colours softens the potentially hard-edged dark silhouettes. The stencil can be cut from card (stock) or transparent mylar and the paint is applied with the same roller that is used for inking the stamps. The theme is extended to the painted wooden key box and the lampshade.

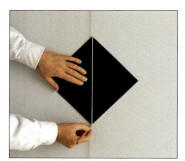

1 Paint the wall with dove-grey paint and leave to dry. Attach a plumbline at ceiling height, just in from one corner. Hold the card (stock) square against the wall so that the string cuts through the top and bottom corners. Mark all the corner points in pencil. Move the card and continue marking the wall to make a grid for the stamps.

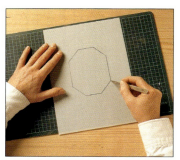

2 Use a pencil and ruler to draw the medallion shape on a sheet of stencil card. Carefully cut out the stencil using a craft knife on a self-healing cutting mat. Spread pale yellow emulsion (latex) paint on to a plate and run the roller through it until it is evenly coated.

3 Position the stencil on one of the pencil marks and use the paint-covered roller to stencil the medallion shape. Paint all the medallions in this way, positioning the stencil in the same place on each pencil mark.

4 Ink one of the cherub stamps with charcoal-grey paint and make a print inside each medallion. Print the cherub in the centre.

5 Paint the wooden box with pale yellow emulsion (latex) paint, inside and out, and leave to dry.

6 Spread some charcoal-grey paint on to a plate and run a roller through it until it is evenly coated. Ink the second cherub stamp and make a print in the centre of the box lid. Print the swag stamp directly beneath the cherub.

7 Measure the sides of the box to determine the number of swag prints that will fit comfortably in a row. Mark the positions in pencil or judge by eye to add swags around the sides of the box. Leave to dry.

8 Rub the corners and edges of the box with fine-grade abrasive paper (sandpaper). Rub the prints in places to add a faded, aged look. Use a cloth to rub burnt-umber artist's oil colour on to the whole box, to give an antique appearance.

9 For the lampshade, stamp several swags on scrap paper and cut them out. Arrange the cut-outs on the lampshade to plan your design. Hold each piece in place with a small piece of masking tape.

10 Spread some dove-grey paint on to a plate and run a roller through it until it is evenly coated. Ink the swag stamp and print swags around the top of the lampshade, removing each paper motif in turn before you stamp in its place.

11 Continue stamping around the base of the shade in the same way, removing each paper motif in turn.

12 Stamp swags around the lamp base to complete the co-ordinated look. Judge the positioning by eye or use paper motifs as before.

RIGHT: Stencilled medallions give an extra dimension to the cherub wall design. The theme is continued with swags and cherubs on other items in the room.

MEDIEVAL DINING ROOM

Decorate your dining room using medieval patterns and colours that will make coming through the door a pleasure for you and your visitors. A dark colour above dado (chair) rail height creates the illusion of a lower ceiling, while a light colour below, combined with a light floor covering, seems to push the walls outwards to give the impression of width. The crown pattern is stamped in a diagonal grid, which is easy, if time-consuming, to draw using a plumbline and a square of card.

You will need

- pencil
- emulsion (latex) paint in dark blue-green, buttermilk yellow and light cream
- paintbrush
- fine-grade abrasive paper (sandpaper)
- masking tape
- ruler
- paint roller
- wallpaper paste (mixed following the manufacturer's instructions)
- plate
- diamond and crown stamps
- foam roller
- plumbline
- card (stock), 15 x 15cm/6 x 6in

1 Draw a horizontal pencil line on the wall, at dado (chair) rail height. Paint the top half of the wall in dark blue-green and the bottom in buttermilk yellow. When dry, lightly sand the blue-green paint. Stick a strip of masking tape along the lower edge of the blue-green, and another 10cm/4in below. Apply light cream paint with a dry roller over the buttermilk yellow.

2 Stick another length of masking tape 2cm/5in below the one marking the edge of the blue-green section. Using a paintbrush and blue-green paint, fill in the stripe between the two lower strips of tape. Leave to dry and peel off the tape. Lightly sand the blue-green stripe to give it the appearance of the upper section of wall.

3 On a plate, mix one part blue-green emulsion (latex) paint with two parts pre-mixed wallpaper paste and stir well. Ink the diamond stamp with the foam roller and stamp a row of diamonds on the narrow cream stripe.

4 Use the plumbline and card (stock) square to mark an all-over grid on the cream half of the wall. This will be used as a guide for the crown stamps.

ABOVE: A simple crown stamp is used here to dramatic effect. You could extend the medieval theme to furniture in the room, for example a wooden box or cabinet.

5 Ink the crown stamp with the blue-green emulsion and wallpaper paste mixture and stamp a motif on each pencil mark. Make several prints before re-inking to create variation in the density of the prints.

CHECKS AND CHERRIES WINDOW

Bring the flavour of the French countryside into your home with checks and cherries. These popular designs are found adorning all kinds of crockery, enamelware, fabrics, pelmets and furniture in rural France. The checked border is applied with an ingenious self-inking rubber roller stamp, which is so easy to use you could get carried away. Be careful, though, because too many checks could become overpowering. Stamp the cherries randomly to make an all-over pattern, leaving plenty of space between the prints in order to prevent the pattern from looking too busy. Keep the whole effect light and airy.

1 Mark the border around the window frame, either applying masking tape along the outer edge or marking it with light pencil guidelines. Paint the border corn-yellow.

2 Mitre the corners for the roller stamp by positioning a sheet of scrap paper at a 45-degree angle, continuing the line of the mitred window frame. Hold the paper in place with tape.

3 Run the blue check-pattern roller stamp down, following the edge of the yellow border and overprinting the mitring paper. Do this in one smooth movement.

ABOVE: Give your kitchen a face-lift with this cheerful, brightly coloured design scheme. Complement the look with blue-and-white checked dishtowels.

4 Flip the paper over, keeping the same angle, and run the roller stamp across the bottom of the border. Overprint the paper then remove it.

5 Use the red stamp pad and the cherry motif rubber stamp to make a well-spaced pattern all over the surrounding wall.

PROVENÇAL KITCHEN

This kitchen is a dazzling example of contrasting colours – the effect is almost electric. Colours opposite each other in the colour wheel give the most vibrant contrast and you could equally well experiment with a combination of blue and orange or red and green. If, however, these colours are just too vivid, then choose a gentler colour scheme with the same stamped pattern. The kitchen walls were colourwashed to give a mottled, patchy background. Put some wallpaper paste in the colourwash to make the job a lot easier – it also prevents too many streaks running down the walls. You can stamp your cabinets to co-ordinate with the walls.

You will need

- emulsion (latex) paint in deep purple and pale yellow
- wallpaper paste (made up according to the manufacturer's instructions)
- household paintbrush
- plumbline
- card (stock) approx. 30 x 30cm/12 x 12in
- pencil
- plates
- foam rollers
- rosebud and small rose stamps
- acrylic paint in red and green
- clear matt (flat) varnish and brush

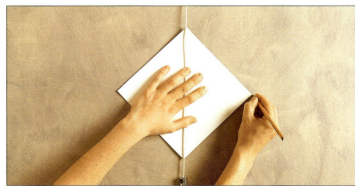

1 To make the colourwash, mix one part deep purple emulsion (latex) with one part wallpaper paste and four parts water. Make it up in multiples of six. It is best to make more than you need. Colourwash the walls. If runs occur, pick them up with the brush and work them into the surrounding wall, aiming for a patchy, mottled effect.

2 Attach the plumbline at ceiling height, just in from the corner. Hold the card (stock) square against the wall so that the string cuts through the top and bottom corners. Mark all four points with a pencil. Continue moving the square and marking points to make a grid pattern.

3 Spread some deep purple paint on to a plate and run a roller through it until it is evenly coated. Ink the rosebud stamp and print a rosebud on each pencil mark until you have covered the entire wall.

4 If you wish to create a dropped-shadow effect, clean the stamp and spread some pale yellow paint on to a plate. Ink the stamp and overprint each rosebud, moving the stamp so that it is slightly off-register.

5 Continue overprinting the rosebud motifs, judging by eye the position of the pale yellow prints. This is known as a dropped-shadow effect.

6 For the cabinet doors, spread some green and red paint on to the plates and run the rollers through them until they are evenly coated. Ink the rose with red and the leaves with green. (If one colour mixes with the other, just wipe it off and re-ink.) Print a rose in the top left-hand corner.

RIGHT: The rosebud print is made to look more subtle by overprinting it in another colour slightly off-register.

7 Print the stamp horizontally and vertically to make a border along the edges of the door panel.

8 When you have printed round the whole border, leave the paint to dry. Apply a coat of clear matt (flat) varnish to protect the surface.

RIGHT: *The traditional rosebud motif is given a new twist by printing it in unusual colours. Choose your own colour scheme to achieve the effect you want.*

ROSE BREAKFAST ROOM

New homes are wonderfully fresh, but the perfectly even walls can look plain if you are used to details such as dado (chair) rails and deep skirting (base) boards. This project shows you how to retain the freshness of new pastel paintwork and add interest with a frieze at dado-rail height and a coat of colourwash below it. Don't worry about painting in a straight line for the frieze – just use two strips of low-tack masking tape and paint between them. You could even try doing it by hand, as it does add character to the decoration, even if you do wobble a bit! Wooden furniture is given a distressed paint finish in toning colours, and stamped with the rose designs to co-ordinate with the walls.

1 To prepare the furniture, rub each piece down with abrasive paper (sandpaper) and apply a coat of cream paint. Make a blue-green glaze by diluting one part paint with three parts water, then brush it on following the direction of the grain. Before the paint has dried, use a cloth to wipe off some of the paint.

2 Spread the dusky-blue paint on to a plate and run the roller through it. Ink the rosebud stamp and print the design on to scrap paper.

3 Referring to the paper pattern, stamp the design in the centre of your chosen piece of furniture.

4 Stamp more rosebuds on either side of the central design. Work with the shape of the individual piece of furniture to decide upon the best position and the number of prints to use.

5 If you are decorating a desk or dresser, unscrew and remove any handles, then stamp the pattern on the drawer fronts. Screw them back after the paint has dried.

6 For a small piece of furniture like this chair, a simple design is best. Paint the chair with cream emulsion (latex) paint, then print a single small rose in peach.

7 To make the colourwash for the walls, mix one part peach emulsion (latex) paint with one part wallpaper paste and four parts water. Make it up in multiples of six. It is best to make more than you need, so that you can do the whole room from the same batch to ensure a colour match. Unless the room has been painted recently, apply a coat of cream emulsion to the walls.

8 Measure about 90cm/36in from the floor and make a pencil mark on the wall. Tape the spirit level to the plank and draw a straight line all round the room 90cm/36in above floor level. Draw another line 3cm/1¼in above it.

9 Apply the colourwash below the line using sweeping random brushstrokes. If runs occur, just pick them up with the brush and work them into the surrounding wall. Aim for a patchy, mottled effect.

10 If you have a steady hand, paint a dusky-blue stripe on the wall with the square-tipped brush, otherwise use masking tape to guide you and remove it when the paint is dry.

11 Spread the dusky-blue and peach paints on to the plates and use the foam roller or paintbrush to ink the large rose stamp, using the colours as shown. Print with the stamp base resting on the top of the dusky-blue stripe. Continue all round the room, re-inking the stamp each time for a regular print.

RIGHT: Three rose stamps look very pretty used as a wall frieze and on matching painted furniture. This is an ideal way to decorate second-hand furniture.

STARRY BEDROOM

At first glance, this bedroom looks wallpapered, but a closer examination reveals the hand-printed irregularity of the star stamps – some are almost solid colour while others look very faded. This effect is achieved by making several prints before re-inking the stamp. The idea is to get away from the monotony of machine-printed wallpaper, where one motif is the exact replica of the next, and create the effect of exclusive, hand-blocked wallpaper at a fraction of the price. The grid for the stars is marked using a plumbline and pencil. If you haven't got a plumbline, make your own by tying a key to a piece of string. You're bound to be delighted with the final result, and feel a great sense of achievement at having done it all yourself.

You will need

- sandy-yellow emulsion (latex) paint or distemper paint
- large paintbrush
- card (stock) 30 x 30cm/12 x 12in
- plumbline
- pencil
- brick-red emulsion paint
- plate
- foam roller
- folk-art star stamp

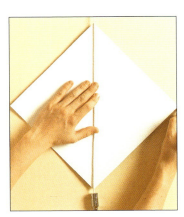

1 Paint the walls sandy yellow with emulsion (latex) paint or distemper paint. You may prefer a smooth, even finish or areas of patchy colour – each will create its own distinct look. Uneven colour will add to the effect of the uneven printing.

2 Hold the card (stock) square diagonally against the wall in the corner at ceiling height. Attach the plumbline at ceiling height so that the string cuts through the top and bottom corners of the square. Mark all four points with a pencil. Continue moving the square and marking points to form a grid all over the wall.

ABOVE: *Sunny colours give this bedroom a warm, welcoming feeling. The simple star design goes perfectly with traditional patchwork quilts and folk-art accessories. Country-style stamped furniture would also be at home in this room.*

3 Spread some brick-red paint on to the plate and run the roller through it until it is evenly coated. Ink the stamp and print a star on every pencil mark, or line the block up against each pencil mark to find your position, whichever you find easiest.

4 Experiment with the stamp and paint to see how many prints you can make before re-inking. Don't make the contrast between the pale and dark too obvious or the eye will always be drawn to these areas.

GRAPE BORDER BEDROOM

Who wouldn't want to sleep in this lovely lavender-grey and white bedroom? The choice of two cool colours has a very calming effect. The frieze is stamped in white at dado (chair) rail height around a lavender-grey wall. The simple reversal of the wall colours on the headboard provides both contrast and continuity. You can stamp on to an existing headboard or make one quite simply from a sheet of MDF (medium-density fiberboard) cut to the width of the bed. Use the stamps to make matching accessories in the same colours. For example, make the most of the stamps' versatility by using only the central part of the tendril stamp on the narrow border of a picture frame.

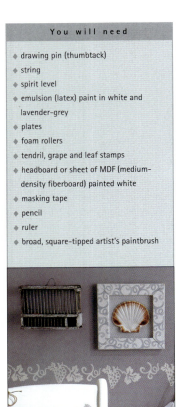

1 Use a drawing pin (thumbtack) to attach one end of the string in a corner of the room at dado (chair) rail height. Run the string along the wall to the next corner and secure the end. Check the string with a spirit level and adjust if necessary.

2 Spread some white paint on to a plate and run a roller through it until it is evenly coated. Ink all three stamps and stamp a tendril, grape and leaf in sequence along the wall. Align the top edge of each stamp with the string and print below it.

3 When the first wall is complete, move the string to the next wall and continue all the way around the room. To decorate the headboard, stick masking tape around the top and side edges of the white board.

4 Spread some lavender-grey paint on to a plate and run a roller through it until it is evenly coated. Ink the leaf and tendril stamps. Align the stamp blocks with the masking tape and stamp alternate leaves and tendrils down both sides of the headboard.

5 Ink all three stamps and stamp a tendril, grape and leaf along the top edge of the headboard. Repeat the sequence to complete the row. Check the spacing before you stamp – wide spacing is better than the motifs appearing squashed together.

6 Measure a central panel on the headboard and lightly draw it in pencil. Stick strips of masking tape around the panel and the border. Mix some lavender-grey and white paint, then paint the border and the central panel in this pale grey colour.

RIGHT: Three stamps are used to create this beautiful border design. If you wish to decorate other pieces of bedroom furniture, you could use one or more of the stamps printed in groups or singly.

COUNTRY GRANDEUR BEDROOM

Redecorating a bedroom can be as refreshing as taking a holiday, and stamping is such fun that it won't seem like work at all. First sponge over a cream background with terracotta emulsion (latex) paint and add a final highlight of pink to create a warm, mottled colour. Any plain light-coloured wall can be covered in this way. The two stamps are then combined to make a border which co-ordinates with an all-over pattern on the wall and a bedside table. You can also decorate matching curtains and cushions, or stamp the border on sheets and pillowcases.

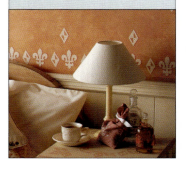

1 Spread some dark salmon-pink paint on to a plate and use a roller to ink the fleur-de-lys stamp. Stamp a row of fleurs-de-lys above the dado (chair) rail, using a piece of card (stock) 7.5cm/3in wide to space the motifs.

2 Ink the diamond stamp with the dark salmon-pink paint, and print diamonds between the fleur-de-lys motifs. Use a card spacing device if you are nervous about judging the positioning by eye.

3 Cut a card square about 25 x 25cm/ 10 x 10in. Attach a plumbline at ceiling height, just in from one corner so that the weighted end hangs down to the border. Use a pencil to mark a grid for the diamond stamps.

4 Ink the diamond stamp with the dark salmon-pink paint. Print a diamond on every pencil mark to make an all-over pattern.

5 Spread some off-white paint on to a plate and run a roller through it until it is evenly coated. Ink both stamps and overprint the border pattern. To create a dropped-shadow effect, stamp each print slightly below and to the left of the motif that has already been printed.

6 Overprint the diamond wall pattern in the same way.

7 Lay the ruler across the table top from corner to corner in both directions to find the central point. Mark the centre lightly in pencil.

8 Set the pair of compasses to a radius of 10cm/4in and lightly draw a circle in the centre of the table top.

9 Increase the radius to 12.5cm/5in. Position the point of the compasses on the edge of the circle, in line with the middle of the back edge of the table. Mark the point on the circle at the other end of the compasses, then move the point of the compasses to this mark. Continue around the circle to make five divisions. Connect the marks with light pencil lines to make a pentagonal shape.

10 Use the black stamp pad to print 15 diamonds on paper then cut them out. Arrange them around the pentagon, as shown. Use the compasses to mark the inner points of the five inward-pointing diamonds.

11 Spread some dusky pink paint on to a plate and run a roller through it until it is evenly coated. Ink the diamond stamp and print the five inward-pointing diamonds at the marked positions.

12 Re-ink the stamp as necessary and print the rest of the pattern. Print an arrangement of three diamonds in each corner of the table top. Paint any moulding and handles on the table in the same shade of pink. Seal the table with a coat of clear matt (flat) varnish.

RIGHT: *Fleurs-de-lys and diamonds make an elegant combination. The circle of diamonds on the bedside table shows how a single simple motif can be positioned at different angles to create a complex design.*

GREEK KEY BATHROOM

This bathroom looks far too elegant to have been decorated by an amateur. The border design is a classic Greek key interspaced with a bold square and cross. The black and gold look stunning on a pure white tiled wall. Every bathroom has different features, so use the border to make the most of the best ones, while drawing attention away from the duller areas. If you like a co-ordinated scheme, you could print the same border on a set of towels, using fabric inks.

You will need

♦ tracing paper
♦ pencil
♦ scissors
♦ spray adhesive
♦ high-density foam rubber, such as upholstery foam
♦ craft knife
♦ acrylic enamel paint in black and gold
♦ plates
♦ wooden batten (furring strip) 2–3cm/ ³/₄–1¹/₄in wide, depending on the bathroom
♦ scrap paper
♦ masking tape

1 Trace, transfer and cut out the pattern shapes from the template section. Lightly spray the shapes with adhesive and place them on the foam rubber. To cut out the shapes, cut the outline first, then undercut and remove any excess, leaving the pattern shape standing free of the foam rubber.

2 Spread an even coating of black paint on to a plate. Place the batten (furring strip) up next to the door frame to keep the border an even distance from it. Make a test print on scrap paper then begin by stamping one black outline square in the bottom corner, at dado (chair) rail height. Print a key shape above it, being careful not to smudge the adjoining edge of the previous print.

3 Continue alternating the stamps around the door frame.

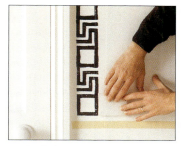

4 Mark the baseline of the design area with masking tape and alternate the motifs along this line.

5 Spread a coating of gold paint on to a plate and dip the cross shape into it. Make a test print on scrap paper, then print the shape in the centre of square frames.

RIGHT: This design would look very dramatic stamped in plain black in a kitchen or bathroom.

SEASCAPE BATHROOM FRIEZE

This really is instant decorating. The sponge shapes come from a child's sea-life painting set. Other themed sets available include jungle, dinosaur, transport and farm animals. Although these are children's sponges, the project is not intended for an exclusively child-oriented bathroom scheme. The shapes are appropriate for grown-ups, too, and they can also be used to decorate other rooms in the home.

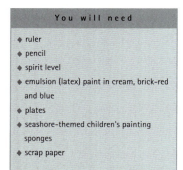

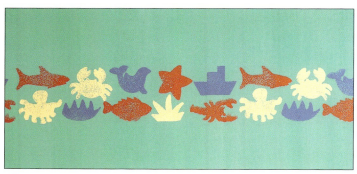

1 Draw a line for the base of your frieze, using a ruler, pencil and spirit level. Spread the paints on to separate plates and press the sponge shapes into the paint following a sequence of cream, brick-red and blue. Make test prints on scrap paper to make sure that the sponges are not overloaded. Print all the sponge shapes across the baseline, then repeat the sequence to make another row.

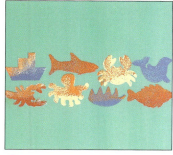

2 Partially overprint each shape by dipping each sponge into a different colour from the one first used.

3 Continue overprinting the shapes. The second colour adds a shadow effect, giving the shapes a more three-dimensional appearance.

FURNITURE AND FURNISHINGS

Make it a rule never to pass by a second-hand furniture shop without glancing in. It's not that stamping is unsuitable for new furniture, just that doing up old junk is so rewarding. You are far less likely to experiment with a new chair than with one that actually needs some life breathing into it! Of course, there are always exceptions. White kitchen units, for example, can be given a new identity with matt (flat) oil-based paint. You can use emulsion (latex) paint on bare wood, and the designs can be protected with varnish. If the wood has previously been painted, use abrasive paper (sandpaper) to give the paint a matt texture to key into.

*ABOVE: Stamping will transform a plain wooden or painted
piece of second-hand furniture such as this kitchen chair.*

*LEFT: Stamps can be simple and traditional, or can be slightly more
quirky to create unique decoration for furniture and furnishings.*

EGYPTIAN TABLE TOP

The beauty of this table top design lies in its simplicity. Just one colour was used on a bold background, with three similar images stamped in regimented rows. The table used here has a lower shelf, but the design would work equally well on any occasional table. The salmon-pink prints show up well on the rich background, making it look even bluer. The stamps are pre-cut and are taken from Ancient Egyptian hieroglyphs. The finished table could be one element of a themed room, or the surprising and eye-catching centrepiece of a room decorated in subdued colours.

You will need

- 3 hieroglyphic rubber stamps
- ruler
- 2 card (stock) strips, for measuring
  stamp positions
- felt-tipped pen
- set square (triangle)
- emulsion (latex) or acrylic paint in
  salmon-pink
- small paint roller
- piece of card or plastic

1 Use the stamp blocks and a ruler to measure out the stamp positions. Place a card (stock) strip along the vertical edge of the table. Mark as many stamp lengths as will fit along it, leaving equal spaces between them. Work out the positioning carefully so that the rows of prints will fit comfortably. Use the second card strip to mark the widths of the stamps.

2 Place the horizontal measure across the table so that it marks the position of the first row. The top of the stamp will touch the measuring strip. Use a set square (triangle) to position the vertical strip at a 90-degree angle to the first row. Move the vertical strip along as you stamp. Coat the roller with paint by running it through a blob of paint on a spare piece of card or plastic.

4 Move the horizontal measure up one stamp space on the vertical measure and stamp a second row of figures. Once again, the tops of the stamps will touch the bottom of the horizontal strip. Check that the card measures remain at a 90-degree angle. Continue until the pattern covers the whole table top.

3 Use the roller to coat the stamps, then print them in sequence all along the first row. Position the stamps following the marks you have made on the card strips.

BELOW: Vibrant colours turn an ordinary table into a main feature. You could also use subtle colours such as beige and brown.

STARFISH BATHROOM CHAIR

Old wooden chairs are not expensive and, with a bit of careful hunting round second-hand shops, you should be able to find yourself a real bargain. Make the effort to strip the old layers of paint – it might take some time, but it gives you a much better base to work on. This chair was given an undercoat of white emulsion (latex) paint, then it was dragged with yellow-ochre in the direction of the grain before being stamped with starfish motifs in light grey. Choose colours that complement your bathroom scheme so that your Starfish Bathroom Chair will blend in with the existing fittings.

You will need

- medium-grade abrasive paper (sandpaper)
- wooden chair
- emulsion (latex) paint in white, yellow-ochre and light grey
- household paintbrush
- plate
- foam roller
- starfish stamp
- clear matt (flat) varnish and brush

1 Sand or strip the chair, then apply a coat of white emulsion (latex) paint. Mix a thin wash of about five parts water to one part yellow-ochre emulsion. Use a dry brush to drag a little glaze at a time in the direction of the grain. Keep drying the brush as you work, to ensure you do not apply too much glaze.

2 Spread some light grey paint on to the plate and run the roller through it until it is evenly coated. Ink the starfish stamp and print around the edge of the chair seat so that the design overlaps on to the sides.

3 Fill in the seat area with starfish stamps, rotating the stamp to a different angle after each print. Space the stamps quite close together to make a dense pattern. Leave to dry thoroughly before applying a coat of varnish to protect the surface.

OPPOSITE: *You can continue the starfish theme with a frieze on the wall.*

BEACHCOMBER'S STOOL

If you stumble across a small milking stool like this one, don't hesitate, just buy it! These sorts of stools were, and still are, used in kitchens, gardens and worksheds for a whole range of tasks. Small children love to sit on them and adults find them invaluable when shelves are just out of reach. They can be used for weeding, sketching, fishing or any activity that requires being close to the ground but not actually on it. This second-hand shop find was painted orange before being stamped with the seashore pattern. It's just the thing to sit on while peeling prawns or cleaning mussels.

1 Paint the stool orange and leave to dry. Spread some deep red paint on to a plate and run the roller through it until it is evenly coated. Ink the shell stamp and make a print in the centre of the stool.

2 Ink the seahorse stamp with purple paint and make a print either side of the shell print. The seahorses face the same direction.

3 Ink the starfish stamp with pale peach paint. Print a starfish border, overlapping the edge so that the design goes down the sides of the stool.

4 When the paint has dried, apply a coat of varnish to the stool. The varnish will dry to a matt (flat) sheen.

BELOW: For a more traditional nautical look, use shades of blue and turquoise.

FISH FOOTSTOOL

This low stool decorated with a leaping fish motif would look good in the bathroom or on the patio for drinks, or it could be used simply for putting your feet on. Any small and useful stool that looks handmade would be a suitable candidate for a make-over. The fish and border blocks are cut from high-density foam and the light and dark blue colour scheme is reminiscent of Balinese batik prints.

You will need

- small stool
- emulsion (latex) paint in dark blue, light blue and off-white
- household paintbrushes
- tracing paper
- pencil
- scissors
- spray adhesive
- high-density foam, such as upholstery foam
- craft knife
- scrap paper
- plate

1 Give the stool two coats of dark blue paint and leave to dry. Trace, transfer and cut out the two pattern shapes from the template section. Lightly spray the shapes with adhesive and place them on the foam. Cut around the outlines with a craft knife, then scoop out the pattern details.

2 Print five fish shapes on to scrap paper and cut them out. Use these to plan the position of the fish design on the stool. The fish should look as if they are swimming at different angles.

3 Spread some light blue and off-white paint on to a plate. Using a paintbrush, apply off-white paint to the top of the fish and light blue to the bottom. Make a test print on scrap paper to make sure the stamp is not overloaded.

4 Using the paper shapes as a guide, stamp the fish lightly on the surface of the stool, printing both colours at the same time.

BELOW: Stamping the fish at different angles gives a lovely illusion of life and movement – they seem to be swimming through deep blue water.

5 Paint the border stamp using the off-white paint. The border is intentionally ragged, so don't go for strict straight edges, but stamp the design in a slightly haphazard fashion.

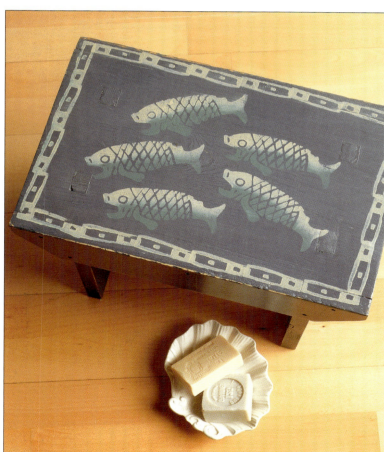

FOLK MOTIF CHAIR

Old kitchen chairs are functional and comfortable but often very plain. This modular style of decoration allows you to unite a non-matching set of chairs by stamping them with similar designs in the same colours. They will look much more interesting than a new set, and will have cost a fraction of the price.

You will need

- wooden kitchen chair
- emulsion (latex) paint in light blue-grey
- small household paintbrush
- abrasive paper (sandpaper) (optional)
- ruler
- pencil
- tracing paper
- scissors
- spray adhesive
- medium-density sponge
- craft knife
- plate
- acrylic or emulsion paint in red, white and dark blue-grey
- scrap paper
- clear matt (flat) varnish and brush

1 Give the chair at least two coats of light blue-grey paint and leave to dry. To achieve a "weathered" look, you could rub down the paint between coats, to let some of the grain show through. Use a ruler to find the centre of the back rest and make a small pencil mark. Trace, transfer and cut out the pattern shapes from the template section. Lightly spray the shapes with adhesive and place them on the sponge. Cut around the outlines with a craft knife.

2 Use a plate as your palette. Spread out an even coating of red, white and dark blue-grey acrylic or emulsion (latex) paint. Press the diamond shape into the red paint and make a test print on scrap paper. Stamp the diamond shape on the marked centre point of the back rest.

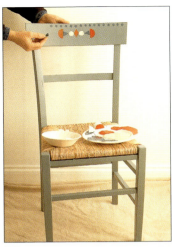

3 Stamp a white circle on either side of the diamond.

4 Stamp a dark blue-grey triangle and finally a red half-moon shape on either side of the stamped motifs, to form a symmetrical pattern.

5 Using the small square shape, stamp dark blue-grey diamonds around the edge of the back rest with equally sized gaps in between.

6 Stamp dark blue-grey squares on the back crossbar, as shown. Then fill in the gaps on the back rest with white diamonds and the gaps on the back crossbar with white squares.

7 Stamp dark blue-grey triangles, pointing outwards, to form a "sawtooth" border down both sides of the chair back.

8 Stamp red circles on the front legs where the lower crossbars meet them. Stamp dark blue-grey triangles above and below the circles, pointing outwards. Add some dark blue-grey and white diamonds to the centres of the lower crossbars. Finally, when all the paint is dry, give the whole chair a coat of clear matt (flat) varnish to protect the design.

GOTHIC CABINET

Visit second-hand shops to find old pieces of furniture with some interesting detailing and panels that would take a stamped heraldic design. This small bedside cabinet looked very gloomy with its original dark woodstain, but has shed its old image and become a complete extrovert as the centrepiece of a medieval entrance hall.

You will need

- small wooden cabinet
- fine-grade abrasive paper (sandpaper)
- emulsion (latex) paint in rust-brown, dark blue-green, lilac and yellow-ochre
- household paintbrush
- medium-sized artist's paintbrush
- black stamp pad
- diamond and fleur-de-lys stamps
- scrap paper
- scissors
- pencil
- ruler (optional)
- plates
- foam rollers
- red-orange smooth-flowing water-based paint (thinned emulsion, poster paint or ready-mixed watercolour)
- lining brush
- shellac and brush
- water-based tinted varnish
- fine wire (steel) wool

1 Sand away the existing varnish or paint. Paint the cabinet in rust-brown on the main body and dark blue-green on any carved details and on the panels. Use the artist's paintbrush to paint the blue-green right into the panel edges, to ensure even coverage.

2 Use the stamp pad to print the diamond and fleur-de-lys motifs on paper and cut them out. Lay them on the panels to plan your pattern. Make a small pencil mark on the panel at the base point of each motif as a guide for stamping. Use a ruler if necessary to make sure the design is symmetrical. Mark the base point of the motif on the back of each stamp block so that you can line up the marks when you print.

3 Spread some lilac paint on to a plate and run a roller through it until it is evenly coated. Ink the diamond stamp and print diamonds using the pencil marks as a guide.

4 Spread some yellow-ochre paint on to a plate and ink the fleur-de-lys stamp. Print the fleur-de-lys motifs, using the pencil marks as a guide.

5 Using red-orange paint and the lining brush, add hand-painted details to the motifs. Support your painting hand with your spare hand resting on the surface of the cabinet and aim to get a smooth, flowing line.

6 Apply a coat of shellac to seal the surface for varnishing and leave to dry. Apply a fairly thick coat of tinted varnish and leave to dry. Rub the raised areas and edges of the cabinet with fine wire (steel) wool to simulate natural wear and tear.

RIGHT: Hand-painted details in red-orange make these heraldic motifs look even more sumptuous. The rich colours are typical of the Gothic Revival furniture made popular by William Morris and the Arts and Crafts Movement in the 19th century.

STAR CABINET

This attractive little cabinet seems to fit in the moment you have finished it. While its style is individual, it does not scream out for attention, and it has that comfortable, lived-in look. The cabinet was painted, stamped, then painted again. Finally, it was given a coat of antique pine varnish and rubbed back with a cloth in places. It glows from all the attention and took just one afternoon to make. This style of decoration is so simple that you might consider transforming other items of furniture in the same way.

1 Paint the cabinet with a coat of olive-green emulsion (latex) paint, applying a second coat if necessary.

2 Trace, transfer and cut out the star shape from the template section. Lightly spray with adhesive and place on the sponge. Cut out with a craft knife. Spread some off-white paint on to a plate. Dip the sponge star shape into the paint and print stars all over the cabinet, quite close together.

3 Make a mixture of two-thirds vermilion paint and one-third PVA (white) glue. When the stars have dried, coat the cabinet with a liberal amount of this colour, daubed on with a brush.

ABOVE: *A simple design is made special by coating it with diluted paint and tinted varnish.*

4 Finish the cabinet with a coat of tinted varnish, then use a cloth to rub some of it off each of the stars. This layering of colour gives the surface its attractive rich patina.

NONSENSE KEY CABINET

If you have a well-developed sense of the ridiculous, then this project will appeal to you. The idea is to use three totally unconnected images of varying scales to form a nonsense design. Our choice was three morris dancers below a large old-fashioned tap, surrounded by stars, but you can choose anything you like. The wooden cabinet was painted with white primer before the stamps were added in dark blue ink. The colour was applied with a fine artist's paintbrush using bright watercolour paint. The streaky paint finish was achieved with yellow watercolour wiped on with a small piece of sponge.

You will need

- small key cabinet
- white primer
- small household paintbrush
- selection of stamps
- permanent ink stamp pad in navy-blue
- scrap paper
- craft knife
- watercolour paints
- fine artist's paintbrush
- small piece of sponge
- medium-grade abrasive paper (sandpaper)
- clear matt varnish and brush (optional)

1 Apply two coats of white primer to the bare wood of the key cabinet, allowing the primer to dry thoroughly between coats.

2 Stamp a selection of motifs on to scrap paper and cut them out. Use them to plan your design by positioning the paper pieces on the central panel of the cabinet door.

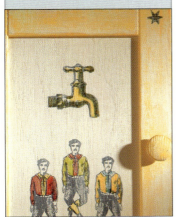

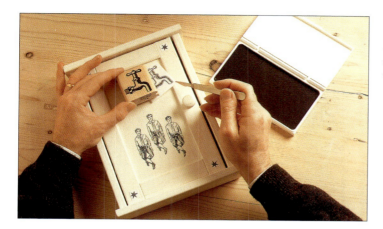

3 When you are happy with your layout, stamp the designs directly on to the cabinet. Use the paper pieces as a guide by moving them out of the way at the last moment.

4 Stamp a small star in each corner of the cabinet door.

5 Begin to paint the details of the illustrated panel using watercolour paints and a fine artist's paintbrush. Fill in the first colour.

6 Continue filling in the details of the prints, adding more colour.

7 Complete the details and leave to dry. When the paint has dried, use a small piece of sponge to wipe yellow watercolour paint over the cabinet avoiding the central, nonsense-illustrated panel.

8 When the paint has dried, lightly rub down the yellow paint with abrasive paper (sandpaper). If desired, seal the surface with a coat of clear varnish.

RIGHT: For a quicker finish, leave the details and background unpainted. The combination of blue and white creates a more cooling effect than vibrant primaries.

COUNTRY CABINET

A popular designer's trick is to paint a piece of furniture in the same colours as the background of the room, but in reverse. This co-ordinates the room without being overpoweringly repetitive. A small cabinet like the one in this project is perfect for such a treatment. Don't be too precise in your stamping – a fairly rough-and-ready technique gives the most pleasing results.

You will need

- wooden cabinet
- emulsion (latex) paint in brick-red and yellow
- small household paintbrush
- plate
- foam roller
- small star stamp
- fine wire (steel) wool or abrasive paper (sandpaper)
- water-based matt (flat) varnish and brush

1 Paint the cabinet with a base coat of brick-red emulsion (latex) paint. Leave to dry.

2 Spread some yellow paint on to the plate and run the roller through it until it is evenly coated. Ink the stamp and print on to the cabinet.

3 Rub around the edges with wire (steel) wool or abrasive paper (sandpaper) to simulate natural wear and tear. This will give an aged appearance.

ABOVE: Rustic-coloured paints, a "distressed" finish and random stamping make this kind of furniture ideal for a country-style interior.

4 Apply a coat of varnish tinted with the brick-red paint (one part paint to five parts varnish) to tone down the contrast between the prints and the background paint.

FABRICS

Making patterns on fabric with rubber or foam stamps is not a new idea and many textiles from small rural communities are still handblocked today. At the other end of the market, very expensive, limited editions of "designer" textiles gain their value because of their labour-intensive style of production. There are a few important rules to obey with fabric: always wash it first; always use permanent inks (some need heat-sealing); and always work with a protective backing sheet under the fabric. Avoid fabrics which have special surfaces that will not absorb the ink and those with very loose weaves and furry materials. You should also avoid using fabric conditioner and starch.

ABOVE: Stamp simple motifs on ready-made items such as these mix-and-match cushion covers – there is no need for sewing!

LEFT: Different fabrics absorb paint at different rates. Those with a close weave are more likely to resist the paint so it sits on the surface.

FLEUR-DE-LYS CUSHIONS

A new set of cushions add comfort and warmth, as well as a homely feel to a room. If you are marking out your own territory, why not do it with vivacious colour contrasts for maximum impact? Choose hard-wearing medium-weight cotton cushion covers. Wash and iron the covers before decorating them and place a sheet of card (stock) inside each cover to protect the other side. The patterns used here, the fleur-de-lys, the crown, and diamond, are very much European in origin but the hemp fringing and the bright colouring give the cushions an unusual tropical flavour.

You will need

- fleur-de-lys, crown and diamond stamps
- black stamp pad
- scrap paper
- scissors
- 3 brightly coloured plain cotton cushion covers
- thin card (stock)
- pencil
- fabric paint in blue, orange and bright pink
- plates
- foam rollers
- long ruler
- iron
- hemp fringing, approximately 5.5m/6yd
- needle and thread or fabric glue

1 Print some fleurs-de-lys on paper and cut them out. Lay a cover on a work surface and arrange the motifs. Here, the bases of the motifs are 10cm/4in apart. Cut the card (stock) to the width of the space between the bases and about 7.5cm/3in high. Draw a line down the centre of the card.

2 Ink the stamp with the blue paint. Place the ruler across the fabric and rest the card on it. Print the first motif above the card. Move the card so that its top left-hand corner rests on the base of the first motif. Line up the centre of the stamp with the right-hand edge of the card to print the next.

3 Continue using the spacer card to print the first row of motifs. Move the ruler down for each new row, keeping it at a right angle to the edge of the cushion cover.

4 Print alternate rows so that the motifs fill the spaces left between the motifs in the row above. Print the other cushion covers using the same technique. Fix (set) the fabric paint with a hot iron, following the manufacturer's instructions. Attach hemp fringing around the covers.

ABOVE: For a more traditional look, use colours such as gold, maroon and cream.

AFRICAN-STYLE CUSHIONS

This glorious pile of cushions is a real stamper's fashion statement with the fabulous animal motifs creating a distinctive African look. The stamps are perfect for making a themed set of cushions to display together. The covers are made from rough homespun fabric that has been vegetable-dyed in rich, spicy shades, and the combination of the primitive stamped shapes and the textured fabric is very effective.

1 Apply the fabric ink directly to the small border stamp and make a test print on a scrap of fabric to ensure that the stamp is not overloaded.

2 Place a sheet of card (stock) to fit inside the cushion cover. This will protect the other side from the black fabric ink.

4 Stamp a row of a larger motif at even intervals above the border. Use a combination of all three stamps in this way to complete the cushion design. Arrange the stamps in different ways on the other covers, either radiating out from the centre, or forming circles and squares.

BELOW: These unusual cushions show how you can build up quite different patterns using the same motifs. Experiment with other designs.

3 Re-ink the stamp and print a row of small motifs round the edges of the cover to create a border.

QUILTED CUSHIONS

A new pile of cushions can change the mood of a room in an instant – so why not update your living room or bedroom with these folk-inspired patterns? You can vary the star design on each cushion to make a co-ordinating mix-and-match set. Don't be daunted by the idea of quilting, as it really is not difficult and cushions present a small size with which to work. Once the painting is complete, simply iron the wadding on to the calico, then sew straight horizontal and vertical, or diagonal, lines through the centres of the stars. Alternatively, buy plain ready-made covers and stamp on the star patterns.

1 Lay the calico on backing paper on a work surface. Spread some of the brick-red paint on to a plate and run the roller through it until it is evenly coated. Ink the folk-art star stamp.

2 Position the stamp in the corner of the calico and print. This square of calico will make the front of one cushion cover.

3 Continue stamping along the row, leaving a space the width of the stamp block between each print. Begin the next row with a blank space, and stamp the star so that it falls between the stars in the bottom row. Repeat these two rows of stars to cover the piece of calico.

4 Using the pear-green paint, ink the small star stamp and print between the red stars. Fix (set) the fabric paint with a hot iron, then iron on the wadding. Stitch horizontal and then vertical lines through the centres of the red stars. Place the calico and the backing fabric wrong sides together and machine stitch, leaving an opening.

ABOVE: These traditional folk-art designs would also look attractive stamped in shades of blue.

ROSE CUSHIONS

Don't get your needle and thread out for this project – just buy plain cushion covers and stamp them with contrasting colours. New cushions revitalize existing decor and they can change the mood of a room in an instant. They are also a clever way to distribute a themed pattern round a room as they subtly reinforce the rosy look. Natural fabrics like this thick cotton weave are perfect for stamping because they absorb the fabric paint easily to leave a good, sharp print. Fabric paints can be fixed (set) with a hot iron after applying to ensure a long-lasting and hard-wearing finish.

You will need

- sheet of thin card (stock)
- natural-fabric cushion covers in 2 different colours
- fabric paint in white and blue
- plates
- foam rollers
- rosebud, large rose and small rose stamps
- scrap paper
- scissors
- iron

1 Place the sheet of card (stock) inside the darker cushion cover. Spread some of the white fabric paint on to a plate and run the roller through it until it is evenly coated. Ink the rosebud stamp and make the first print in the bottom right-hand corner of the cover.

2 Continue stamping in rows, using the stamp block as a spacing guide – use the top edge as the position for the bottom edge of the next print. You should be able to judge by eye after a couple of prints. Fill the cover with a grid pattern of rosebuds.

3 For the second, paler-coloured cushion cover, ink all three stamps with the blue fabric paint. Stamp each one on to scrap paper and cut them out. Use the paper patterns to work out the position of the rows of motifs.

4 Re-ink the large rose stamp and make the first print in the top left-hand corner. Use the paper pattern to help with the spacing between the motifs. Complete the row.

5 Ink the small rose stamp and complete the next row, again using the paper pattern for spacing.

ABOVE: *Fabrics with woven stripes make it very easy to position the rose prints, and add to the overall effect.*

6 Stamp another row of large roses, then print the rosebud stamp in the same way to complete the pattern. Finally, fix (set) the fabric paints on both covers with a hot iron, following the manufacturer's instructions.

WHITE LACE PILLOWCASES

Attractive lace-edged pillowcases are now mass-produced and imported at very reasonable prices. You can buy many different designs ranging from hand-crocheted cotton to machine-made broderie-anglaise style cutwork. Choose a selection of different lace cushions for your room, then stamp delicate pink hearts in soft colours on to their centres to make a romantic display for the bedroom. Fabric paints work very well on cotton fabric, but it is advisable to wash and iron the pillowcases before you stamp them. This removes the glaze that might block the paint's absorption.

You will need

- lace-edged, white pillowcases
- iron
- ruler
- pencil
- sheet of thin card (stock)
- fabric paint in pale pink
- plate
- foam roller
- small heart stamp

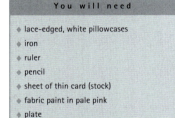

1 Wash and iron the pillowcases to give a crisp, flat surface and remove any dressing in the fabric.

2 Using a ruler, measure between the corners to find the centre of the pillowcase. Make a small pencil mark at this point.

3 Place the sheet of card (stock) inside the pillowcase between the two layers so that the colour does not pass through to the other side.

4 Spread some pale pink fabric paint on to the plate and run the roller through it until it is evenly coated, then ink the small heart stamp. Print a group of four hearts so that the points meet at the central pencil mark.

5 Stamp another four hearts in line with the first, but with the points facing outwards. Leave to dry before fixing with a hot iron according to the manufacturer's instructions.

BELOW: Experiment with other patterns using different heart stamps to make alternative versions of the lace pillowcase.

TUMBLING ROSE CHAIR COVER

R eady-made slip covers for director's and wicker chairs provide an innovative way of restyling a room. It is rather like putting on a new jacket and changing your image. The design of the roses follows the curve of the chair and the direction of the seat. One of the advantages of these covers is that you can use them to disguise less than perfect chairs that are still structurally sound. Look out for old Lloyd loom chairs with sprung seats – their appearance may have been spoiled by coats of gloss paint over the years, but they're still ideal for a slip cover.

You will need

♦ fabric paint in green and red
♦ plate
♦ foam rollers
♦ large rose stamp
♦ ready-made calico slip cover
♦ sheet of thin card (stock)
♦ iron

1 Spread some green and red paint on to the plate and run the rollers through them until they are evenly coated. Ink the rose part of the stamp red and the stalk and leaves green.

2 Place the sheet of card (stock) behind the front panel of the slip cover and begin stamping the roses. Rotate the stamp in your hand after each print to get the tumbling rose effect.

3 Place the sheet of card behind the seat section and stamp the roses in the same way as the front.

4 Place the sheet of card inside the top section and stamp the top row, following the shape of the slip cover. Continue stamping to fill the cover, rotating the stamp as you did before. Fix (set) the fabric paint with a hot iron, following the manufacturer's instructions.

ABOVE: Tumbling roses would also look very pretty stamped on bedroom curtains or a large laundry bag.

COUNTRY-STYLE THROW

I
t's hard to imagine a home without a throw. Throws not only hide a multitude of sins like stains and worn patches, but they can instantly change the mood of a room with their colours and patterns. A casually draped throw gives off a wonderful sense of relaxation and comfort. The textured throw used in this project illustrates how well stamp prints can work on all sorts of surfaces, and most fabrics would be suitable. Fabric paints are easy to use, in fact most fabrics absorb the colour instantly, which means there is less chance of smudging than there would be on a smooth, non-porous surface such as wood or shiny paper. Always use a piece of backing paper when printing on fabric.

You will need

- plain-coloured throw, or suitable length of fabric with a hemmed edge
- iron
- backing paper, such as thin card (stock) or newspaper
- fabric paint in red, blue and purple
- plate
- paintbrush
- foam roller
- trellis heart stamp
- sheet of scrap paper

1 Press the throw or length of fabric with a hot iron so that it lies flat. Place it on some backing paper on a large work surface such as a wallpaper-pasting table.

2 Put the three fabric paints on to the plate and mix them together to create a violet-blue colour. Run the roller through the paint until it is evenly coated, then ink the stamp.

3 Starting in the top left-hand corner, about 4cm/1½in in from the edge, stamp a row of hearts. If you don't have a chequerboard pattern to follow, space them about 5cm/2in apart. Stamp the next row between the hearts in the first row. Overlap the rows by 2cm/¾in.

4 Take the design right up to the edge, printing part of the heart where it overlaps the edge. Have a sheet of scrap paper in place to take up the unwanted paint. Leave the design to dry before fixing (setting) it with a hot iron, following the manufacturer's instructions.

RIGHT: The textured fabric of this throw complements the pattern on the trellis hearts beautifully. It also helps you to position the stamp.

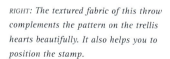

SEASHORE THROW

Throws are indispensable accessories in every home – while adding glorious swatches of colours to any room, they also cleverly disguise any worn or stained patches on household furniture. Throws can be thick and wintry or light and airy like this one, which could also double up as a sarong for a quick wrap-around. Crêped cotton has a fine, crinkled texture, which adds volume to the fabric and makes it drape well. Cotton or other natural fibres are the best choice as they absorb the fabric paint easily. So, have a go at this throw and make a luxurious gold design for your home.

1 Protect your work surface with backing paper. Lay the crêped cotton fabric over this and pin down with drawing pins arond the edges.

2 Spread some gold fabric paint on to the plate and run the roller through it until it is evenly coated. Ink the seahorse stamp and make the first print in one corner of the fabric.

3 Print a border along the top and bottom edges of the fabric, alternating the shells and seahorse stamps.

4 Stamp widely spaced rows of seahorses between the borders, turning the stamp 180 degrees each print. The prints in each row should fall between those of the previous row. Fix (set) the fabric paint with a hot iron, following the manufacturer's instructions. Press directly down on to the fabric, ensuring the crêped cotton retains its texture.

ABOVE: *Stamping is possible on many different fabrics, even the crinkled surface of crêped cotton.*

NO-SEW STAR CURTAIN

This is a quick and stylish solution to window dressing, especially if you don't like sewing. Light muslin (cheesecloth) drapes beautifully and its transparency allows the star pattern to show through the gathered layers. The motif is cut from medium-density sponge which is quite absorbent and makes several prints before you need to re-charge your stamp. You can use gold fabric paint but a more brilliant, glittering result is achieved by mixing bronze powder into a PVA (white) glue and water base.

You will need

- pencil
- tracing paper
- scissors
- spray adhesive
- medium-density sponge, such as a kitchen sponge
- felt-tipped pens
- craft knife
- bowl
- PVA (white) glue
- bronze powder
- paintbrush
- plate
- sheet of paper, the width of the muslin
- white butter muslin (cheesecloth)

1 Trace, transfer and cut out the pattern shape from the template section. Lightly spray the shape with adhesive and place it on the sponge. Draw around it in felt-tipped pen.

2 Cut out the star shape with a craft knife. First cut around the outline, then part the sponge and cut all the way through.

3 Mix up the gold colour in a bowl, using two spoonfuls of PVA (white) glue to one spoonful of water and half a spoonful of bronze powder. You can make a large or small amount of the mixture, just keep the proportions the same. Spread an even coating of the gold mixture on the plate.

OPPOSITE: This lovely airy window dressing could also be stamped with romantic cherubs.

4 Place the paper underneath the muslin (cheesecloth). Make a test print to ensure that the sponge is not overloaded, then print the first star just in from the corner. Measure the position of the next stamp with the width of three or four splayed fingers.

5 Measure upwards in the same way, and print the first star of the second row. This should be evenly spaced between the first two stars on the first row. Continue in this way, alternating the two rows, until you have covered the whole of the muslin fabric with evenly spaced stars.

SPRIGGED CALICO CURTAINS

atural calico has a lovely creamy colour, especially when the sun shines through it. However, it is usually used as an upholsterer's lining fabric and this association can make calico curtains look basic. This stamped floral sprig lifts the humble calico into another dimension, giving it a sophisticated finish. Calico is prone to shrinkage, so wash the fabric before you stamp it and make up the curtains. Refer to the section at the beginning of the chapter for instructions for making the linocut stamp. You will find the sprig pattern in the template section.

You will need

- ◆ calico fabric
- ◆ backing paper, such as thin card (stock)
  or newspaper
- ◆ linocut stamp
- ◆ fabric stamping ink in green
  and dark blue
- ◆ scrap paper
- ◆ scissors
- ◆ ruler
- ◆ card (stock)
- ◆ pencil

1 Lay the fabric out on a flat surface, such as a wallpaper-pasting table, with the backing paper underneath. Make several prints of the linocut stamp on scrap paper, cut these out and use them to plan the position of the motifs on the fabric.

2 Decide on the distance between the sprigs and cut out a square of card (stock) with the same dimensions to act as a measuring guide. Use it diagonally, making a pencil mark at each corner all over the surface of the fabric.

3 Apply green ink directly to the edges of the linocut stamp.

4 Fill in the middle of the stamp with dark blue ink. Make an initial print on a scrap of fabric to determine the density of the stamped image.

5 Stamp the floral sprig on to the calico, using the pencil marks to position the base of the stamp. You need to apply gentle pressure to the back of the stamp and allow a couple of seconds for the ink to transfer. Don't rush; the result will be all the better for the extra time taken.

RIGHT: Calico tie-backs can be made to match the main fabric. You may find it easier to make the tie-backs before stamping, to determine the best position for the design.

STELLAR TABLECLOTH

These starry rubber stamps are the perfect way to add a heavenly aspect to your dining table, and it could not be easier to achieve. Fabric or paper napkins, placemats and tablerunners can all be stamped to match with the same treatment. The tablecloth used here has a scalloped edge which makes for very easy spacing – simply count the scallops and then decide to stamp on, say, every third one. If you have a straight-edged cloth, measure the length and width of the cloth, and the length and width of the stamp to discover how many will fit comfortably along the edge. If the cloth isn't very big, find the centre by folding it in half and then in half again. Begin with a print at each corner, then one at the halfway mark, and space the other prints in between.

1 Plan the position of your motifs, using one of the methods described above. Coat the smaller stamp with fabric ink and make a test print on to a scrap of fabric to ensure that the stamp is not overloaded.

2 Make the first print by positioning the small star rubber stamp in one corner of the tablecloth.

3 Stamp a large star on either side of the small star. Continue along the edges of the tablecloth, alternating the sizes of the stars.

4 Stamp one widely spaced square of small stars approximately 10cm/4in in from the first row (depending upon the size of your cloth) and then another square of large stars another 10cm/4in closer to the centre. It should look like an all-over pattern with a border.

ABOVE AND RIGHT: *Scalloped edges and star motifs create a contemporary look for a dining room or occasional table.*

STARFISH HAND TOWELS

These seashore-style hand towels are made from a cotton/linen mix, similar to the fabric used for glass cloths. Fabric paints are ideal for the job because the colour is permanent once fixed with an iron and you can use the towels again and again. The stamps have been given a three-dimensional look by stamping firstly in green and then overprinting some areas in white. They're perfect for a seashore themed room.

1 Wash the towels to remove any glaze from the fabric as this may block the absorption of the colour. Press each towel flat with an iron.

2 Place a towel on the backing paper. Spread some green paint on to the plate and run the roller through it until it is evenly coated. Ink the stamps and print a border, alternating starfish with seahorses.

3 Stamp two rows of green starfish down the length of the towel. Ink half the stamp edges with white paint. Overprint each stamped starfish and seahorse by lining up one point of the stamp with the green stamped image, then positioning the rest of the stamp.

LEFT: Making and decorating your own hand towels is surprisingly simple, and the towels will be very pleasant to use.

VINEYARD TABLE NAPKINS

hese stamped table napkins look great with rush mats on a wooden table top. They bring together even the most casual collection of plates, glasses and cutlery to look like a deliberate choice. You can buy a set of plain table napkins or make your own by sewing straight seams along the edges of squares of cotton fabric. The fabric paints can be heat-treated with a hot iron to make the pattern permanent. Always follow the manufacturer's instructions, which may vary from brand to brand.

1 Wash and iron the napkins to remove any glaze which may block the paint's absorption. Lay the first napkin on top of several sheets of newspaper. Spread some cream fabric paint on to a plate and run the roller through it until it is evenly coated. Ink the grape stamp and print a bunch of grapes in each corner of the napkin.

2 Stamp a bunch of grapes halfway along each edge, then ink the tendril stamp and print tendrils between the grapes. Stamp all the napkins in this way and leave to dry. Seal the designs with an iron, following the paint manufacturer's instructions.

LEFT: You could stamp a tablecloth border to match the napkins.

STARRY FLOORCLOTH

A floorcloth is a sheet of canvas, painted and varnished and used in place of a rug. Canvas is hard-wearing, especially after a few coats of varnish, and it feels cool and smooth underfoot. Artist's canvas comes in all widths – just think of the paintings you've seen – and it is available through arts and crafts suppliers.

You will need

- plain cream artist's canvas
- pencil
- ruler
- scissors
- fabric glue and brush
- white acrylic primer
- household paintbrush
- emulsion (latex) paint in dark blue, lime-green and light blue
- plate
- foam roller
- starburst stamp
- matt (flat) varnish and brush

1 Draw a 4cm/1½in border around the edge of the canvas, then fold this back to make a seam. Mitre the corners by cutting across them at a 45-degree angle, then apply the glue and stick down the edges. Prepare the canvas by painting it with white acrylic primer.

2 Paint the primed floorcloth dark blue, applying two coats if necessary. Measure and draw a 10cm/4in border around the edge.

3 Paint the border lime-green, applying two coats to give a good coverage.

4 Spread some light blue paint on to the plate and run the roller through it until it is evenly coated. Ink the stamp and begin printing the stars in one corner. Judge the spacing visually, stamping a random arrangement of stars to cover the cloth.

5 Apply several coats of matt (flat) varnish, leaving each one to dry thoroughly before applying the next.

RIGHT: *Create your own colour scheme to complement the furnishings in the rest of the room.*

ROSE FLOORCLOTH

Here is an unusual alternative to buying an expensive runner-rug – simply make a floorcloth out of plain artist's canvas. Floorcloths were originally used by American settlers who found that sailcloth could be stretched over a bed of straw to cover their hard floors, and make an inexpensive and hard-wearing surface. They decorated them to imitate chequered marble floors and fine carpets, and found that the paint and varnish added to their durability. They were eventually replaced by the invention of linoleum, but have recently come back into fashion. Artist's canvas comes in many widths and is available through arts and crafts suppliers.

You will need

- plain cream artist's canvas (cut to the required size)
- pencil
- ruler
- scissors
- fabric glue and brush
- white acrylic primer
- paintbrush
- emulsion (latex) paint in black
- plate
- foam roller
- rosebud, small rose and large rose stamps
- large sheet of paper

1 Draw a 4cm/1½in border around the edge of the canvas, then fold this back to make a seam. Mitre the corners by cutting across them at a 45-degree angle, then apply the fabric glue and stick the seams down flat. Turn the canvas over and paint with one or two coats of white acrylic primer.

2 Spread some black paint on to the plate and run the roller through it until it is evenly coated. Ink all the stamps and print a circular repeat pattern on to the paper. You could use a plate to help draw an accurate circle.

3 Stamp six small roses along the bottom edge of the floorcloth, three in each corner. Place them at an angle, as shown.

4 Place the paper pattern over the floorcloth and lift it up as you stamp each element of the pattern on to the canvas. After you have printed the first rose circle pattern, you will get to know the order of the prints, and you may not need to refer to the paper pattern so often.

5 Leave the first completed circle to dry thoroughly before placing the paper pattern on to the next section and stamping the pattern as before. When you have repeated the pattern along the length, finish off the top edge of the floorcloth with the same six small roses that you started with.

RIGHT: A single circle of roses would look very attractive stamped in the centre of a tablecloth, using fabric paint.

CHERUB SHOPPING BAG

Large canvas shopping bags with shoulder straps are both fashionable and useful. They come in a range of plain colours that seem to cry out to be given an individual touch with your choice of motifs and colours. Stamping works well on canvas and you can choose from fabric paint, acrylics or household emulsion (latex) paint. Bear in mind that you will not be able to wash the bag if you use emulsion or acrylic, while fabric paint can be fixed (set) with an iron to make it permanent and washable.

You will need

- blue canvas shopping bag
- backing card (stock)
- cherub and swag stamps
- black stamp pad
- scrap paper
- scissors
- emulsion (latex), acrylic or fabric paint in white and pale blue
- plate
- foam roller
- iron (optional)

1 Lay the bag on a flat surface and insert the backing card (stock) to prevent the paint from passing through to the other side.

2 Make several cherub and swag prints on scrap paper using the black stamp pad. Cut them out and arrange them on the bag to plan your design.

3 Spread some white paint on to the plate and run the roller through it until it is evenly coated. Ink the cherub and swag stamps and print the pattern, removing each paper motif and stamping in its place. Leave to dry, then ink the edges of the stamps with pale blue paint. Overprint the white design to create a shadow effect. If using fabric paint, follow the paint manufacturer's instructions to fix (set) the design with an iron.

TWO-TONE SCARF

Wrap yourself in garlands of roses by stamping a silk scarf with this red and green pattern. Scarves are wonderfully versatile and they really can make an everyday outfit look very special. When you're not wearing your scarf, drape it over a chair or hang it on a peg to add dashes of colour to a room. The scarf shown here was originally cream but it was then dipped in pink dye for an attractive two-tone effect – a light-coloured scarf would work just as well, though.

You will need

- fabric paint in red and green
- plates
- foam rollers
- small rose and rosebud stamps
- sheet of white paper
- silk scarf
- backing paper

1 Spread the red and green paint on to the plates and run the rollers through them until they are evenly coated. Ink the small rose red and its leaves and the rosebud stamp green. Stamp them on the corner and edges of the paper. Slip the paper pattern under the scarf on top of the backing paper.

2 Print alternating small roses and rosebuds around the border.

3 Fill in the middle of the scarf with two parallel rows of small roses.

TRAILBLAZER SCARF

Beginners are often nervous about printing on fabric for the first time. Here is a no-risk method of fabric printing which allows you to make all the design decisions and complete the stamping before you go near the fabric with stamp and paint. The stamp is inked with fabric-transfer colour and the pattern arranged on paper first. The paper is then placed printed side-down on the fabric and a light pressure is applied to the back of it with a heated iron. When the paper is removed, the design will be transferred to the fabric in reverse. If you are still hesitant, rest assured that the printing must be done on synthetic fabric, so the project is relatively inexpensive.

1 Measure the width of the scarf and cut paper strips of the same length. Make a border along each paper strip, using two alternating stamps and the red and blue inkpads. You will need four borders.

2 Cut a piece of paper to fit in the central area of the scarf. Stamp a widely spaced pattern using the third stamp and the green inkpad.

3 Place the scarf on a flat surface and turn the stamped paper patterns face-down in position along all four edges to make a border.

BELOW: Choose your own favourite motifs and colour scheme to make a scarf to match a particular outfit.

4 Apply light pressure with a dry iron, following the manufacturer's instructions on timing and temperature. Lift the iron between motifs – a sliding iron will blur your print.

5 Transfer the central pattern with the iron in the same way.

ANGEL T-SHIRTS

Fabric paints are very easy to use, come in a wide range of colours and can be fixed (set) with a hot iron to make them washable and permanent. The cherubs can be used in many ways, including the funky colour combinations chosen here. Strong contrasts, complementary shades or dayglo colours will all give the cherub motif a new image. By overprinting the cherubs slightly off-register in a second colour, you can add a three-dimensional look, too. Wash and iron the T-shirt before printing to remove any glazes that may block the absorption of the fabric paint.

You will need

- plain-coloured T-shirts
- backing card (stock)
- cherub and swag stamps
- black stamp pad
- scrap paper
- scissors
- fabric paint in various colours
- plate
- foam roller
- ruler (optional)
- iron

1 Lay a T-shirt on a flat surface and insert the backing card (stock) to prevent the paint from passing through to the other side.

2 Stamp several cherubs or cherubs and swags on scrap paper. Cut them out and arrange them on the T-shirt to plan your design.

3 Spread some fabric paint on to a plate and run the roller through it until it is evenly coated. Ink the cherub stamp and print the pattern, removing each paper motif and stamping a cherub in its place. Re-ink the stamp after each print and press down firmly with the stamp to allow the fabric paint to penetrate the fabric.

4 Use a ruler to help align the pattern if necessary. Stamp swag motifs around the neckline, if desired. Follow the paint manufacturer's instructions to fix (set) the design with an iron.

BELOW: *Experiment with other stamps and colours to create your own individual T-shirts for family and friends.*

CHINA AND GLASS

Stamping a motif gives the same print every time and this will enable you to make matching sets of crockery and glassware. Several brands of paint on the market are designed to be used on these surfaces at home. They don't need firing in kilns at high temperatures, but the paint can be made more resilient by baking in a domestic oven. The one drawback is that this paint is not recommended for food use, which means avoiding mouth contact, so don't paint around the lip of a glass or cup. Ceramic paints or acrylic enamels make crisp, opaque prints which are particularly effective on glass, tiles wooden plates and plain white china.

ABOVE: Humble utilitarian objects such as flowerpots will be transformed with colourful stamped borders and motifs.

LEFT: Acrylic enamel paint is used for stamping a bold design on china. Curved glass surfaces are best printed with foam stamps.

GOTHIC DISPLAY PLATE

Large china display plates look great mounted on the wall, or set high on a beautifully polished dresser, and they don't have to be confined to country kitchen-type interiors, as demonstrated by this bold pattern. The plate used here is a larger platter with a pale blue border outlined in navy blue, although the design can also be stamped on a plain plate. Use acrylic enamel paint to stamp on ceramics and glassware. It can be baked in a household oven according to the manufacturer's instructions. The resulting patterns are very hard-wearing and even seem to stand up to dishwashers and scouring pads, but the paints are recommended for display rather than for food use.

You will need

- black stamp pad
- diamond and crown stamps
- scrap paper
- scissors
- display plate
- acrylic enamel paint in navy blue and deep orange
- plates
- foam rollers
- ruler

1 Use the stamp pad to print eight diamond motifs and one crown on paper and cut them out. Arrange them on the plate to plan the design of the border pattern and central motif.

2 Spread some navy blue acrylic enamel paint on to a plate and run a roller through it until it is evenly coated. Ink the diamond stamp, then remove one of the paper shapes and stamp a diamond in its place.

OPPOSITE: *Choose a display plate with a wide border and select a diamond stamp that will fit neatly inside it.*

3 Place a ruler under the plate, so that it runs centrally from the printed motif to the one opposite. Line up the stamp with the edge of the ruler to print the second motif. Print diamond motifs on the other two sides of the plate in the same way, then fill in the diamonds in between, judging by eye.

4 Ink the crown stamp with deep orange paint and stamp a single crown in the centre of the plate. Bake the plate in the oven, following the paint manufacturer's instructions.

GRAPE JUG

Awhite ceramic jug (pitcher) like this one seems to be crying out for some stamped decoration, and the grape vine stamps do the trick in minutes. Choose a well-proportioned plain jug and transform it into something that is decorative as well as practical. Acrylic enamel paint is relatively new on the market and, although it resembles ordinary enamel, it is in fact water-based and does not require harmful solvents for cleaning brushes and stamps. Follow the manufacturer's instructions to "fire" the stamped jug in a domestic oven to add strength and permanence to the pattern. Without "firing", the paint will only stand up to non-abrasive cleaning.

You will need

- white ceramic jug (pitcher)
- detergent and clean cloth
- grape, tendril and leaf stamps
- black stamp pad
- scrap paper
- scissors
- acrylic enamel paint in black and ultramarine blue
- plate
- foam roller

1 Wash the jug (pitcher) in hot water and detergent, then wipe dry with a clean cloth to ensure that there is no grease on the surface.

2 Print a grape, a tendril and a leaf on to scrap paper and cut them out. Arrange them on the jug to plan the finished design.

3 Mix together the black and ultramarine blue acrylic enamel paint on a plate. Run the roller through the paint until it is evenly coated and ink the stamps. Stamp the motifs following your planned arrangement as a guide.

4 The leaf stamp may be used to fill any gaps, and the pattern may be repeated on the other side of the jug. Follow the manufacturer's instructions if you wish to make the design permanent by "firing" it in the oven.

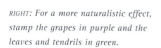

RIGHT: For a more naturalistic effect, stamp the grapes in purple and the leaves and tendrils in green.

PERSONALIZED FLOWERPOTS

Commercially decorated flowerpots can be very expensive but you can customize ordinary clay pots very easily – and the designs will be uniquely yours. The sunwheel motif used here is an ancient symbol with real energy. The colours chosen create a vibrant display that is best complemented by bright, attractive pot plants. Change the plants according to the season or to suit your mood. Three stamps, three colours of paint and a roll of masking tape are all you need to turn plain flowerpots into a sensational display.

You will need

- pencil
- tracing paper
- fine-tipped pen
- craft knife
- spray adhesive
- high-density foam, such as upholstery foam
- acrylic enamel paint in navy blue, red and cream
- plates
- glazed and plain terracotta flowerpots
- masking tape

1 Trace, transfer and cut out the pattern shapes from the template section. Lightly spray the shapes with adhesive and place them on the foam.

2 Use a craft knife to cut around the outlines of the large sunwheel motif. Scoop out the background and the pattern details.

3 Cut out the small motif, then scoop out the centre circle in the same way as the large sunwheel motif.

4 Spread an even coating of navy blue acrylic enamel paint on to a plate and press the large sunwheel motif into it. Make a test print to make sure that the stamp is not overloaded.

5 Stamp the large motif around the flowerpot four times. If you are using a larger flowerpot, you will be able to fit in more prints.

6 Spread an even coating of red acrylic enamel paint on to a plate and press the small motif into it. Make a test print to make sure the stamp is not overloaded. Stamp the small motif in groups above and below the large ones.

7 Cut out a small stepped triangle from foam using a craft knife.

8 Place two parallel strips of masking tape around the top end of a blue-glazed flowerpot. Leave a 1cm/½in gap between the two strips.

9 Squeeze some cream acrylic enamel paint on to a plate. With an offcut of foam, apply the paint to the gap between the two strips of masking tape.

10 Allow time for the paint to dry, then peel off the masking tape to reveal the cream border around the top of the pot.

11 Make sure the cream paint is spread evenly on a plate. Press the stepped triangle shape into it. Make a test print first, then stamp the pattern above and below the cream line, matching up the points of the triangle.

RIGHT: Make a mix-and-match set of stamped flowerpots, using coloured glazed pots or plain terracotta ones. One of these flowerpots, planted with spring flowers or bulbs, would make a lovely home-made gift.

DECORATED TILES

These days you can buy wonderful decorated tiles in all shapes and sizes, but they cost a fortune! So, why not use stamps and paint to make your own set of exclusive decorated tiles? Acrylic enamel paint resembles ordinary enamel, but it is in fact water-based and does not include harmful solvents. If you are decorating loose tiles, bake them in a domestic oven following the manufacturer's instructions to "fire" the colour and give added strength and permanence. The fired tiles will be waterproof and resilient to non-abrasive cleaning. If you are stamping on to a tiled wall, it is best to position the design where it will not need too much cleaning – the paint will certainly withstand an occasional soaking and can be wiped with a damp cloth.

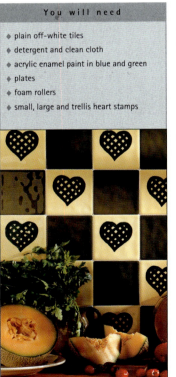

You will need

◆ plain off-white tiles
◆ detergent and clean cloth
◆ acrylic enamel paint in blue and green
◆ plates
◆ foam rollers
◆ small, large and trellis heart stamps

1 Wash the tiles with detergent and hot water, then dry them thoroughly with a clean cloth before you apply any paint. The tiles must be clean and grease-free.

2 Spread some blue paint on to the plate and run a roller through it until it is evenly coated. Ink the small heart stamp and print two hearts side by side at the top of the tile, with equal spacing on either side.

3 Align the next two stamps directly below the first. Take care not to smudge the first two when stamping the second row. Acrylic enamel paint dries fast, so you only need to wait a few minutes to avoid smudges.

4 To make another design, ink the large heart stamp and make a single print on another off-white tile. Press the stamp down, then lift it off immediately to get an interesting surface texture.

5 Ink the large heart stamp and print overlapping the edges, so that the point is at the top edge of the tile and the curved part is at the bottom.

6 Ink the large heart stamp and make a first print with the heart angled to the left. Leave it to dry, then print another heart angled to the right as shown.

7 Spread some green paint on to a plate and run a roller through it until it is evenly coated. Ink the trellis heart stamp and print a single heart in the centre of a tile.

8 Continue printing a single trellis heart in the centre of each tile. The texture will be different on every print, making the tiles look far more interesting and giving an expensive hand-painted effect.

RIGHT: If you prefer, stamp less tiles with the heart motifs and use them as individual highlights on a chequerboard pattern of plain tiles. See the Country Kitchen project for an example of how to position the stamped tiles.

COUNTRY KITCHEN

Specialist suppliers sell beautifully decorated tiles but they can be very expensive. So why not use stamps and paint to make your own set of exclusive tiles? The grape stamp is inked with two shades of green that blend in the middle in a slightly different way each time. Small touches such as the rustic hanging rail and the wooden plate add rustic authenticity to a country kitchen. The wood for the rail needs to be old and weathered. The nails banged into the rail as hangers are called "cut" nails, which are used for floorboarding. Attach the rail to the wall and hang fresh herbs from it, conveniently close to the cooker (stove). The wooden plate is stamped with different parts of the tendril motif to make a decorative border and central design.

You will need

- plain tiles
- detergent and clean cloths
- acrylic enamel paint in blue-green and yellow-green
- plates
- foam rollers
- grape, leaf and tendril stamps
- emulsion (latex) or acrylic paint in olive-green
- scrap paper
- weathered piece of wood, maximum 30cm/12in long
- long "cut" nails or hooks
- hammer or drill
- black stamp pad
- scissors
- wooden plate, sanded to remove any stain or varnish
- vegetable oil

1 Wash the tiles in hot water and detergent, then wipe dry to ensure that there is no grease on the surface.

2 Spread some blue-green acrylic enamel paint on to one plate and some yellow-green paint on to another. Run the rollers through the paint until they are evenly coated.

3 Ink the leaf stamp and the top and right side of the grape stamp with the blue-green roller. Ink the rest of the grape stamp with the yellow-green roller.

4 Stamp a bunch of grapes in the centre of each tile. Remove the stamp directly, taking care not to smudge the print. If you do make a mistake, you can simply wipe off the paint with a clean cloth and start again. Follow the manufacturer's instructions to "fire" the tiles in the oven if required.

5 For the hanging rail, spread some olive-green emulsion (latex) or acrylic paint on to a plate and run a roller through it until it is evenly coated. Ink the leaf stamp and stamp twice on to scrap paper to remove some of the paint.

6 Stamp on to the length of weathered wood without re-inking the stamp. The resulting print will be light and faded-looking, like the wood itself. Make as many prints as you can fit along the length. Hammer in the nails or drill and screw in the hooks to complete the hanging rail.

7 For the wooden plate, stamp several tendrils on to scrap paper using the black stamp pad and cut them out. Arrange them on the plate to work out the spacing and positioning of the motifs.

8 Spread some olive-green emulsion or acrylic paint on to a plate and run a roller through it until it is evenly coated. Ink the corner of the tendril stamp comprising the two curls that will make up the border pattern. Carefully begin stamping these motifs around the edge of the plate.

9 Ink the whole stamp and stamp two tendrils in the centre of the plate. Leave the paint to dry.

10 Dip a clean cloth into some vegetable oil and rub this into the whole surface of the plate, including the stamped pattern. You can repeat this process once all the oil has been absorbed into the wood. Each time you rub oil into the plate, the colour of the wood will deepen.

RIGHT: Stamp co-ordinating motifs on tiles and wooden accessories, using different paints and techniques appropriate to each surface. Position the grape tiles as highlights or create an all-over effect, as illustrated in the Decorated Tiles project.

STARRY VASE

Plain glass vases are relatively inexpensive to buy. The transparency of glass gives a new dimension to the stamped stars. The colour is applied to one surface, but the design is visible from all sides. You could try the stamps on any plain glass vase – this one was particularly easy to work with because of the flat surfaces. There are now some paints available called acrylic enamels. These are suitable for use on glass and ceramics and they give a hard-wearing finish that stands up to non-abrasive washing. The selection of colours is great, so take a look at them and try some glass stamping.

1 Wash the vase to remove any grease from the surface. Dry it thoroughly.

2 Spread some paint on to the plate and run the roller through it until it is evenly coated. Ink the stamp and make a test print on a piece of glass.

3 Stamp the stars randomly on to the glass vase. Apply gentle pressure with a steady hand and remove the stamp directly to avoid it sliding on the slippery surface.

FOLIAGE VASE

These stamped leaves will definitely add a designer touch to a plain glass vase, making it worthy of display with or without flowers or an arrangement of decorative leaves. The transparent glass allows the print to be seen from all sides, and the paint disperses on the smooth surface, adding texture to the leaves. Acrylic enamel paints are suitable for both glass and ceramics, and they have a consistency which works well with stamps. They also leave a glossy, hard-wearing finish that can be strengthened in an oven, if the manufacturer's instructions are followed carefully.

You will need

- plain rectangular glass vase
- detergent and clean cloth
- acrylic enamel paints in black and white
- plates
- foam rubber rollers
- leaf stamp

1 Wash the vase and wipe it dry with a clean cloth to ensure that there is no grease on the surface. Spread some black and white paint on to two plates. Run a roller through the white paint, and use it to ink the leaf stamp.

2 Print the first stamp on to the top half of the vase. Remove the stamp directly, taking care that it does not slide on the surface and smudge the print. If you make mistakes, they can be wiped off with a clean cloth.

3 Clean the leaf stamp and ink it with the black paint in the same way as with the white paint. Stamp a black leaf below the white one, so that it faces in the opposite direction. Allow to dry. If you wish to strengthen the paint in the oven, do so following the paint manufacturer's instructions.

HEARTS VASE

Take a plain vase and stamp it with rows of primary-coloured hearts to create a bright and cheerful display piece for a sunlit kitchen window. Instead of being purely functional, the vase becomes artistic and decorative – you could also put this one on the mantelpiece with or without cut flowers. There are now some paints available called acrylic enamels. These are suitable for use on glass and ceramics and they give a hard-wearing finish that stands up to non-abrasive washing. The selection of colours is great, so choose your own combination to suit the decor of your room.

You will need

- plain rectangular glass vase
- detergent and clean cloth
- acrylic enamel paints in yellow, blue and red
- plate
- foam roller
- small heart stamp

1 Wash the vase to remove any grease from the surface and dry it thoroughly. This will give you a better surface for stamping and will ensure a more successful print.

2 Spread a small amount of yellow paint on to the plate and run the roller through it until it is evenly coated. Ink the stamp and print a diagonal row of hearts on to the glass, starting at the top left-hand corner. Lift the stamp directly so that the prints are crisp and do not smudge.

3 Clean the stamp and ink it with blue
paint. Add blue hearts in between
the yellow ones as shown.

4 Clean the stamp and ink it with red
paint. Then complete the design by
adding the red hearts in the spaces left
on the vase.

*RIGHT: Repeating a simple motif in bright
primary colours creates a very modern
cheerful effect.*

VALENTINE VASE

Present a dozen red roses in this beautiful stamped vase and you won't need Cupid's arrow to get your point across! There are a number of different types of glass paint on the market, but this vase is stamped with acrylic enamels, which work on glazed ceramics as well. The cupid is first stamped in cream, then painted over with a mottled white, achieved by dabbing paint on with a brush. A heart stencil is cut from card (stock) and used in combination with the cherub to complete the romantic valentine theme.

You will need

- pencil
- stencil card (stock) or plastic
- craft knife
- self-healing cutting mat
- plain rectangular glass vase
- acrylic enamel paint in red, cream and white
- plate
- foam roller
- stencil brush (optional)
- cherub stamp
- artist's paintbrush

1 Draw a heart shape on to a small piece of stencil card (stock) or plastic. Cut out the stencil with a craft knife on a self-healing cutting mat.

2 Position the heart stencil on the vase. Use red acrylic enamel paint and either the foam roller or the stencil brush to stencil the heart.

3 Spread some cream acrylic enamel paint on to a plate and run the roller through it until it is evenly coated. Ink the cherub stamp and make a print above the heart. Remove the stamp directly to prevent it from sliding. Use the artist's paintbrush to stipple a mottled coating of white paint over the cherub. Do not cover the whole print.

BLACK ROSE VASE

The transparency of this plain glass vase creates the illusion that the black rose is floating in mid-air, somewhere above the mantlepiece. Glass is an interesting surface to stamp on because it is so smooth that the paint disperses as soon as it is applied. It is a good idea to have a spare piece of glass handy so that you can practise your stamp before committing yourself to the final print. This way, you can find out how much paint you need to get the desired effect. The single colour print lends a sophisticated touch.

You will need

- glass vase
- detergent and clean cloth
- acrylic enamel paint in black
- plate
- foam roller
- large rose stamp
- piece of glass

1 Wash the vase to remove any grease from the surface, then dry it thoroughly with a clean cloth.

2 Spread some black paint on to the plate and run the roller through it until it is evenly coated. Ink the stamp and make a test print on the glass.

3 Stamp the black rose in the centre of the vase front. Apply gentle pressure with a steady hand and remove the stamp directly to avoid it sliding on the slippery surface. If you are not happy with the print, you can wipe it off before it begins to dry, clean the glass with a cloth and try again.

JAPANESE-STYLE VASE

Transform a plain glass vase with some chic calligraphic stamping. For this project, high-density foam was cut into strips, then dipped into acrylic enamel paint. The strips were then twisted into different shapes to make a series of quick prints. Don't make too many prints – the end result should look like an enlargement of a Japanese calligraphic symbol. The paint finish is tough enough to withstand gentle washing, but take care, because all unfired surface decoration such as this is prone to chipping and peeling.

You will need

- set square (triangle)
- felt-tipped pen
- high-density foam, such as upholstery foam, 25 x 10 x 5cm/10 x 4 x 2in
- craft knife
- plain rectangular glass vase
- detergent and clean cloth
- acrylic enamel paint in black
- plate

1 Using a set square and felt-tipped pen, draw lines 1cm/½in apart along the length of the foam.

2 Cut along the lines using a craft knife, then part the foam and cut all the way through it.

3 Clean the vase thoroughly with a clean cloth to remove any surface grease and dry it well.

4 Spread an even coating of paint on to a plate. Curl up a strip of foam and dip it into the paint.

5 Use both hands, positioned just above the glass surface, to curl the foam strip into an open-ended shape. When the curve looks right, press it on to the vase. Lift it off straight away to avoid any smudging.

6 Press a straight strip of foam into the paint, then use it to continue the line around the side of the vase.

BELOW: Strips and curls of foam make good stamps for curved glass surfaces.

7 Complete the calligraphic design with a series of these straight black lines. Use different width strips of foam if necessary. Applying the pressure unevenly will give a more authentic effect.

SNOWFLAKE STORAGE JARS

Almost every kitchen could do with the occasional facelift. Rather than pay for a completely new look, why not just cheer up your storage jars and give your kitchen a breath of fresh air? You can create a whole new atmosphere by stamping patterns on your jars with acrylic enamel paint. The finish is quite tough and will stand up to occasional gentle washing, but will not withstand the dishwasher. Choose a design that suits your kitchen, or copy the pattern for the motif used here.

You will need

- pencil
- tracing paper
- spray adhesive
- high-density foam, such as upholstery foam
- craft knife
- detergent and clean cloth
- glass storage jars
- acrylic enamel paint in white
- plate
- tile

1 Trace and transfer the pattern shape from the template section. Lightly spray the shape with adhesive and place it on the foam. Cut around the outline with a craft knife.

2 Cut horizontally into the foam to meet the outline cuts then remove the excess foam.

3 Clean the glass jars thoroughly with detergent and a cloth, then dry them well. This will remove any grease and will provide a better surface.

4 Spread an even coating of paint on to the plate. Press the stamp into it and make a test print on a tile to make sure that the stamp is not overloaded.

5 Holding the jar steady with your spare hand, press the foam stamp around the side of the jar.

6 Rotate the stamp 90 degrees and make a second print directly below the first. Continue in this way, alternating the angle of the stamp with each print. Cover the whole surface of the jar with the snowflake motifs.

RIGHT: A flexible foam stamp is ideal for printing on a rounded glass surface. Experiment with other simple shapes.

VINTAGE GLASS BOWL

Turn a plain glass bowl into an exquisite table centrepiece, to be filled with floating candles, by stamping a white tendril pattern on the outside. Stamped glassware looks wonderful because the opaque pattern seems to intermingle as you look through the transparent glass. Another advantage is that you can see the stamp as the print is being made, which helps you to position it correctly and avoid overlaps and smudges. Glass painting has become popular recently and there are several brands of specialist glass paint available. Acrylic enamel paint has a good consistency for stamping and is water-based, allowing you to simply wipe it off and start again if you make a mistake.

You will need

- plain glass bowl
- detergent and clean cloth
- acrylic enamel paint in white
- plate
- foam roller
- tendril stamp

1 Wash the bowl in hot water and detergent, then wipe dry to ensure that there is no grease on the surface. Spread some white acrylic enamel paint on to the plate and run the roller through it until it is evenly coated.

2 Ink the tendril stamp and stamp the first row of prints around the base of the bowl. Remove the stamp directly, taking care that it does not slide or smudge the print. If you do make a mistake, wipe off the paint with a clean cloth and start again.

3 Turn the stamp the other way up to stamp the second row of motifs. Position the prints in between the tendrils on the first row, so that there are no obvious gaps in the design.

4 Stamp one more row with the stamp the original way up. Allow the stamp to overlap the edge of the bowl, so that most of the stem is left out. Leave the bowl to dry or "fire" it in the oven to fix the design, following the paint manufacturer's instructions.

BELOW: *The delicate tendril design would also look attractive in a pale shade of green for a more modern effect.*

ACCESSORIES

A ccessories are probably the ideal starting-point if you have never considered a rubber stamp as a decorating tool. You can transform a lampshade, picture frame or wooden tray in minutes, with minimal effort and even less mess. All you need is a stamp and an inkpad to create an all-over pattern, then a quick rinse with water to clean the stamp. What could be easier? Starting a new craft activity is often the most difficult part, so it makes sense to begin with something small, until you have built up the confidence to attempt more ambitious projects. This shouldn't take long, because stamping is so easy and so little can go wrong.

ABOVE: A wide range of accessories are suitable for stamping, for example giftwrap, book covers, lampshades, as well as this tray.

LEFT: A leaf pattern transforms a plain painted cutlery box.

GLORIOUS GIFTWRAP

If you want to make a gift extra special, why not print your own wrapping paper, designed to suit the person to whom you are giving the present? All you need is a selection of rubber stamps, inkpads or paint, and plain paper. Your home-made giftwrap will show that you really wanted to make the gift memorable. Stamped paper is great at Christmas when you need to wrap lots of presents at the same time. Your gifts will look very individual, particularly if you continue the motif on to the labels.

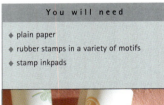

You will need

- plain paper
- rubber stamps in a variety of motifs
- stamp inkpads

1 To make a non-regimented design, like this clover-leaf pattern, first stamp at one edge of the paper. Then rotate the stamp in your hand to change the direction of each print. Continue stamping the design, judging the spacing by eye and printing the motifs close together. Re-charge the stamp with ink as required.

2 Turn the paper and continue stamping the shapes. The end result should have roughly an even amount of background to pattern.

3 To achieve a more formal pattern, like this bird design, begin by stamping a row of shapes along the bottom edge.

4 Build up the design, alternating between two colours if you like, as shown here, to make an all-over pattern of closely spaced shapes.

RIGHT: Experiment with different motifs, repeating them to make all-over patterns. Try different kinds of paper, for example brown parcel wrap or tissue paper.

STARRY WRAPPING PAPER

Here is a way to print your own wrapping paper that will look better than any paper available in the high street. The design will be unique and it hardly costs anything at all, unlike the hand-printed top-of-the-range designs available commercially. People have always enjoyed the satisfying activity of making repeat patterns, and nowadays we only really get a chance to do so at nursery school. But now you can grab some sheets of plain paper or colourful tissue paper, clear the kitchen table and start stamping lots of different patterns to your heart's delight.

You will need

- ruler
- pencil
- brown parcel wrap
- acrylic paint in brown, blue, white and cream
- plate
- foam roller
- starburst, folk-art and small star stamps

1 Use the ruler and pencil to mark one edge of the brown parcel wrap at approximately 12cm/5in intervals.

2 Spread a small amount of brown paint on to the plate and run the roller through it until it is evenly coated. Ink the starburst stamp and print on to the parcel wrap, using the pencil marks as a guide for the first row and judging the next rows by eye.

3 Ink the folk-art stamp with blue paint and stamp these stars in the spaces between the brown stars.

ABOVE: Create your own designs using different star stamps. Use different colours for specific occasions, for example red and gold paints would be ideal for Christmas.

4 Ink the small star stamp with white paint and carefully fill in the centres of the blue stars.

5 Stamp cream stars along diagonal lines between the rows of blue and brown stars.

CHRISTENING PARTY

The giftwrap, cards and table setting of this project will create a strong visual theme that is appropriate for a traditional christening or naming-day party. Use the cherubs to announce the baby's birth and herald the start of the celebrations. Buy a good-quality white paper or card blanks for the cards. Some papers are deckle-edged, while others are textured. The choice is a personal one and a textured surface will give interesting stamped effects, so experiment on samples of paper. Set off the hand-printed wrapping paper by tying the parcels with white satin ribbons and bows.

1 Lay the tablecloth or sheet on to the backing card (stock). Ink the swag stamp with bottle-green fabric paint and print across one corner of the cloth, so that the tassels are about 2.5cm/1in from the edges. Stamp swags all around the edge of the cloth to create a scalloped effect.

2 Spread some silver fabric paint on to a plate and run a roller through it until it is evenly coated. Ink both cherub stamps and, alternating the two designs, make a print above every other swag all round the edge of the cloth.

3 Continue to stamp a widely spaced cherub pattern in the centre of the cloth, alternating both stamps and rotating the direction of the prints. Follow the manufacturer's instructions to fix (set) the fabric paint with an iron.

4 For the napkins, spread some bottle-green acrylic paint on to a plate and run a roller through it until it is evenly coated. Ink the cherub stamps and make one print on each white table napkin.

5 Spread some white acrylic paint on to a plate. Use a roller to ink the cherub stamps. Stamp a white cherub on each green napkin.

6 To make the cards, cut and fold the paper to the required size, at least 14 x 11.5cm/5½ x 4½in. Draw pencil lines on the back of the stamp block to mark the mid-points on each side to help position the stamp accurately. Spread some blue-grey acrylic paint on to a plate and run a roller through it until it is evenly coated. Ink the stamp and print cherubs on the cards. Leave to dry.

7 Spread water-based size on to a plate and run a roller through it until it is evenly coated. Ink the cherub stamps with size and overprint the blue-grey prints. Leave to dry for the time recommended by the manufacturer until the size becomes tacky. Lay sheets of silver leaf on to the size and burnish the backing paper with a soft cloth.

8 Remove the backing paper and use wire (steel) wool to rub away excess silver leaf still clinging to the paper.

9 To make the wrapping paper, lay the silver paper on some newspaper on a flat surface. Using the black stamp pad, stamp several cherubs and swags on scrap paper and cut them out. Arrange the paper motifs on the silver paper to plan your design. Cut a card strip as a guide to the spacing between the motifs.

10 Spread some bottle-green acrylic paint on to a plate and run a roller through it until it is evenly coated. Ink the cherub stamp and print cherubs on the silver paper. Use the card strip to space the stamps.

11 Ink the swag stamp with white acrylic paint and print the linking swags between the cherub motifs.

RIGHT: Your guests will be delighted with hand-printed co-ordinating invitations and table linen for a special occasion such as a christening, wedding or silver wedding. For a golden wedding party, use gold fabric paint and gold wrapping paper.

BOHEMIAN BOOK COVERS

Brown parcel wrap is perfect book-covering material – it is strong, folds crisply and costs very little. The paper usually has a shiny side and a matt side, with the matt side more absorbent to paint. Pattern making with potato cuts is great fun, and the elements used here – a small solid square, a square outline, and a triangle – can be used in different combinations to make a variety of designs. Use the three paint colours to make your own design. These papers would make ideal covers for a row of cookbooks on a kitchen shelf. The watercolour paint is mixed with PVA (white) glue which dries transparent, leaving a slight sheen that looks great combined with the characteristic potato-cut texture.

You will need

- knife
- 2 potatoes
- bowl
- PVA (white) glue
- paintbrush
- watercolour paint in brick-red, brown and yellow-ochre
- plate
- craft knife
- brown parcel wrap

1 Cut the potatoes in half with a knife, then trim the edges to give them all the same square shape.

2 In a bowl mix PVA (white) glue and water in equal amounts, then add a drop of watercolour paint. The texture should be thick and sticky.

3 Spread an even coating of the paint mixture on to a plate then dip a potato into it – this will make it easier to see the design as you cut it out. Leave a square border around the edge of the potato shape, then divide the rest of the surface diagonally. Scoop out one triangular section with a craft knife.

4 Print a row of this pattern along the bottom edge of the paper.

RIGHT: A humble potato cut can be repeated to build up sophisticated geometric designs and create a co-ordinating set of book covers.

5 Stamp the following row with the same stamp the other way up. Add variety to the design by rotating the stamp for each new row, to form different patterns.

6 To make a chequerboard pattern, leave a gap between the prints. Dip a small piece of potato into the paint and stamp dots in the middle of the blank squares. Experiment with your own combinations.

WEDDING ALBUM COVER

Custom-made wedding photograph albums are never as special as one you make yourself. For most of us, a wedding is the only time we are photographed professionally looking our very best, so the presentation should do the pictures justice. The album should have a solid spine, so don't choose the spiral-bound type. Visit a specialist paper dealer and discover the wonderful range of textured papers. The paper is stamped with gold size and gold leaf is laid on to it to create gleaming golden cherubs and swags. Initials or the date of the wedding add the finishing touch.

1 Lay the opened album on the sheet of paper and trim the paper to size. Allow a border round the edges to fold over the paper inside the cover. Cover the album with the paper, sticking down the overlaps on the inside of the cover.

2 Stamp several cherubs and swags on scrap paper and cut them out. Lay them out on the album cover with any initials or dates to plan your design. When you are happy with the design, use the paper cut-outs as a guide for positioning the stamps.

3 Spread some gold size on to the plate and run the roller through it until it is evenly coated. Ink the stamps with size and stamp the design on the album cover. Leave to dry for the time recommended by the manufacturer until the size becomes tacky.

5 Brush away any excess gold leaf still clinging to the paper. Add initials and the date, if required, using gold transfer letters or paint them freehand in size and gild as before.

4 Lay sheets of gold leaf on to the size and burnish with a soft brush.

BELOW: Gold leaf stamped on textured white paper is a beautiful way to remember a very special day.

STATIONERY, NOTEBOOKS AND FOLDERS

Have fun experimenting with stamp designs and create your own range of stationery at the same time. The stamps can be used alone or in combination with each other to make a whole range of patterns linked by the use of colour to form a set. Here, the plain books, folders and stationery are all a neutral brown and the pattern is stamped in a sepia tone, which complements the faded colour of the paper. Mixing extender or PVA (white) glue into the paint will make the paint dry more slowly, giving you extra time to put your design together. Hand-printed stationery is very quick and easy to make and will give great pleasure for your own use or as an individual gift.

You will need

- sepia acrylic paint
- plates
- extender or PVA (white) glue
- foam rollers
- grape, tendril and leaf stamps
- scrap paper
- notebooks
- brown parcel wrap
- craft knife
- self-healing cutting mat
- acrylic or emulsion (latex) paint in off-white
- folder
- square-tipped artist's paintbrush
- small file
- handmade paper folded into cards
- natural brown envelopes

1 Spread some sepia acrylic paint on to a plate. Add extender or PVA (white) glue and mix together.

2 Run a roller through the paint until it is evenly coated and ink the grape stamp. Make several test prints on scrap paper to gauge the way the paper absorbs the paint and how much paint you will need to apply to the stamp to achieve the desired effect.

3 Stamp the first bunch of grapes in the middle of one of the notebook covers.

4 Ink the tendril stamp and surround the grapes with tendril motifs. The pattern can be repeated on the back cover of the notebook.

5 Stamp a bunch of grapes on to a small piece of brown parcel wrap. Carefully cut around the outline with a craft knife on a self-healing cutting mat to make a stencil.

6 Spread some off-white paint on to a plate and run a roller through it until it is evenly coated. Position the stencil on a notebook cover and run the roller over the stencil to make a solid grape shape. Leave to dry.

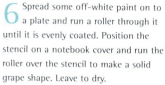

7 Ink the grape stamp with sepia acrylic paint and overprint the stencilled shape to add the detail.

8 For the folder, cut a window out of a sheet of scrap paper the same size as the folder cover to make a paper frame.

9 Lay the window frame on the cover. Ink the leaf stamp with sepia paint and stamp leaves all over the cover, overlapping the frame. Leave to dry, then remove the frame to reveal a plain border around the leaf pattern.

10 Mix some off-white paint into the sepia to make a lighter brown. Using a brush, apply the lighter brown paint to one side of the grape stamp and sepia to the other.

11 Stamp a single bunch of grapes on to the cover of a small file. The bunch of grapes will be shaded on one side, creating an interesting three-dimensional effect.

12 Place the folded cards of handmade paper on sheets of scrap paper. Stamp an all-over pattern of sepia tendrils, overlapping the edges so that the cards look as if they have been cut from a larger sheet of stamped paper. The texture of the paper will show through in places and the colour will vary as the paint gradually wears off the stamp, adding to the rich, handmade effect.

RIGHT: Once you realize how easy it is to make stamped stationery, notebooks and folders, there will be no turning back. For example, you could also print the grape stamp at the top of sheets of notepaper.

HERALDIC STATIONERY

Design and print a personalized set of stationery to add a touch of elegance to all your correspondence. Heraldic motifs have been used for centuries to decorate letters and secret diaries, but it is no longer necessary to live in a palace to be able to use them. This project demonstrates the variety of ways in which a single stamp can be used to produce different effects. The resulting stationery is based on a common theme but with plenty of individual flourishes. Experiment with your favourite colour combinations and try all-over or border patterns to add even more variety. Many craft shops sell special embossing powders that can be heated to produce a raised print.

You will need

- dark blue artist's watercolour paint
- plates
- foam rollers
- diamond, fleur-de-lys and crown stamps
- brown parcel wrap
- craft knife
- self-healing cutting mat
- small notebook, folder, postcards and textured and plain white notepaper
- gold paint
- dark blue paper
- ruler
- set square (triangle)
- paper glue
- fine artist's paintbrush

1 Spread some dark blue watercolour paint on to a plate and run a roller through it until it is evenly coated. Ink the diamond stamp and print one motif on to a small piece of the brown parcel wrap.

2 Cut out the diamond shape with a craft knife on a self-healing cutting mat. Try not to over-cut the corners because the shape will be used as a stencil and the paint may bleed through.

3 Position the paper stencil in the middle of the notebook cover and use the roller to apply dark blue watercolour paint through it. Leave to dry.

5 Cut a rectangle the size of the fleur-de-lys stamp block out of dark blue paper. Measure and divide it in half lengthways. Cut away one side with a craft knife, leaving a narrow border around the edge to make a window in one side.

4 Spread some gold paint on to a plate and run the roller through it until it is evenly coated. Ink the diamond stamp and stamp a gold print directly over the solid blue diamond, lining up the edges as closely as possible.

6 Using a ruler and set square (triangle) to position the stamp, print a dark blue fleur-de-lys in the centre of the folder. Glue the blue paper over the print so that half the fleur-de-lys motif shows through the window.

7 Ink the fleur-de-lys stamp with gold paint. Cover the cut-out side of the design with a straight-edged piece of parcel wrap. Stamp a gold fleur-de-lys to align with the sides of the blue print. Remove the piece of parcel wrap to reveal the final design, which will be half gold and half blue.

8 Stamp a blue fleur-de-lys on a notebook cover or postcard. Cover one half of it with a straight-edged piece of parcel wrap and overprint in gold to make a two-colour print.

9 Fold a piece of textured notepaper to make a card. Stamp a blue fleur-de-lys on the front of the card. The texture of the paper will show through in places. Add flourishes of gold paint using a fine artist's paintbrush.

10 Stamp a gold crown at the top of textured and plain white sheets of notepaper.

RIGHT: Experiment with other stamps and colours to create your own personalized stationery.

BOOK COVERS AND SECRETS BOX

This project evokes another era, when time appeared to pass more slowly and leisure time had nothing to do with aerobic exercise. Diaries and scrapbooks were kept and lovingly covered with printed papers, and secret mementoes were hidden in locked wooden caskets. Recapture the spirit of a bygone age by stamping patterned papers and using them to bind sketchbooks, albums and diaries. Preserve the battered antiquity of an old wooden box by stamping it and lining it in warm muted shades of red and green, then rubbing back the paint to simulate years of wear and tear.

1 For the book cover, use the stamp pad to print four tulips on scrap paper. Cut them out and arrange them in a row along the top edge of the sugar (construction) paper, side by side and alternately facing up and down. Use these paper prints as a guide for stamping.

2 Spread some deep red watercolour paint on to a plate and dip the stamp into it. Lay the ruler across the paper and use to align the stamp to print the first row. Re-ink the stamp after three prints for an irregular hand-printed effect.

3 Move the ruler down the width of a stamp block for each new row. Stamp the rows so that the tulips lie between the prints in the previous row. Cover the paper completely and leave to dry. Print more sugar paper, using the leaf and pineapple stamps and the leaf-green and black paint.

4 Cover the books with the stamped paper, sticking down any mitred corners with PVA (white) glue. Place a strip of bookbinding tape along the spine to cover the paper edges so there is an equal width of tape on the front and back cover. Trim away the tape at the top and bottom with a craft knife.

5 For the secrets box, use the stamp pad to print some tulips and leaves on scrap paper and cut them out. Arrange them on the wooden box to plan your design, deciding which motifs will be red and which green.

6 Spread some brick-red emulsion (latex) or acrylic paint on to a plate and run the roller through it until it is evenly coated. Ink the stamps and remove one paper shape at a time to stamp a leaf or tulip motif in its place.

7 Ink the leaf stamp with sage-green paint and stamp green leaves on the secrets box in the same way.

8 Place the wooden batten (furring strip) along the edge of the box and use the sage-green paint and the lining brush to paint an outline around the box and corner motifs. Slide your hand along the batten to keep an even line.

9 Leave the paint to dry completely, then lightly distress the stamped prints with abrasive paper (sandpaper) or wire (steel) wool. The secrets box can then be polished with furniture polish, if desired.

RIGHT: Sugar paper makes an effective background to the "distressed", aged stamp designs and is the ideal weight for book covers. If sugar paper is not readily available, you could use brown parcel wrap.

TREASURE BOXES

Sets of lidded round boxes made from lightweight wood, card (stock) or papier-mâché are often imported from the Far East and are readily available in the stores. The plain ones, sometimes called blanks, are not expensive and they make the ideal base for some imaginative stamping work. The hearts in this project have been grouped to form a larger motif, with some of them only partially stamped, so they don't look like hearts. As you can see, experimentation produces all sorts of variations on the heart theme.

1 Paint the lid of the box light grey with emulsion (latex) or acrylic paint. Leave to dry. If extra coverage is needed, apply more than one coat, leaving to dry between coats.

2 Spread some orange paint on to the plate and run the roller through it until it is evenly coated. Then ink the large heart stamp. Print the top half of the hearts around the side of the lid. Do not print the hearts too closely together – use the stamp to estimate the spacing before you begin.

3 Align the stamp with the pattern printed on the side of the lid, then print the pointed part of each heart around the top of the lid. This gives the impression that the hearts have been folded over the lid.

5 Still using the orange paint, stamp one complete large heart in the centre of the lid. Ink the small stamp with black paint and stamp a circle of hearts with their points radiating outwards between the yellow "V" shapes.

4 Use the same pointed part of the heart to print a zigzag border around the bottom edge of the box.

BELOW: It is amazing how many different patterns can be created using a couple of simple motifs.

MATISSE PICTURE FRAME

You can create instant art by combining stylized stamp leaf prints with bold blocks of bright colour on a picture frame. Matisse's stunning cut-outs were the inspiration for this project. In his later life, Matisse used paper cuttings to create collage pictures that are as bold and fresh today as when they were first made. For the framed image, print a single leaf in the same style on to paper and enlarge it on a photocopier. Make a printing block and print it on to coloured paper and to make a simple decorative motif.

You will need

◆ broad wooden picture frame
◆ emulsion (latex) paint in black
◆ paintbrush
◆ set square (triangle)
◆ pencil
◆ artist's acrylic, gouache or poster paints
  in lime-green and fuchsia
◆ plate
◆ foam roller
◆ leaf stamp
◆ clear matt (flat) varnish and brush

1 Paint the frame in black (latex) emulsion and let it dry. Use a set square (triangle) and pencil to mark four squares in the corners of the frame, with sides the same as the width of the wood.

2 Paint the corner squares lime-green. You will need to apply several coats of paint for the most intense colour. Make sure that none of the black background shows through the lime-green.

3 Spread some fuchsia paint on to a plate and run the roller through it until it is evenly coated. Ink the leaf stamp and stamp one leaf in each lime-green corner. Rotate the stamp each time, so that the stem of the leaf always points inwards.

ABOVE: *This work of art is surprisingly easy to achieve. Matisse's cut-outs will give you other ideas for colour schemes.*

4 Let the paint dry, then apply a coat of clear matt (flat) varnish to seal and protect the picture frame.

STARRY PICTURE FRAME

This project combines many of the creative possibilities of stamping. It involves four processes: painting a background, stamping in one colour, overprinting in a second colour and rubbing back to the wood. These processes transform a plain wooden frame and they are neither time-consuming nor expensive. It is surprisingly difficult to find small, old frames that are broad enough to stamp. Fortunately, a wide range of basic, cheap frames can be found in do-it-yourself stores.

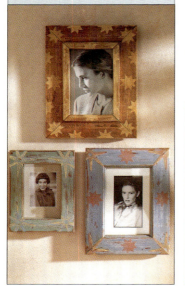

1 Paint the picture frame with sky-blue emulsion (latex) paint and leave it to dry thoroughly.

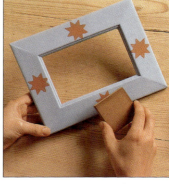

2 Spread a small amount of red-brown paint on to the plate and run the roller through it until it is evenly coated. Ink the small star stamp and print it in the middle of each side.

3 Using the red-brown paint, stamp a large star over each corner of the frame. Leave to dry thoroughly.

4 Ink the large stamp with gold paint and overprint the red-brown corner stars. Leave to dry before rubbing the frame gently with wire (steel) wool or abrasive paper (sandpaper) to give it a slightly aged appearance.

BELOW: *Experiment with other stamps, choosing one to suit the frame. Large stars overlap the sides of this deep frame.*

GRAPE PICTURE FRAME

A decorated frame draws attention to the picture within, while providing another opportunity to add colour and pattern to a room. This frame can be hung with the broad end at either the top or the bottom, depending on the nature of the picture it surrounds. The balance of the grape, leaf and tendril motif is reinforced by using the same colours to paint the border lines. Practise using a long-bristled lining brush on paper first before you paint the fine lines on the frame. The "hands-on" style does not require perfection – slightly wavy lines add character.

1 Stamp all three motifs on to scrap paper and cut them out. Position them on the broad end of the picture frame to plan your design.

2 Use a set square (triangle) and pencil to draw a line around the frame, just inside the green border. Draw a second line around the centre of the frame.

3 Spread some olive-green paint on to one side of the plate and blue on to the other. Run the roller through the paint until it is evenly coated, allowing the colours to blend slightly in the middle. Ink the stamps and print the motifs in the planned positions.

4 Use the lining brush to paint the pencil lines ultramarine blue. Steady your hand by sliding it along the raised border as you work. If you make a very obvious mistake, wipe off the paint immediately with a damp cloth, but you may need to touch up the background colour when the new line has dried.

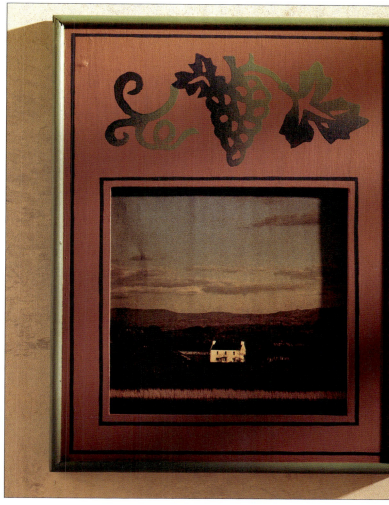

RIGHT: Choose stamp motifs and a colour scheme to complement your favourite picture.

SEEDPOD LAMPSHADE

Unusual lampshades can be very expensive. The solution is to take a plain lampshade and apply some surface decoration that will transform it from a utility object into a stylish focal point. This design, which resembles a seedpod, is easy to cut from high-density foam. It makes a bold, sharp-edged print and the flexibility of the foam means that it can bend around the curved surface. Remember to extend the pattern beyond the edges of the lampshade, so that only parts of the motifs appear. The lampshade will look as if it has been made from hand-printed fabric.

You will need

- pencil
- tracing paper
- spray adhesive
- high-density foam, such as upholstery foam
- craft knife
- thinned emulsion (latex) paint in creamy yellow and pale blue
- plates
- small rubber roller
- plain-coloured lampshade

1 Trace and transfer the seedpod pattern shape from the template section. Lightly spray the shape with adhesive and place it on the foam. Cut out the motif using a craft knife. Cut around the outline first, going all the way through the foam. Cut around the centre detail to a depth of about 1cm/½in, then under-cut and scoop out this section, and cut away the background.

2 Spread some creamy yellow paint on to a plate and coat the roller evenly. Use it to apply a coating of paint to the stamp.

3 Make the first print a partial one, using only the top end of the stamp. Continue to print at random angles, leaving plenty of spaces for the second colour. Wash the stamp, removing all traces of yellow paint.

BELOW: The outline shape looks like a stencil, but it is in fact all part of the home-made foam stamp.

4 Spread some pale blue paint on a second plate and coat the roller. Use it to apply an even coating of paint to the stamp.

5 Stamp blue shapes at random angles in between the yellow ones. Be sure to make some partial prints so that the pattern continues over the edges.

FLORAL LAMPSHADE

Anew lampshade can work wonders, freshening up a dull corner and providing as much in the way of style as in illumination. This paper shade has a good shape with interesting punched edges. However, a plain shade would work equally well for this project. In this design it is essential to space the rose pattern accurately, so make a quick paper pattern to ensure perfect results with every print.

You will need

- emulsion (latex) or fabric paint in pink and green
- plate
- 2 square-tipped paintbrushes
- large rose stamp
- scrap paper
- scissors
- masking tape
- plain lampshade (either paper or cloth)

1 Spread some pink and green paint on to the plate. Using the square-tipped paintbrushes, ink the leaves of the rose stamp green and the flower pink. (If one colour mixes with the other, just wipe them off and re-ink the stamp.)

2 Print five rose motifs on to scrap paper and cut them out.

3 Using masking tape, stick the paper
roses round the lampshade. Make
sure that they are spaced the same
distance apart and not too close
together. Depending on the size of
the shade, you should be able to fit
four or five roses round it.

4 Re-ink the stamp and lift off each
paper rose individually as you stamp
on to the lampshade itself. Hold the
lampshade firmly with your spare hand
and roll the stamp across the curved
surface to get an even print.

RIGHT: *This would be an ideal accessory
for one of the rose fabric projects in
this book.*

STARFISH LAMP

This project transforms a plain, ordinary lamp into an individual and stylish accessory. Buy the cheapest lamp you can find because, once the base has been painted and the shade stamped, you won't be able to recognize the item you bought originally. The deep red stamps on the pink background not only give out a lovely coloured glow when the lamp is switched on, but cheer up a dull corner even when switched off.

You will need

♦ lamp with fabric shade and wooden base
♦ emulsion (latex) paint in deep red and light grey-blue
♦ paintbrush
♦ plates
♦ pencil
♦ foam roller
♦ starfish stamp

1 Paint the base of the lamp with deep red emulsion (latex) paint and leave to dry thoroughly.

2 Using a dry brush and a small amount of light grey-blue paint, lightly brush on the colour to shade the shape of the turned wood.

3 Use the stamp block to work out the spacing of the starfish round the shade. Lightly mark the design in pencil. Spread some deep red paint on to a plate and run the roller through it until it is evenly coated. Ink the stamp and begin by printing the bottom row of the pattern, following the pencil marks.

4 Stamp a row of starfish around the top of the shade. Remember to check the spacing as you go – you will fit fewer around the top than the bottom.

ABOVE: Simple stamping on the lampshade is given extra interest by painting and overpainting the base in two colours. Choose a colour scheme to suit your room.

FOLK COFFEE CANISTER

Rescue an old kitchen canister and give it a new identity as a piece of folk art. Painted tinware was very popular with early American settlers, and for years peddlers roamed the countryside loaded down with brightly painted cans, pitchers and bowls they sold from door to door. All these years later tinware is still a popular way of brightening up kitchen shelves. Prepare this canister by rubbing down the old paint with abrasive paper (sandpaper) to provide a surface for a fresh coat of emulsion (latex) paint. After stamping, bring out the colour and protect the surface with several coats of clear varnish.

You will need

- empty coffee canister
- abrasive paper (sandpaper)
- small household paintbrush
- emulsion (latex) paint in brick-red, black and bright red
- fine artist's paintbrushes
- plates
- foam roller
- tulip stamp
- clear gloss varnish and brush

1 Sand the canister. Paint the canister and lid brick-red. Leave to dry, then paint the rim of the lid black using a fine artist's paintbrush.

2 Run the roller through the black paint until it is evenly coated. Ink the tulip stamp and print a tulip on the side of the canister, tilting the stamp block around the curve of the canister.

3 Fill in the tulip shape carefully, using bright red paint and a fine artist's paintbrush.

ABOVE: *Stamping works well on tin surfaces. In this project, the tulip shape is filled in using a fine artist's paintbrush.*

4 Apply several coats of gloss varnish to seal and protect the canister. Allow each coat to dry completely before applying the next.

VINE LEAF CUTLERY RACK

A small wooden cutlery rack like this one provides another ideal surface for stamping. Use the stamps to loosely co-ordinate your kitchen or dining room without being swamped by matching patterns and colours. The wood has been stained blue and is then rubbed back to reveal some of the natural grain underneath. The two colours of the pattern are stamped separately using thinned emulsion (latex) paint for a light and airy finish.

BELOW: This design would look very attractive stamped on the top of a pine shelf unit or kitchen dresser.

1 Sand the surface of the cutlery rack to reveal some of the grain. Spread some dark olive-green paint on to a plate and thin it with water until it is a runny consistency.

2 Use the roller to ink the leaf stamp. Print two leaves side by side on the back and front of the rack as shown. Print two leaves one above the other on the sides. Leave to dry.

3 Spread some light olive-green paint on to a plate and run the roller through it until it is evenly coated. Ink just the tips of the leaves and overprint all the darker green prints. If some of the prints are slightly off-register, this will only add to the rustic appearance of the cutlery rack.

CANDLE BOX

A long time ago every home would have had a candle box hanging on the kitchen wall, kept full to meet the lighting needs of the household. Although rarely needed in quite the same way today, candle boxes are still popular and add to a comfortable atmosphere. Candle boxes can be bought, but are quite easy to make from five pieces of wood. The open top allows you to see when your supply is running low and the sight of the new candles is somehow reassuring as well as attractive.

1 Sand away any varnish and smooth any rough edges on the box.

2 Paint the bare wood with a single coat of shellac.

BELOW: This box has a heraldic theme.

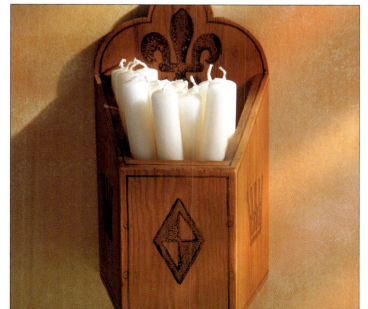

3 Spread some woodstain on to a plate and run the roller through it until it is evenly coated. Ink the stamps and print a single motif on each side of the box. Print the fleur-de-lys so it will be visible above the candles. Use the lining brush to paint a thin border on all sides of the box.

WOODEN WINE CRATE

Old wood usually looks best with a faded rather than freshly painted pattern. The grape design here does not detract from the crate's rustic quality because it has been stamped in a muted green, then rubbed back to blend with the existing lettering on the wood. If you are lucky enough to find a custom-made wine crate like this one, it will simply need a good scrubbing with soapy water, then be left to dry before you stamp it.

You will need

- old wine crate or similar wooden box
- scrubbing brush (optional)
- emulsion (latex) paint in olive-green
- plate
- foam roller
- grape stamp
- fine abrasive paper (sandpaper)

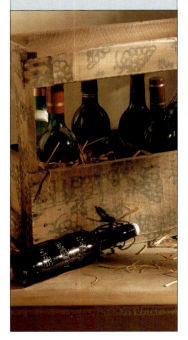

1 If necessary, scrub the wine crate or box well with soapy water and a scrubbing brush. Leave the wood to dry.

2 Spread some olive-green paint on to a plate and run the roller through it until it is evenly coated. Ink the stamp and begin stamping a random pattern of grapes. Stamp at different angles to add variety.

3 Cover all the surfaces of the crate or box, overlapping the edge if the planks are too narrow to take the whole motif.

ABOVE: Look out for a wooden crate or box with plenty of character. Your local wine merchant may be able to help.

4 Leave the paint to dry, then rub back the pattern with abrasive paper (sandpaper) so that it becomes faded and blends with the original surface decoration or lettering. Rub gently and aim for a patchy, distressed appearance.

GILDED TRAY

This simple wooden tea tray is transformed into an item of historic grandeur by using an easy gilding technique. Begin by sanding away any old paint or varnish and painting the base of the tray in black and the sides in red-ochre emulsion (latex) paint, applying two or three coats. The heraldic motifs make up a central panel design, and the fine outline is repeated around the edge of the tray. The tray is stamped twice, first with the red-ochre paint and then with gold size, which is a transparent glue used for gilding. Dutch metal leaf is then applied over the size.

1 Measure out and mark in pencil the six-sided central panel. Draw a border around the edge of the tray. Print eight fleurs-de-lys and five diamonds on to scrap paper and cut them out. Use them to plan your design, marking the base point of each motif in pencil on the tray. Spread some red-ochre paint on to a plate and run the roller through it until it is evenly coated. Ink the stamps and print the fleur-de-lys and diamond pattern.

2 Using the wooden batten (furring strip) to support your hand, use the lining brush and the red-ochre paint to paint a fine line around the design, following the pencil lines of the central panel. Paint another fine line just inside the edge of the tray. If you have never used a lining brush, practise making lines on scrap paper until you are confident with the technique.

3 Paint the sides of the tray with size. Leave the size to become tacky, according to the time specified by the manufacturer. Place one sheet of Dutch metal leaf on to the size at a time and burnish with the back of a soft brush. Spread the gold size on to a plate and use the roller to ink the stamps with size. Overprint the red-ochre patterns, stamping each print slightly down and to the left of the already printed motif to create a dropped shadow effect. Leave the size to become tacky and gild with Dutch metal leaf in the same way as before. Use a stiff paintbrush to sweep away the excess leaf. Seal the whole tray with a protective coat of shellac.

BELOW: This opulent treatment would also transform a plain wooden side table in a medieval-inspired drawing room.

TULIP TRAY

Paint and stamp a tray like this one and you will be tempted to display it rather than put it to practical use. You can in fact do both, if you apply several coats of varnish to give the tray a washable surface. The tulips and leaves are stamped on bold geometric shapes to give them added impact. The colours used here are not typical of folk art and give the tray a dramatic, contemporary look. You could use a more traditional colour combination, such as black, red and green, for a completely different effect.

1 Paint the tray with dusky blue emulsion (latex) paint and leave to dry. Use a ruler and pencil to draw a square in the centre of the tray, then draw a square on the diagonal inside it. Add two rectangular panels on either side of the central square. The size of the panels will depend on the tray.

2 Paint the diagonal square and the two rectangles in buttermilk-yellow, and the remaining area of the larger square in dark blue. If your tray has cut-out handles, paint inside them in dark blue.

ABOVE: Cheerful colours and bold shapes make a breakfast tray or television supper tray a pleasure to use. Choose a tray with high sides like this one.

3 Spread some dark blue paint on to a plate and use the roller to ink the tulip and leaf stamps. Print two leaves on the side panels and two tulips in the central square, both end to end.

4 Apply at least three coats of clear satin varnish, allowing each coat to dry thoroughly before applying the next. The stamping will become more resistant with each coat of varnish.

SEASIDE PICNIC

Picnics in cookbooks and magazine articles always look irresistibly inviting and miles away from the reality of hastily made sandwiches on an assortment of unbreakable plates. One of the challenges with picnics is that they tend to be spontaneously arranged on a sunny day, so presentation gets forgotten. The trick is to prepare your picnic set in advance ready for the next time the sun shines. For this project, you don't need to buy new picnic gear – old plates and napkins will look perfect jumbled together when they are all stamped with the same seashore design theme.

You will need

- wooden tray
- acrylic enamel paint in deep red and light blue
- plates
- foam rollers
- starfish, shell and seahorse stamps
- selection of plates and platters
- scrap paper
- scissors
- pencil
- checked napkins and tablecloth
- backing paper
- fabric paint in sea-green
- iron

1 To stamp the tray, spread some of the deep red paint on to a plate and run a roller through it until it is evenly coated. Ink the starfish stamp with the roller and make the first print in a corner of the tray.

2 Print a starfish in the other three corners, then ink the shell stamp and make one print in the centre of the tray. Print seahorses all along the outside edges of the tray.

3 To stamp the plates, ink the seahorse stamp with deep red paint and print on to a piece of scrap paper. Cut out the motif and plan your design by positioning the seahorse round each plate and marking with a pencil where each stamp will go.

4 Ink the stamp and print the first seahorse, following your pencil marks as a guide for positioning.

5 Re-ink the stamp and turn it the other way round for the next print. Continue turning the stamp each time you print so that heads meet heads and tails meet tails.

6 To stamp the platters, spread some light blue paint on to a plate and run a roller through it until it is evenly coated. Ink the starfish stamp and print in two opposite corners of each platter.

7 Ink the shell stamp with the light blue paint and make a print next to one of the starfish.

8 Print one more shell motif as shown, then complete the platter design by adding two seahorse motifs in the remaining spaces.

9 Protect your work surface with backing paper and lay a napkin over this. Count the checks to decide on the spacing of your design. Spread some sea-green fabric paint on to a plate and run a roller through it until it is evenly coated. Ink the shell stamp and make the first print in one corner.

10 Stamp a shell in each corner of the napkin, then ink the seahorse stamp and make a print by the side of each shell.

11 Ink the starfish stamp and complete the border pattern by printing a starfish in the remaining spaces on the border. Stamp the tablecloth to match the napkins. Fix (set) the fabric paint with a hot iron, following the manufacturer's instructions.

RIGHT: It is easy to make this co-ordinated picnic set. Stamping on to checked fabric gives even simple motifs extra interest. It also provides a grid which makes positioning the stamps very straightforward. Now all you need is the food!

CHILDREN'S ROOMS

Children grow up and change their ideas very quickly, so decorating on their behalf presents its own particular problems. Realistically you must expect them to demand a completely new decor around every five years. This can be quite liberating, however, as you don't have to think in the very long term, so throw caution to the wind and enjoy yourself. While the decor of their room might be important to some children, most – especially younger ones – will be happy for you to make the decorating decisions for them. Whether you are decorating for a baby, a young child or a young adult, these rooms should inspire you to be creative and individual.

ABOVE: Decorate whole walls or individual pieces of furniture to give your child's room a truly individual look.

LEFT: One single stamp and two paint colours transform the look of a plain toy box.

NURSERY WALLS

Children are often bombarded with a riot of primary colours or surrounded in pretty pastels, so this dark colour scheme provides an unusual and refreshing change. It gives the room a wonderful period feel and the deep blue-green shade is known for its calming effect. You can offset the dark colour by painting a light colour above the dado (chair) rail and laying a lighter, natural floor covering like sisal or cork tiles. The effect is rich and intense. This idea can be adapted to any colour scheme and you can reverse the effect by using a light background with darker stamps. Experiment with colours and shades and you'll often find that unusual combinations create the most stunning impact.

You will need

- emulsion (latex) paint in deep blue-green, sap-green and red
- household paintbrush
- plates
- foam roller
- large heart stamp
- water-based matt (flat) varnish and brush (optional)

1 Paint the wall below the dado (chair) rail in deep blue-green. Leave to dry. Spread a small amount of sap-green paint on to a plate and run the roller through it until it is evenly coated. Ink the stamp and begin printing the pattern in groups. Re-ink the stamp only when the print is very light.

2 Gradually build up the pattern all over the wall. The first prints after inking will be solid and bright; the last ones will fade into the background. This is a feature of the design, so make the most of the natural irregularities.

3 This is an optional step. If you find that the contrasts are too strong, mix some varnish with the blue-green paint (one part paint to five parts varnish) and brush it all over the pattern. Leave to dry.

4 Ink the stamp with red paint and overprint every third heart in the top row. Then overprint every third heart in the next row, this time starting one in from the edge. Repeat these two rows to overprint the whole pattern. Only re-ink the stamp when the colour has faded.

BELOW: A single repeated motif will look varied and interesting if you only re-ink the stamp occasionally.

POLKA-DOT BEDROOM WALLS

Deciding on the bedroom decor for older children can sometimes be difficult. They are definitely not babies and probably don't want a themed room. However, something light-hearted and not too fussy can be hard to achieve. A spot is the simplest of motifs and can be used on its own or in combination with other shapes. Stars can be added as a variation, or darker spots stamped below the dado (chair) rail. The end result is far from childish but neither is it too sombre. The colours used here are quite sophisticated but another combination would change the mood completely.

You will need
◆ pair of compasses
◆ scrap paper
◆ scissors
◆ low-density sponge, such as a bath sponge
◆ felt-tipped pen
◆ craft knife
◆ emulsion (latex) paint in dusky blue
◆ plate
◆ plumbline (optional)
◆ ruler (optional)
◆ emulsion paint in black and yellow (optional)

1 Use a pair of compasses to draw a circle with a diameter of 8cm/3¼in on scrap paper. Cut it out.

2 Using this circle as a template, draw two circles on the sponge with a felt-tipped pen.

3 Cut out the circles with a craft knife. First cut around the outline, then part the sponge and cut right through to the other side.

4 If you are using star motifs as well as the spots, draw out a star shape on another piece of sponge and cut it out with a craft knife.

5 Spread an even coating of dusky blue paint on to a plate and press the spot stamp into it. Make a test print on to scrap paper to ensure that the stamp is not overloaded. If you trust your eye, then begin printing the spots in evenly spaced rows. If you need a guide, attach a plumbline at ceiling height and stamp the spots alongside it, measuring the distance between the spots with a ruler. Move the line along a measured distance and repeat the process.

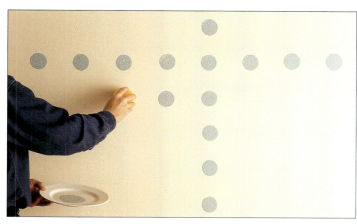

6 For a more dramatic effect, darken the blue down a tone by adding some black, then stamp more spot motifs below the dado (chair) rail.

▶

7 If you are using the star motif too,
dip the sponge into yellow paint,
test on scrap paper, and stamp stars at
equal intervals between the spots. For
further interest, you could mix a darker
yellow, and stamp over the original stars,
slightly off-centre, to create a dropped
shadow effect.

RIGHT: Position the sponge stamps by
eye or, if you are nervous about this,
use a plumbline and a ruler to mark
out an evenly spaced pattern.

CARIBBEAN BATHROOM

Bathtime should be a fun-filled part of a child's day but sometimes there is a certain reluctance on the part of the child to enter the bathroom. Make the room appealing for your child by decorating the walls with bright and cheerful motifs. This bathroom has a tropical seaside theme. The intense sky-blue of the background is separated from the sandy yellow by a bright red peg rail, a feature that is both decorative and extremely functional. The stamps are pre-cut bath sponges. We have copied the sponge colours here, but you could choose any colour combination you wished.

You will need

- emulsion (latex) paint in viridian-green, pink and yellow
- plates
- scrap paper
- set of tropical-theme sponges

1 Spread even coatings of viridian-green, pink and yellow paint on to separate plates. Press the palm tree sponge into the green, then make a test print on scrap paper to ensure that the sponge is not overloaded with paint. Stamp the first print at a 45-degree angle, just above the peg rail.

2 Press the fish sponge into the pink paint and make a test print on scrap paper. Then stamp the fish beside the palm tree. Once again avoid an upright print, angle it slightly.

3 Press the pineapple sponge into the yellow paint, make a test print on paper, then stamp it above the others, once again at a 45-degree angle.

4 Continue stamping the three shapes until they fill the wall. Position the prints close to one another, and change the angle of the print each time so that the pattern is densely packed and completely random.

BELOW: *This design uses pre-cut children's bath sponges. Many other shapes are readily available to buy.*

APPLE TREE MURAL

It is advisable to undertake this project when the children are out of the way. This sort of decorating is very appealing to young people and they will want to join in. However, if you are willing to let them help you, be prepared for a less stylish and more spontaneous result. The apple tree mural is perfect for a playroom or for a new baby's room. It is the kind of design that will last throughout childhood, as it will not appear babyish too quickly. The mural was painted with pieces of sponge instead of a brush to harmonize all the textures, so that the tree, leaves and fruit all have the same soft finish. The colours are muted to prevent the design becoming too overbearing.

You will need

- stiff card (stock)
- pencil
- craft knife
- felt-tipped pen
- low-density sponge, such as a bath sponge
- diluted emulsion (latex) paint in pink, brick-red, yellow, sap-green, blue-grey, ochre and olive-green
- plates
- paintbrush
- scrap paper

1 Draw the branch, trunk and base shapes on to a sheet of stiff card (stock). Carefully cut out the shapes with a craft knife.

2 Using a felt-tipped pen, draw a circle and a leaf on to the sponge. Cut around the outline, then part the sponge and cut right through.

3 Decide where to position the trees on the wall, then draw around the base template in pencil.

4 Draw the tree trunk above the base, using a long, rectangular shape as a template.

5 Add six curved branches. Stagger three branches up one side of the tree trunk, then flip the template over to draw three matching branches opposite them.

6 Spread the paints out on to separate plates using a paintbrush. For the tree's base you will need pink, brick-red, yellow and sap-green. Starting at the skirting (base) board, use a piece of sponge to fill in the pencil outline drawn on the wall. Make a test print on scrap paper first to ensure that the sponge is not overloaded.

7 Fill in the tree trunk and the branches with the blue-grey paint. The sponging should not look perfect; it should be textured and rough. Cut the sponge into a point at one end to print the ends of the branches.

8 Stamp the leaves in ochre and olive-green. Over-stamp one colour with the other occasionally, to give a three-dimensional effect.

9 Finally, use the sponge circle and pink paint to stamp the apples. Space them randomly in the foliage. Print some apples to overlap the leaves and print others partially, as if obscured by the leaves. Apply more pressure to one side of the sponge; it will print darker and give the fruit a shaded effect.

RIGHT: *A mixture of sponge painting and stamping gives this beautiful mural a lovely delicate appearance.*

"COUNTRY QUILT" FRIEZE

Stamp this friendly, folk-style frieze in a child's bedroom in soft pinks and a warm green. The pattern is reminiscent of antique American appliqué quilts. The overlapping edges and jauntily angled birds accentuate its naive charm. The colour scheme avoids the harshness of primaries which are so often chosen for children. Green is a calming colour available in many different tones and shades. For this project use a sap-green, which contains a lot of yellow, for warmth. The finished effect is bright enough to be eye-catching without being overpowering.

1 Divide the wall by painting the lower section sap-green, up to dado (chair) rail height. Measure 24cm/9½in up from the green section and draw a straight line using a pencil, ruler and spirit level to act as a guide for the top of the border. Cut a straight strip of foam, 2cm/¾in wide, using a craft knife.

2 Trace and transfer all the pattern shapes from the template section, then spray with adhesive. Stick them on to the foam and cut out with a craft knife. Press the straight strip into the green paint and make a test print. Print a line along the pencil guideline, then another just above the green wall section.

3 Press the curved strip into the green paint, make a test print, then stamp curved lines to form a branch.

4 Press the leaf shape into the green paint, make a test print, then stamp the leaves in groups, as shown, two above and one below the branch.

5 Stamp pale pink birds along the branch – you need two prints, one facing each direction. Do not make the prints too uniform; aim for a patchy, textured effect.

6 Clean the bird stamp, then press it into the crimson paint. Stamp the rest of the birds along the branch, alternating the direction of the motif as before.

7 Stamp a row of pink and crimson hearts above the top line to complete the frieze pattern.

HEARTS TOY BOX

This project gives instant appeal to the most ordinary of wooden boxes. It works just as well on old as new woods, but if you are using an old box give it a good rub down with medium- and fine-grade abrasive paper (sandpaper) before you begin. This will remove any sharp edges or splinters. The box is given a rust-red background before being stamped with three different heart shapes in four colours. The stamps are rotated so that they appear at different angles and the pattern turns out quite randomly. It is best to follow the spirit of the idea rather than adhering rigidly to the instructions. That way, you will end up with a truly individual design.

You will need

- hinged wooden chest/box with a lid (suitable for storing toys)
- emulsion (latex) paint in rust-red
- household paintbrush
- emulsion or acrylic paint in maroon, sap-green, bright green and dark blue
- plates
- foam rollers
- small, large and trellis heart stamps
- fine-grade abrasive paper (sandpaper)
- matt (flat) varnish and brush

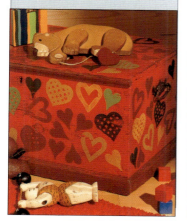

1 Paint the box with rust-red paint, applying two coats to give a good matt background. Leave the paint to dry between coats.

2 Spread some maroon paint on to a plate and run a roller through it until it is evenly coated. Use the roller to apply a border round the edge of the lid. Leave to dry.

3 Spread some sap-green paint on to a plate and coat a roller. Ink the small heart stamp and print a few hearts randomly over the lid of the box.

4 Ink the large and the trellis heart stamps with the sap-green paint. Print some hearts close together and others on their own to create a random pattern. Cover the whole box in this way.

5 Clean all three stamps and ink with the bright green paint. Build up the pattern by adding this colour in the gaps, leaving enough space for the last two colours.

6 Clean the stamps. Using the dark blue paint, continue stamping the three hearts over the box.

7 Clean the stamps. Finally, fill in the remaining background space with the maroon paint and the three heart stamps. No large spaces should remain. Leave to dry completely.

8 Use fine-grade abrasive paper (sandpaper) to rub down the box where you think natural wear and tear would be most likely to occur.

9 You can preserve the comfortable "weathered" look of the toy box by applying two coats of matt (flat) varnish. Leave to dry between coats.

RIGHT: Unusual colours give this design real impact. If you prefer, you can stamp the hearts in primary or pastel colours to fit in with the rest of the room. Paint the box in a background colour that will show off the motifs.

MINIBUS TOY BOX

Every child should be encouraged to tidy away his or her toys at the end of the day and this eye-catching toy box might just do the trick! The pastel-coloured toning patches behind the bus stamps give the box a 1950s look and are stencilled on to a light turquoise background. Stamp the buses on quite randomly so that some extend beyond the patch shapes. Change the angle of the stamp while you work to add visual interest. This is a project where you could ask the child to help.

You will need

- hinged wooden box
- emulsion (latex) paint in light turquoise
- household paintbrush
- pencil
- ruler
- sheet of stencil card (stock) or mylar
- spray adhesive
- craft knife
- emulsion or stencil paint in yellow, pink and pastel blue
- plates
- small paint roller
- stamping ink in brown
- minibus rubber stamp
- rubber roller

1 Apply two coats of light turquoise emulsion (latex) paint to the box. Leave to dry. Draw and cut out a stencil for the background shape. It should be large enough to contain the whole stamp image plus a small border.

2 Spread the yellow, pink and pastel blue paints on to separate plates. Using a small paint roller, paint the first colour through the stencil on to the box. You will need an equal number of shapes for each colour.

3 Wash the roller and apply the two remaining colours, painting through the stencil as before. Balance the shapes with an equal amount of background colour. Leave to dry.

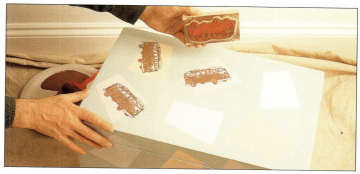

4 Pour some brown stamping ink on to a clean plate. Coat the rubber stamp with ink using a rubber roller.

5 Stamp the bus motifs on to the pastel patches. Allow the stamps to overlap some of the patches and vary the angle of the stamp.

ABOVE: Use a stamp that will reflect your child's interests and hobbies. There is a wide selection of ready-made stamps to choose from. Position the stamps at jaunty angles, with some overlapping the box lid.

TEMPLATES

The templates on the following pages may be resized to any scale required. The simplest way of doing this is to enlarge them on a photocopier, or trace the design and draw a grid of evenly spaced squares over your tracing. Draw a larger grid on another piece of paper and copy the outline square by square. Draw over the lines to make sure they are continuous.

**TROMPE L'OEIL
PLATES**
page 38

GREEK URNS
page 36

**FRENCH COUNTRY
KITCHEN**
page 46

KITCHEN ALCOVE
page 42

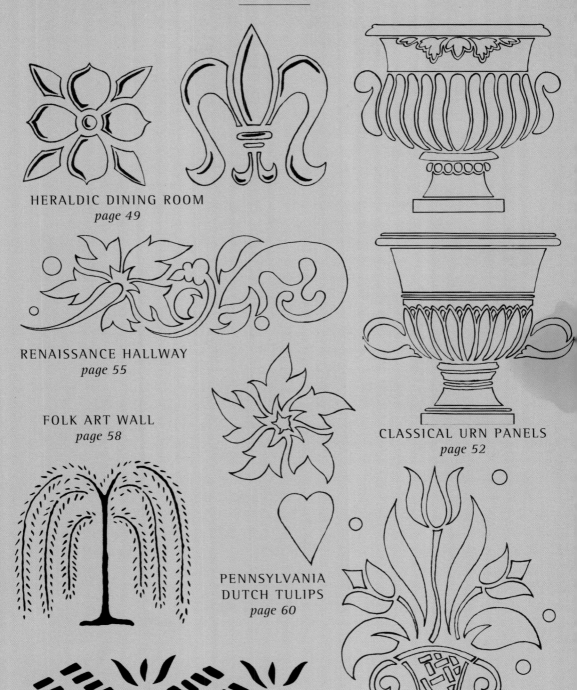

HERALDIC DINING ROOM
page 49

RENAISSANCE HALLWAY
page 55

FOLK ART WALL
page 58

CLASSICAL URN PANELS
page 52

**PENNSYLVANIA
DUTCH TULIPS**
page 60

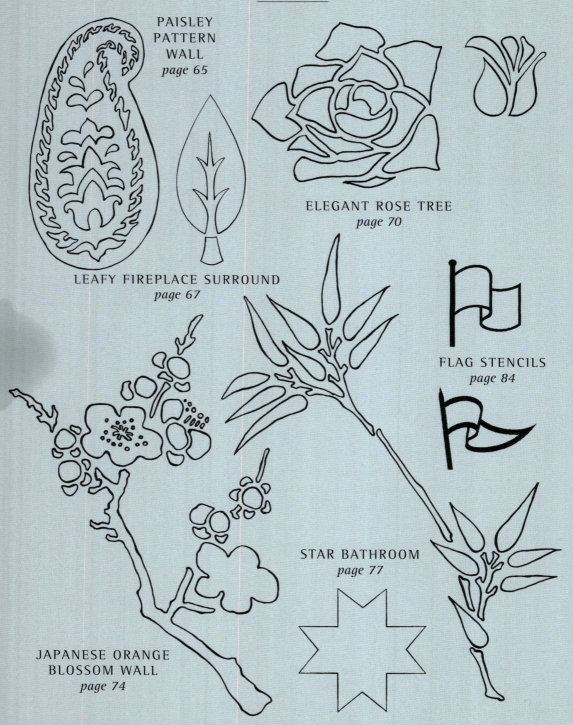

PAISLEY
PATTERN
WALL
page 65

LEAFY FIREPLACE SURROUND
page 67

ELEGANT ROSE TREE
page 70

FLAG STENCILS
page 84

STAR BATHROOM
page 77

JAPANESE ORANGE
BLOSSOM WALL
page 74

BATHROOM FRIEZE
page 80

MAKING SANDCASTLES
page 82

**CHILD'S SEASIDE
ROOM**
page 86

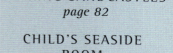

ANIMAL BEDROOM
page 90

**BRIGHT
TRANSPORT
BORDER**
page 94

ART NOUVEAU TILES
page 100

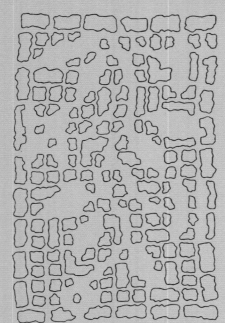

MEDALLION STENCILLED FLOOR
page 102

VICTORIAN WINDOW
page 98

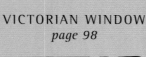

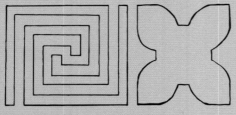

**GREEK KEY FLOOR
BORDER**
page 104

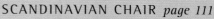

SCANDINAVIAN CHAIR *page 111*

BRONZE CHAIR *page 108*

PAINTED
DRAWERS
page 114

TRAIN TOY
BOX
page 117

HAWAIIAN HIBISCUS
CABINET *page 120*

SCANDINAVIAN CHAIR *page 111*

CELTIC
KNOT BOX
page 124

DAISY STOOL
page 127

AFRICAN BEDSIDE CHEST
page 133

STRIPED TABLE
AND CHAIRS
page 136

ORGANZA
CUSHION
page 144

FLOWER POWER CHAIR
page 140

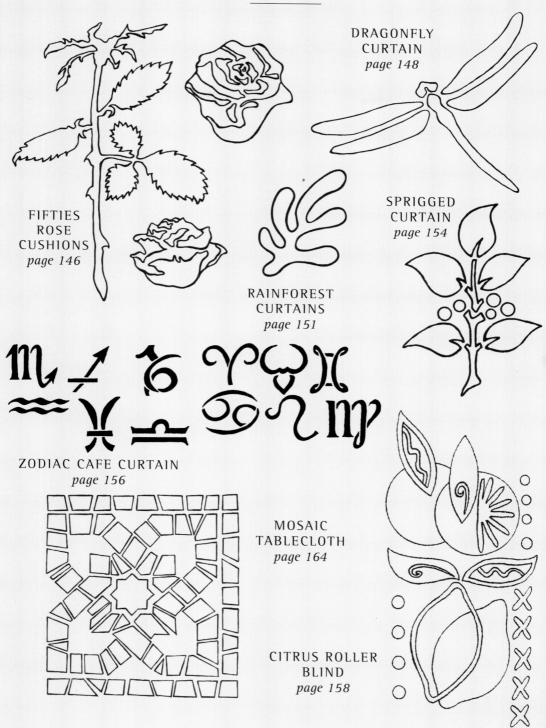

DRAGONFLY
CURTAIN
page 148

FIFTIES
ROSE
CUSHIONS
page 146

SPRIGGED
CURTAIN
page 154

RAINFOREST
CURTAINS
page 151

ZODIAC CAFE CURTAIN
page 156

MOSAIC
TABLECLOTH
page 164

CITRUS ROLLER
BLIND
page 158

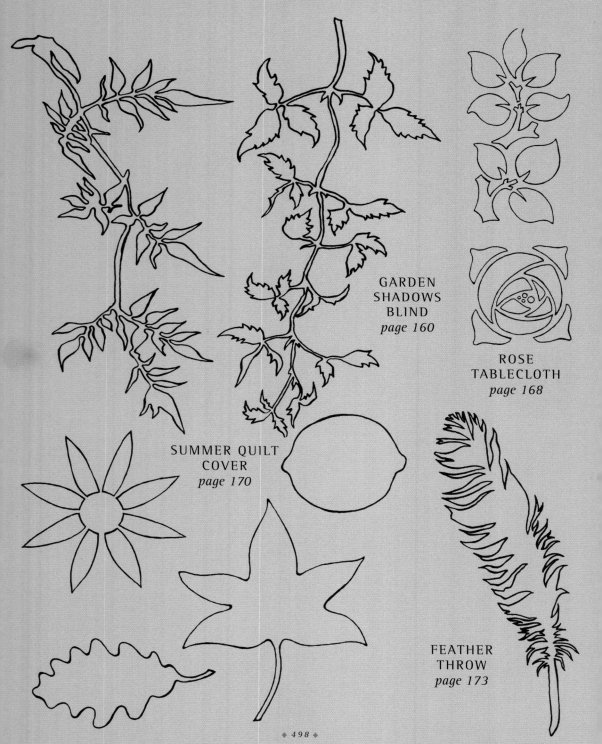

GARDEN
SHADOWS
BLIND
page 160

ROSE
TABLECLOTH
page 168

SUMMER QUILT
COVER
page 170

FEATHER
THROW
page 173

AE
OL
MR
UV

LOVE PILLOWS
page 176

GIRL'S BED CANOPY
AND CUSHION
page 178

SEASHELL
BEACH
BAG
page 182

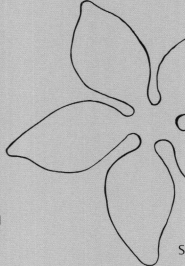

GINGERBREAD APRON
page 184

SEVENTIES FLOWER CANVASES
page 187

LEAFY PICTURE FRAMES
page 208

STARS AND STRIPES
FLOORCLOTH
page 193

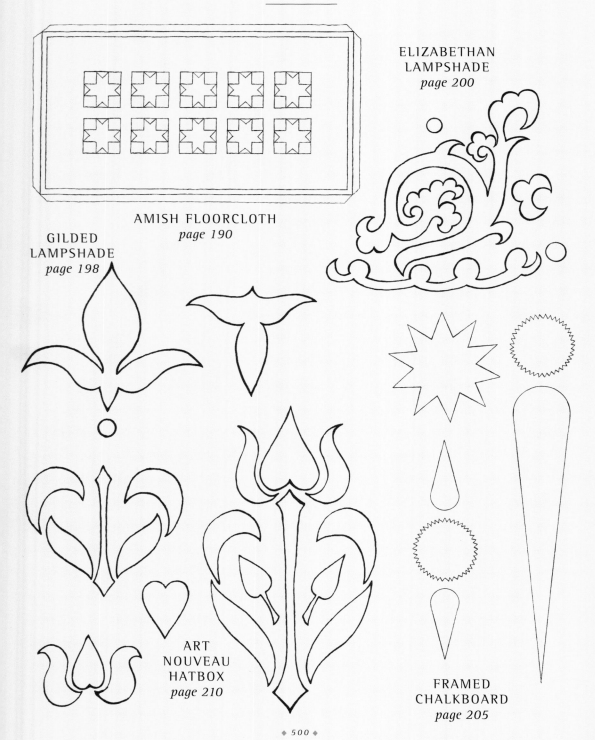

ELIZABETHAN
LAMPSHADE
page 200

AMISH FLOORCLOTH
page 190

GILDED
LAMPSHADE
page 198

ART
NOUVEAU
HATBOX
page 210

FRAMED
CHALKBOARD
page 205

LEAF-ETCHED VASE
page 218

CITRUS FRUIT TRAY
page 212

BUTTERFLY GIFT WRAP
page 223

GILDED
CANDLES
page 214

PASTEL PAPER
LANTERNS
page 239

BUTTON GIFT WRAP
AND GIFT TAGS
page 228

A

C

B

SEAWEED GIFT WRAP
page 224

SHOE BOX
page 242

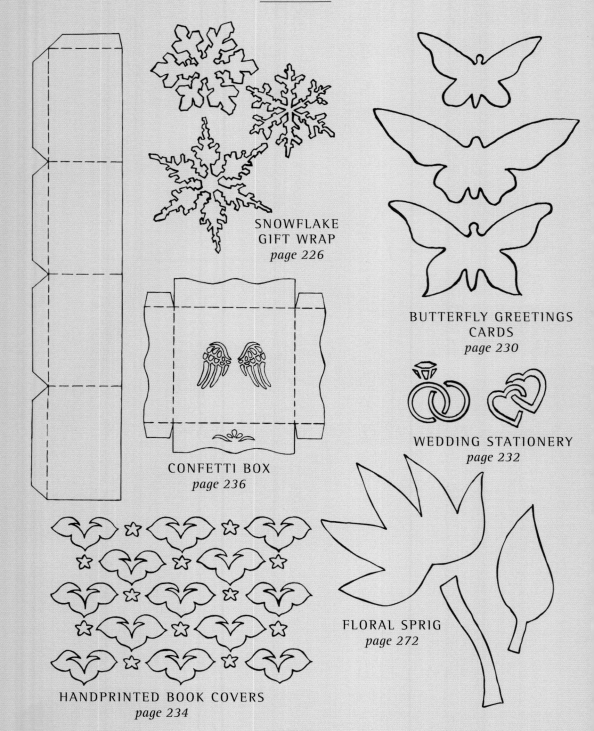

SNOWFLAKE
GIFT WRAP
page 226

BUTTERFLY GREETINGS
CARDS
page 230

WEDDING STATIONERY
page 232

CONFETTI BOX
page 236

FLORAL SPRIG
page 272

HANDPRINTED BOOK COVERS
page 234

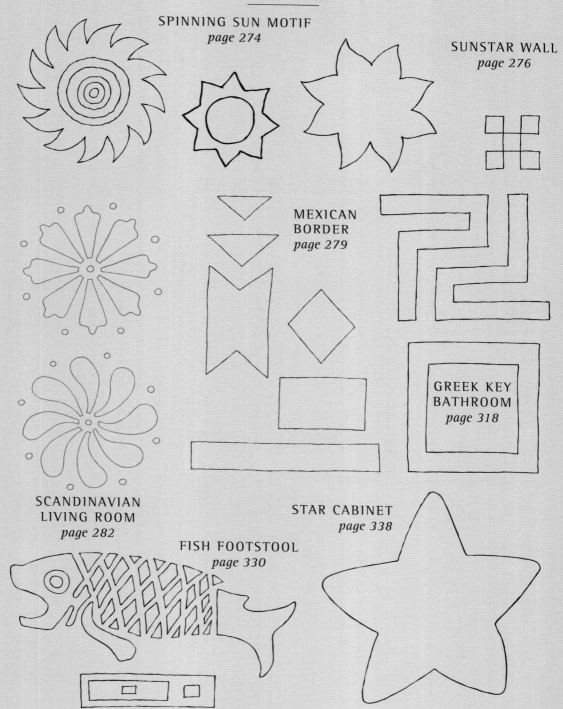

SPINNING SUN MOTIF
page 274

SUNSTAR WALL
page 276

MEXICAN BORDER
page 279

GREEK KEY BATHROOM
page 318

SCANDINAVIAN LIVING ROOM
page 282

STAR CABINET
page 338

FISH FOOTSTOOL
page 330

1

FOLK MOTIF CHAIR
page 332

**SPRIGGED CALICO
CURTAINS**
page 366

NO-SEW STAR CURTAIN
page 364

PERSONALIZED FLOWERPOTS
page 390

SNOWFLAKE STORAGE JARS
page 410

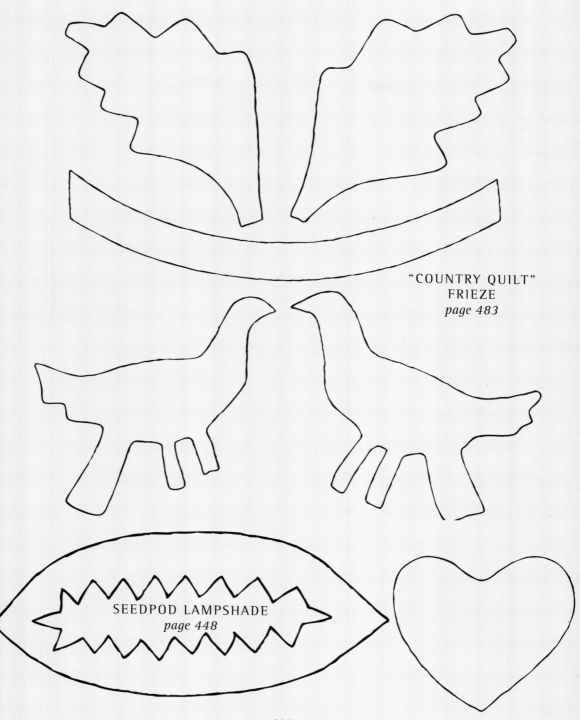

"COUNTRY QUILT"
FRIEZE
page 483

SEEDPOD LAMPSHADE
page 448

INDEX

This edition is published by Lorenz Books an imprint of Anness Publishing Ltd Hermes House, 88–89 Blackfriars Road London SE1 8HA tel. 020 7401 2077; fax 020 7633 9499

www.lorenzbooks.com
www.annesspublishing.com

If you like the images in this book and would like to investigate using them for publishing, promotions or advertising, please visit www.practicalpictures.com for more information.

UK agent: The Manning Partnership Ltd; tel. 01225 478444; fax 01225 478440; sales@manning-partnership.co.uk

UK distributor: Grantham Book Services Ltd; tel. 01476 541080; fax 01476 541061; orders@gbs.tbs-ltd.co.uk

North American agent/distributor: National Book Network; tel. 301 459 3366; fax 301 429 5746; www.nbnbooks.com

Australian agent/distributor: Pan Macmillan Australia; tel. 1300 135 113; fax 1300 135 103; customer.service@macmillan.com.au

New Zealand agent/distributor: David Bateman Ltd; tel. (09) 415 7664; fax (09) 415 8892

Publisher: Joanna Lorenz
Editorial Director: Helen Sudell
Editors: Doreen Gillon and Felicity Forster
Production controller: Steve Lang

A CIP catalogue record for this book is available from the British Library.

Previously published in two separate volumes, *The Complete Book of Decorative Stencilling* and *The Complete Book of Decorative Stamping*

ETHICAL TRADING POLICY
Because of our ongoing ecological investment programme, you, as our customer, can have the pleasure and reassurance of knowing that a tree is being cultivated on your behalf to naturally replace the materials used to make the book you are holding. For further information about this scheme, go to www.annesspublishing.com/trees

ACKNOWLEDGMENTS

The stencilling projects were created by Lucinda Ganderton, and the stamping projects were created by Stewart and Sally Walton, with the following exceptions:

Petra Boase: Making sandcastles, Painted drawers, Leafy picture frames.
Penny Boylan: Citrus roller blind.
Sacha Cohen: Greek urns, Heraldic dining room.
Emma Hardy: Trompe l'oeil plates, Organza cushion, Gilded candles.
Alison Jenkins: Rainforest curtains, Mosaic tablecloth.
Cheryl Owen: Kitchen alcove, Classical urn panels, Elegant rose wall, Bathroom frieze, Child's seaside room, Bright transport border, Scandinavian chair, Train toy box, Hawaiian hibiscus cabinet, Daisy stool, African bedside chest, Striped table and chairs, Dragonfly curtain, Girl's bed canopy and cushion, Leaf-etched vase, Button gift wrap and gift tags, Wedding stationery, Confetti box, Pastel paper lanterns.
Sandra Partington: Elizabethan lampshade.
Marie Perkins: Citrus fruit bowl.
Judy Smith: Flag stencils.
Suzie Stokoe: Summer quilt cover, Gold leaf picture frame.
Liz Wagstaff: Gilded lampshade.
Stewart and Sally Walton: Folk art wall, Star bathroom, Animal bedroom, Victorian window, Medallion stencilled floor, Bronze chair, Love pillows, Amish floorcloth, Stars and stripes floorcloth, Framed chalkboard.
Josephine Whitfield: Taurus gift wrap, Butterfly gift wrap, Seaweed gift wrap.